URBAN STRUCTURE AND THE LABOUR MARKET

URBAN STRUCTURE AND THE LABOUR MARKET

*Worker Mobility, Commuting, and
Underemployment in Cities*

WAYNE SIMPSON

CLARENDON PRESS · OXFORD
1992

Oxford University Press, Walton Street, Oxford OX2 6DP
Oxford New York Toronto
Delhi Bombay Calcutta Madras Karachi
Petaling Jaya Singapore Hong Kong Tokyo
Nairobi Dar es Salaam Cape Town
Melbourne Auckland
and associated companies in
Berlin Ibadan

Oxford is a trade mark of Oxford University Press

Published in the United States
by Oxford University Press, New York

British Library Cataloguing in Publication Data
Data available

Library of Congress Cataloging-in-Publication Data
Simpson, Wayne.
Urban structure and the labour market : worker mobility,
commuting, and underemployment in cities / Wayne Simpson
p. cm.
Includes bibliographical references and index.
1. Labour mobility. 2. Urban economics. 3. Underemployment.
4. Commuting. I. Title.
HD5717.S56 1991 331.12' 09173'2—dc20 91–32146
ISBN 0–19–828358–X

Typeset by Pure Tech Corporation, Pondicherry, India

Printed and bound in
Great Britain by Bookcraft (Bath) Ltd,
Midsomer Norton, Avon

To my parents, Wes and Bernice

PREFACE

AS a young graduate student searching for meaningful issues to study, I was fascinated by the role that cities—especially great cities—play in modern civilization. This fascination led me to a great city, London, and the urban economics programme at the London School of Economics for four years. Those are years that I will always remember fondly and which engendered both a Ph.D. dissertation and a lasting interest in urban economics and urban labour markets. This line of enquiry has often been solitary not only because interest in urban economics has declined since its peak in the 1970s but also because I have encountered very few researchers specializing in urban labour market analysis. Reflection has always reaffirmed my initial judgement that cities are about work as well as play (consumption) and that understanding the urban economy meant understanding its labour market. I finally decided that I should attempt to assemble the ideas and research that had grown out of my Ph.D. manuscript, some of which have appeared in articles in various journals. The result is a completely reworked, updated and, I believe, much more thoughtful analysis of the urban labour market that is intended to be of interest to urban and labour economists, geographers, planners, policy-makers, and others interested in urban and labour studies.

This book is written to appeal not only to economists but also to others with a serious interest in urban studies and labour markets. For this reason, I have confined the more technical and mathematical treatment of the analysis to specific asterisked subsections in Chapters 2–6. Those who wish to avoid a mathematical treatment may skip these subsections and, I hope, lose very little of the rigour of the argument. Others, especially economists, inclined toward a mathematical treatment, will find a succinct presentation of the ideas in those subsections. The book is aimed at the level of senior undergraduate and graduate students as well as researchers and teachers. The mathematical sections may be understood by anyone with intermediate calculus or the equivalent of an undergraduate course in mathematics for economists.

I would like to thank once again my graduate supervisors, Christopher Foster and Ray Richardson, for their guidance during the formation of this research programme and the writing of my Ph.D.

dissertation at the LSE. Christopher Foster told me in 1977 that there was a book in my dissertation work and I am belatedly acknowledging his good judgement. I owe a special debt of gratitude to Norm Cameron of the University of Manitoba who hired me to teach labour economics when academic jobs were scarce and gave me the opportunity to pursue this research over the past eleven years. I would also like to thank William Watson of McGill University and two anonymous referees for reading the manuscript and providing useful comments to improve the exposition, and Anne van der Veen of the University of Twente whose collaboration over the past year has undoubtedly influenced and stimulated my revision of the first draft of the manuscript.

Finally, I must thank my wife, Jeannine, who shared those years in London with me, bore our three children, and created the happy family environment in which long-term projects such as this one are sustained. I hope that we will share many more of the world's great cities together.

W.S.

Winnipeg, Canada
September 1990

CONTENTS

List of Tables   xi

1. INTRODUCTION   1

   1.1 *Defining Urban Economic Problems*   2
   1.2 *Labour Markets in Urban Economies*   5
   1.3 *An Outline of the Study*   9

2. THEORY OF URBAN SPATIAL STRUCTURE   12

   2.1 *Basic Residential Location Theory*   14
   2.2 *Refinements to Basic Residential Location Theory*   17
   2.3 *Employment Decentralization and the Location of
        Industry*   28
   2.4 *Residential Location with Decentralized Employ-
        ment*   35
   2.5 *Critics of Urban Spatial Theory*   41
   2.6 *Workplace Choice and Urban Structure*   46

3. INFORMATION, SEARCH, AND MATCHING: A SURVEY   50

   3.1 *Information and the Labour Market*   51
   3.2 *Basic Theory of Job Search*   52
   3.3 *Job Matching*   56
   3.4 *Spatial Considerations—The Island Economy*   58
   3.5 *Enterprise Search for Workers and Job Matching*   62
   3.6 *Concluding Remarks*   68

4. JOB–WORKER MATCHING IN URBAN SPACE   69

   4.1 *Behaviour of Workers*   69
   4.2 *Behaviour of Employers*   78
   4.3 *Skill, Search, and Spatial Matching*   81

5. JOB–WORKER MATCHING AND URBAN COMMUTING   90

   5.1 *Explaining Residential Location and Workplace
        Choice*   91
   5.2 *Determinants of Residential Location*   92
   5.3 *Determinants of Workplace Choice*   96

5.4 Evidence on Workplace Choice, Residential Location, and Commuting   101
5.5 Further Evidence—Commuting Differences by Sex
and Race   109
5.6 Concluding Remarks   114

6. JOB–WORKER MATCHING AND UNDEREMPLOYMENT   116
6.1 Underemployment and Labour Market Theory   118
6.2 Underemployment and the City   123
6.3 Urban Structure and Underemployment   128
6.4 Empirical Evidence   134
6.5 Extensions: Spatial Mobility, Job Availability, and
Underemployment   139
6.6 Concluding Remarks   149

7. EMPLOYMENT POLICIES AND URBAN
REDEVELOPMENT   152
7.1 Conventional Urban Employment Programmes   155
7.2 Local Job–Creation Programmes   163
7.3 Finding the Optimal Local Policy Mix   170

8. FINAL THOUGHTS . . . FOR NOW   173
8.1 Workplace Choice and Traditional Urban Issues   174
8.2 Workplace Choice and Traditional Labour Market
Issues   180

References   183
Index   197

LIST OF TABLES

2.1 (*a*) Distance of the household from the city centre by household income for Greater London, 1971–2   17
(*b*) Distance of the household from the city centre by household income for Toronto, 1979   17

2.2 Distance of the household from the city centre by various household characteristics for Greater London, 1971–2, and Toronto, 1979   20

2.3 Density of employment and population with distance from the city centre for Greater London, 1971–2, and Toronto, 1979   32

2.4 Density of employment with distance from the city centre for Greater London, 1971–2, by industrial category   33

5.1 Full sample regression estimates of residential and workplace location for Greater London and Toronto   104

5.2 Subsample regression estimates of residential and workplace location for Greater London and Toronto   107

5.3 Regression estimates of residential and workplace location for females and males in Toronto   112

6.1 Regression estimates of unemployment rates by sex for Greater London, 1971   137

1

INTRODUCTION

URBAN economics is only three decades old. It developed from concerns about economic problems in urban areas, including 'poverty, slums, pollution, segregation, suburban sprawl, and the financing of local public services' (Mills, 1972a: 1). These concerns were translated into public funding for urban research and urban policy initiatives, which in turn attracted economists to apply existing theories and to develop new theories with specific urban applications. Textbooks were written; courses were developed and often integrated with urban and regional planning programmes; journals specializing in urban economics were created; and urban economics became a respectable subdiscipline within economics.

Urban economics and urban problems may seem less prominent today than they did then, but they are no less serious. Leach (1985) documents the rise and fall of urban policy during the 1970s in the United States, Canada, and Australia and Higgins et al. (1983) tell a similar story for the United Kingdom. The authors of both books see the demise of urban policy as unfortunate, since the initial problems remain important, largely unresolved, and likely to recapture public attention in the future. Public attention and funding has shifted to other issues but will return to urban problems eventually. Urban economics must therefore continue to develop if solutions to these enduring urban problems are to be found.

Labour economics is a much older discipline than urban economics, but one that has been revolutionized in the last three decades. This revolution reflects the widespread application of microeconomic theory to the study of the labour market. It also reflects the development of new microeconomic concepts particularly relevant to the labour market, including human capital theory and the economics of information. Regardless of the techniques used, labour economics remains an important part of social and economic thought, and concern with problems of unemployment, underemployment, and earnings inequality ensures a prominent place for labour economics in future scholarship.

This book combines the study of urban and labour economics. It studies labour markets from a unique urban perspective. It is not a complete theory of the labour market, since there are many textbooks for that purpose (Addison and Siebert, 1979; Hammermesh and Rees, 1984; Fleisher and Kniesner, 1984; Wachtel, 1984), nor is it a complete treatment of urban economics in the usual sense (Richardson, 1971; Mills, 1972*a*; Evans, 1984; Henderson, 1985). It is instead a theory of the labour market that applies to the special character of urban areas and urban problems. It is thereby intended to be a contribution to the study of both urban economics and labour economics of interest to students of urban and labour market problems.

1.1 DEFINING URBAN ECONOMIC PROBLEMS

Most people live and work in cities, particularly in developed economies. Each city may be conceived to be a small, open economy with almost the full spectrum of economic activities and problems—public and private resource allocation, income distribution, unemployment and underemployment, inflation, and balance of payments. Monetary policy, agriculture, and mining are not direct urban concerns, but there is little else that is not.

Since the urban economy is almost a microcosm of the national economy, understanding its problems requires the application of many economic subdisciplines including economic growth and development, welfare economics, transportation, public finance, environmental economics, regional economics, and labour economics. During the 1960s and 1970s, when urban economic problems were in the limelight, these subdisciplines were often used to identify urban problems and suggest policies. This exercise may have been useful but it did not usually identify uniquely urban problems, since the urban case was simply treated as an application of another subdiscipline.

The application of labour economics to the study of the urban economy provides a good example. Many inner cities were, and still are, deteriorating at an alarming rate. This deterioration, and the human misery that it implied, was a focus for the War on Poverty programme started in 1964 in the United States. The American economy, despite low unemployment rates by today's standards, contained *spatially concentrated areas* with very high rates of unemployment and underemployment, poverty, and general economic despair among residents. The standard tools of labour economics plus the burgeoning theory of segmented labour markets (Cain, 1976; Harrison and Sum, 1979) were used to analyse these problems, but this analysis did not help us to understand why these problems were spatially concentrated within cities nor what urban planners and urban politicians could be expected to do to alleviate them. The problems seemed to have no uniquely urban characteristics; they simply occurred in cities.

Sifting through economic theory did provide the basis for a subdiscipline called urban economics, however. This basis was spatial economics. Economies of spatial agglomeration were used to provide a theory of the formation and growth of urban areas and the development of an urban hierarchy within regions and nations. The economics of residential and industrial location was developed to provide a theory of the urban land market and of the spatial organization of economic activity within the city. A glance at a recent urban economics text, such as Evans (1984) or Henderson (1985), or at articles in the *Journal of Urban Economics* indicates that spatial economic theory is now commonly defined to be the core of urban economics.

Spatial economics provides a unique urban view of the spatial concentration of high rates of unemployment and underemployment, poverty, and general economic despair among residents. Residential location explains the spatial segmentation of families within the city according to income and preferences (Alonso, 1964). Poor families, beset by chronic unemployment and underemployment, tend to be confined to older inner-city areas by the competition for land and the lack of affordable housing elsewhere and by discrimination in the housing market (Kain, 1975). This process may in turn be reinforced by zoning arising from externalities in land pricing and from political considerations.

In this view labour markets generate poverty and poor residents are assigned by the urban land market to older inner-city areas. Labour economics is non-spatial and provides no insight into the urban problem other than to explain poverty, which occurs in rural areas as well. The analysis suggests a general policy response to deal with underemployment and poverty, such as aggregate demand stimulus (Cheshire, 1979, 1981).

Some urban scholars have argued, however, that urban structure—the spatial distribution of people and jobs within the city—affects labour market performance. They observe that the poor lack employment opportunities near by as employment growth is concentrated in suburban areas far from the inner city. This separation of the underemployed from employment opportunities aggravates poverty in cities. This 'spatial mismatch' problem requires measures to improve worker mobility, such as improvements in core-to-suburb transportation facilities (Rees, 1966*b*; Kain 1968*a*), or at least special attention to the employment needs of inner-city residents (Needham, 1981). Their arguments are criticized, however, because they lack an explicit theoretical framework to explain how urban structure affects labour market activity (Cheshire, 1979; Lillydahl and Singell, 1985).

Others have argued that the conventional model of residential location and urban structure itself is flawed. The commuting patterns in cities appear to reflect considerations other than finding the best residential location from a predetermined workplace (Kain, 1975; Hamilton, 1982). Considerations often mentioned include decisions about workplace location (Siegel, 1975; Weinberg, 1979) since workplace location decisions occur more frequently than residential location decisions. Moreover, workplace location decisions may be particularly important in today's multiple-earner families (Beesley and Dalvi, 1974). This criticism of the theory of urban structure again suffers from lack of a clear analytical framework and supporting evidence.

The crucial issues in this debate are spatial and concern the mobility of workers within cities. If workers are perfectly mobile within cities, then one can ignore workplace location behaviour as in the current theory of urban structure and the welfare implications of the spatial concentration of underemployment within cities are trivial. Special studies of the inner cities would not then be warranted as Cheshire (1981) claims. If, on the other hand, the current approach to urban analysis is unsatisfactory and the spatial mismatch of jobs and workers is a problem, the source and nature of limitations to worker mobility in the urban labour market need considerable elaboration if effective policies are to be devised. What seems to be missing is a clear assessment of the theory and evidence regarding the mobility of the urban workforce.

This book provides an economic analysis of the spatial mobility of workers within cities to address these issues in as clear a fashion as possible. The study takes the view that worker mobility is not costless and that these mobility costs may be important in understanding urban labour markets. It is true that an urban area is characterized by high population density and a transportation infrastructure designed to connect workers and workplaces relatively inexpensively, but mobility problems remain. Gayer (1971) found, for example, that inner-city workers were unlikely to search for vacant jobs in suburban areas despite the lack of employment opportunities in the inner city and despite wages for suburban jobs which more than compensated for the additional commuting costs from the inner city to the suburbs. In other words, neither inadequate labour demand nor transportation cost appears to account for inner-city unemployment and underemployment. As a result, spatial immobility of inner-city workers requires further investigation.

These issues have important policy implications. A recent example is provided by Leonard (1987), who notes that many courts have placed the burden of racial integration on employers. If races are residentially segregated and if workers are not mobile, then the supply of labour to many employers is not racially mixed. Employers may not discriminate and the labour force may still be racially segregated. Yet the cause of labour-force segregation is not employment discrimination alone but residential segregation and worker immobility as well. Effective policy to provide equal employment opportunities requires a better understanding of each of these elements of economic and social behaviour.

A theory of the spatial mobility of urban workers provides labour economics and the study of urban labour markets with a new and uniquely urban focus. Urban worker mobility interacts with residential and industrial location patterns to determine the urban spatial structure. In turn, the urban spatial structure influences the labour market through worker mobility. Problems arising from the spatial development of an urban area may be considered and urban initiatives may be formulated. While many studies and authors have promoted this view, no theoretical basis for it has been provided. Thus the study of the spatial mobility of workers seems warranted to investigate the basis for this view and to improve our understanding of the spatial development of urban areas.

1.2 LABOUR MARKETS IN URBAN ECONOMIES

Our focus is the urban labour market, an important and sometimes neglected element in urban analysis. This focus provides a new perspective to analyse traditional urban concerns including poverty, transportation, housing, and local government finance. There are few urban economic issues that do not involve the labour market in a fundamental way.

Urban areas are often defined in labour market terms. Commuting patterns provide a common criterion to delineate urban boundaries in the United States (the Standard Metropolitan Statistical Area or SMSA), the United Kingdom (the Standard Labour Market Area or SMLA), and Canada (the Census Metropolitan Area or CMA). The criterion requires a stipulated percentage of workers in each county or other administrative area to commute to the designated central business district or core of the urban area. Underlying this definition is the concept of an urban area as a large labour market, providing employers with access to a large and varied workforce and workers with access to a variety of employment opportunities.

One can think of the urban area as a labour market in two ways. First, one can think of the urban area as a single labour market. Many empirical analyses use urban areas as the unit of observation for distinct labour markets (Bowen and Finegan, 1969; Freeman, 1982; Topel, 1986). Secondly, the urban area may be viewed as a group of local labour markets which interact and which have a common employment centre or central business district. The manner in which these labour markets interact depends upon the spatial mobility of workers within the urban area. Attention then shifts to residential and workplace location decisions, transportation and commuting decisions, and the spatial structure of an urban area. It is this second perspective which is featured in this study.

Labour market analysis is crucial to understand such important urban problems as poverty. Physical deterioration of neighbourhoods and communities, lack of services, and the tax revenue constraints that limit public response to these problems reflect the spatial concentration of the poor within urban areas. This poverty is in turn closely associated with inadequate earning opportunities—a labour market problem. Chronic unemployment, low wages, and sporadic work patterns are the norm rather than the exception in these areas. While some of the poverty may be short-lived, in other cases it is a way of life sometimes referred to as the poverty trap.

Many argue, however, that the problem is not only a poverty trap but a cultural trap as well (Moynihan, 1968; Doeringer and Piore, 1971). Inadequate earnings opportunities foster social alienation, including loss of self-esteem, personal ambition, and respect for social values. This alienation in turn makes it difficult for the poor to take advantage of the few good employment opportunities that do arise. Criminal activity and idleness are the common responses to the surplus time available, rather than neighbourhood rejuvenation even if funds are available. In this view, better employment opportunities can provide both the funds and the social climate for urban renewal. Improvements in transportation and other local services would be expected to follow in response to increased demand and greater local tax revenue. It would be inappropriate, however, to expect these service improvements to generate employment opportunities themselves.

The importance of the labour market as a component of urban analysis reflects its general significance in economic and social analysis. The labour market is a crucial element in modern macroeconomic analysis. The roles of transaction costs and institutions in the labour market as impediments to the wage flexibility needed to reduce unemployment have been studied extensively, although considerable controversy remains. This controversy extends to microeconomic analysis where a vigorous academic and policy debate about the extent and significance of labour market segmentation and job rationing has been sustained. Explicit or implicit theories of the labour market—reflecting views on the nature of unemployment, the distribution of earnings, and real and nominal wage growth—form an integral part of modern economic and social thought.

It is not surprising, therefore, that many researchers concerned with urban problems should turn to the analysis of urban labour markets. In one of the early studies of the urban economy, Thompson (1965) concludes that

[T]he local labour market is a (perhaps the) main arena in which urban economic issues must be resolved . . . Urban managerial economics seems destined to become heavily involved in labour market analysis and employment planning, the perfunctory role accorded to it at present notwithstanding.

Thompson emphasizes information services to assist job search, general career education, and vocational training—all of which are important aspects of the treatment of the urban labour market in this study. Other American studies include Rees and Shultz's (1970) pioneering study of wages in Chicago and Ginzberg's (1968, 1973) extensive and thoughtful analysis of employment problems and policies in New York City. In the United Kingdom it would include Metcalf and Richardson's (1980) study of unemployment in London. In developing countries it would include Mohan's (1986) study of Bogotá, Colombia for the World Bank. The list is too long to attempt to be comprehensive.

In a sense, however, urban labour market analysis has been neglected. These studies primarily use existing labour market theory to analyse a particular urban area and a uniquely urban perspective is not formulated. As a result no uniquely urban insights are obtained. The conclusions are generally applicable to large and small urban areas and rural communities alike. The urban area is a useful data base and convenient policy focus but nothing more.

This neglect is directly related to the issues raised in the previous section. Workplace location decisions have been cited as an important factor ignored by conventional analysis of urban structure and commuting. The spatial mismatch hypothesis postulates that labour market performance somehow depends upon urban structure. In each of these cases, however, a model of the urban labour market and worker mobility is needed to explain how workers find, or do not find, jobs within cities. Until such a model is developed and tested, these arguments will remain justifiably weak in the eyes of most urban analysts.

Ginzberg (1985: 686) warns us of the serious consequences of this neglect:

Although Adam Smith warned about the immobility of labour, most of his followers have used a labor market model that assumes that people, like capital, will flow quickly to wherever the returns are higher. We have learned during these last several decades, however, that large and persistent differences in the population-to-employment ratio and the unemployment rate can persist between central cities, with their large concentration of poor minorities, and the suburbs ... What is clear is that if society decides not to intervene, many vulnerable workers may be forced into a marginal relationship to the labor market for the whole of their working careers, since the market adjustment process may require a generation or two.

The question remains whether there is a uniquely urban aspect to labour market problems that occur in cities. Hall's (1981) report of the Inner Cities Working Party in the United Kingdom summarizes the research issues quite well. The report sees economic progress, involving growth and decline, as concentrated spatially both within and among urban areas. A major problem in this context is labour market adjustment, or worker mobility, in which 'many of the so-called rigidities ... have a specific local and spatial dimension ... including for example the location of homes and workplaces' (p. 133).

The important research questions, from a uniquely urban standpoint, are the influence of urban structure on these labour market problems and the scope for urban or local policies to combat these problems in ways that national programmes cannot. This is the neglected issue that this study seeks to address by providing an urban context to labour market analysis.

It is worth noting that the Hall report anticipates and approves the approach taken in this study. In one particularly lucid passage the report states:

Especially within the conurbations, there is a need to study the phenomenon of local labour markets—the areas within which workers will normally look for work. At any one moment these are fixed absolutely by the time and money that members of the labour force are willing and able to expend on the journey to work, but may also be constrained by their perceptions of employment opportunities. A very large conurbation like London may not be by any means a single local labour market in this sense, particularly for the less-skilled and lower-paid occupational groups: in the economic jargon, they may have tight spatial indifference curves. (p. 140)

In other words, the urban area consists of a series of local labour markets within which worker mobility is limited by their perceptions of employment opportunities.

A recent thoughtful assessment of the spatial mismatch problem for young workers in inner cities agrees with the perspective taken by the Hall report:

The key question, then, is whether search and commuting costs for young people in the inner city are costly. And certainly, such a scenario is plausible. Transportation costs may be very high . . . An even more plausible story is one that emphasizes the high cost of initial job search outside the neighborhood . . . the job search process of teenagers may rely heavily on informal networks, which may dissipate with distance. (Ellwood, 1986: 155–6)

We now turn to this research agenda, beginning with a chapter-by-chapter outline of the study.

1.3 AN OUTLINE OF THE STUDY

The defining characteristic of cities is their spatial concentration of population, and spatial structure is fundamental to any urban theory. Chapter 2 examines urban spatial economic theory as a foundation for the remainder of the study. It reviews the well-developed theories of residential choice and enterprise location and concentrates on the important and pervasive phenomenon of employment decentralization within cities. The evidence for this approach is broadly assessed by the introduction of a very useful data source that has been under-utilized in urban research—household transportation survey micro-data. The chapter then identifies a neglected area of research in this approach to spatial structure—the theory of workplace choice in the urban labour market. The development of this theory and its implications for urban economic behaviour in the remainder of the study seeks to fill this void and to answer many of the unanswered questions in the analysis of urban spatial structure as it pertains to the labour market.

Chapter 3 considers those aspects of modern labour economics that are useful to develop a model of workplace choice in an urban labour market. The focus of the chapter is a survey of the economics of information and job search. The contribution of this chapter is an explicitly spatial treatment of this literature as the basis for the analysis in the remainder of the study. At the same time, the more general spatial elements of this model and its applicability to the regional migration literature are noted.

Chapter 4 develops a specific model of search and job–worker matching for workers and employers in the urban labour market. The crucial relationship between skill acquisition and spatial mobility is developed and considerable supporting literature is cited. The nature of spatial equilibrium in the labour market is considered.

Chapter 5 combines the theories of residential location and urban structure in Chapter 2 with the model of job–worker matching in Chapter 4. The contribution of job–worker matching to the analysis of urban spatial structure is identified and implications for commuting behaviour are derived and compared to those from the conventional model of Chapter 2. Econometric tests of the theories using the transportation survey microdata introduced in Chapter 2 are assessed. Commuting patterns are examined, first in a general way and then by reference to a specific, simultaneous-equations model that attempts to incorporate the essential features of the combined theories. Careful analysis of the evidence on commuting behaviour from the transportation survey microdata and other sources supports the view that the job–worker matching model of Chapter 4 is an important component of the analysis of urban spatial structure. This view is reinforced by consideration of the literature on discrimination and commuting.

Chapter 6 extends the analysis to consider specific labour market problems. A theory of underemployment in the urban economy is developed from the job–worker matching model of Chapter 5. The theory provides an explicit framework for the literature concerned with labour market problems arising from the spatial mismatch of urban jobs and workers. The theory is tested with reference to data and studies from the United Kingdom, Canada, and the United States. New links are made between mainstream economic analysis and the literature on segmented labour markets and the culture of poverty from an urban spatial perspective. A clear distinction is drawn between the underemployment explained by this theory of urban spatial structure and other aspects of underemployment, particularly those related to job rationing and inadequate aggregate demand.

Chapter 7 looks at the policy implications of the analysis in Chapter 6 for employment and urban redevelopment. The basic approaches to employment policy—counselling, training, information, and mobility programmes, and job creation—are reviewed and evaluated in the light of this study. The role of the urban economy in employment analysis and employment policy development is identified. The appropriate policy focus is considered in terms of both programmes and level of control.

Chapter 8 provides a summary of the argument and directions for further research. In particular, the chapter examines the potential links between the research in this study and such traditional urban economic concerns as spatial structure, transportation, housing and redevelopment, and dynamic urban models. It also considers the implications of the study for traditional analysis of labour markets. Since the study seeks to initiate a new approach to certain issues in urban and labour market analysis, it is hoped that the research agenda with which the reader concludes this book is considerably larger than the one with which he or she began it.

2

THEORY OF URBAN SPATIAL STRUCTURE

SPATIAL structure is a central feature of the study of urban economics. Spatial structure means not only the location of households and enterprises within the city but also the various spatial interactions between households and enterprises. These interactions may be social interactions between households, business interactions between enterprises, or work–residence commuting trips between households and their employers. A city is a spatial concentration of population designed to economize on these interactions; hence understanding these interactions is necessary to understand the urban economy.

How can these interactions be understood? Urban residential location theory provides an explanation of many of the stylized facts—why the rich live in the suburbs and the poor in the central city, how commuting costs and transportation infrastructure matter, and why families move as they grow and change. In recent years the theory has provided a richer analysis by considering residential location decisions when employment is decentralized. Like any prominent theory, however, residential location theory has critics and many of their objections remain unresolved. Can the theory explain the land rent patterns in cities? Can it explain commuting patterns, or does much of actual commuting behaviour appear to be wasteful? If the theory is inadequate, what is missing—housing externalities? fiscal incentives? dynamics? In this chapter we examine the theory of urban spatial structure and its problems to define the scope for labour market analysis in the remainder of the book.

In an age of rapid urban growth it is natural to think of urban spatial structure as dynamic. Rapid urban growth can only arise from a large net in-migration of people from rural areas, other cities, and other countries. This influx is normally accompanied by a rapid growth of employment as enterprises relocate from elsewhere or new enterprises begin. Rapid urban growth leads to a shortage of land sites, which induces a conversion of old land sites to new uses and an expansion of suburban areas of the city. Changing land values, in particular rising central city rents, induce dramatic changes in spatial structure as new firms and households seek appropriate land and buildings and as existing firms and households adjust their accommodation.

Yet one need not have rapid urban growth to observe dramatic changes in urban spatial structure. Even if net in-migration is modest, gross in-migration and out-migration from a city may be substantial. Moreover, dramatic changes in the accommodation needs of a stable urban population may occur in only a few years—a large youth population seeking apartments near the centre of the city may become a large population of families with young children seeking suburban housing and amenities. Technological innovation ensures that firms will not only grow and decline rapidly but often need to change land sites to produce efficiently. The rapid development of suburban industrial parks has not been confined to rapidly growing cities. Cities with slow growth may find it even more important to accommodate changing industrial needs to prevent out-migration of jobs.

Truly dynamic models are complex, however. One may simplify the model by reducing it to a series of snapshots using a static equilibrium model. A static model can focus upon the forces shaping urban spatial structure at a particular point in time as if the past and future did not matter. Given a set of initial conditions, which may reflect past urban development, the model determines the equilibrium spatial structure of the city. This spatial structure would be sustained forever if conditions remained unchanged. As conditions change, for example as population grows or technology advances, a new snapshot of urban spatial structure is provided by the static model. Comparison between snapshots, or comparative statics, provides insights into the forces shaping the spatial structure of the city without the details of the path of adjustment. The model must then be judged on the basis of its ability to capture the major influences on urban spatial development.

Our analysis begins with a simple, but insightful, static equilibrium model of urban spatial structure which focuses on the choice of residential location and work–residence commuting patterns. We then consider extensions of the model which are important for empirical applications. The comparative statics of this model, as it has been applied to the analysis of metropolitan growth, are set out. We then review the critics' arguments to establish a common view of one major weakness of the standard theory—its treatment of the workplace choice of urban residents. This weakness provides motivation for the remaining chapters.

2.1 BASIC RESIDENTIAL LOCATION THEORY

A conventional starting-point for analysis of urban spatial structure is Alonso's (1964) formal model of residential location choice from a predetermined, central workplace.[1] The model extends consumer demand theory to incorporate spatial considerations by distinguishing the location of urban land sites in terms of distance to the central workplace or 'access'. Distance to the workplace is important because commuting costs are assumed to be proportional to distance so that consumers who choose sites closer to the workplace incur lower commuting costs. Other costs of spatial interaction are ignored.

Each household-consumer prefers to be closer to the central workplace, generating excess demand for central land sites which will increase their unit price. Households are therefore faced with a choice between more expensive land and lower commuting costs (better access), or less expensive land and higher commuting costs. Alonso solves the household's problem to derive its bids for land at each location, called the bid-rent curve. Households that prefer good access to inexpensive land will bid for expensive central land sites; households that prefer to forgo access for inexpensive land will bid for suburban land sites. The actual land-price structure—the price per unit of land at each distance from the central workplace—is determined by successful land bids until urban fringe land prices match agricultural land prices at those locations.[2] The urban land-use pattern is a series of concentric zones with 'access hungry' households occupying smaller, more expensive sites in more central zones and 'land-hungry' households consuming larger amounts of inexpensive land in more distant zones.

Household consumption is restricted by real income. In a large city, land prices are high because of the increased competition for central locations. If household incomes are not commensurately higher in a large city, households must economize on land by relying on smaller lots for housing or on multiple-household dwellings such as high-rise apartments or shared accommodation. Households cannot solve the problem of high prices simply by moving farther out since commuting

---

[1] The model extends to urban spatial organization a tradition of spatial analysis which can be traced to von Thunen's theory of agricultural land use in the 19th century. Ponsard (1983) traces the historical development of this approach.

[2] The price structure, a hedonic price index, is determined by supply and demand for the attribute, in this case access to work. Rosen (1974) has generalized the approach to a model of hedonic or implicit prices for any heterogeneous good or service.

costs will increase. Hence, out-migration from large cities can be prevented only by higher incomes which compensate for higher land prices near the centre or the increased cost of access in large cities (Richardson, 1973).

Real income will differ among city residents. Since rich consumers can afford both more access and more land than poor consumers, it is not clear whether rich households will opt for central or suburban land sites without additional assumptions. Indeed, if preferences are unrelated to income then rich and poor households will locate in each zone with rich households occupying larger land sites (and bigger houses) whether they are 'access hungry' or not. To explain the observed pattern of rich households locating in the suburbs, Alonso (1964: 108) assumes that 'the desire for land is strong and not easily satisfied'. Specifically, as income rises the marginal utility of land decreases at a slower rate than land acquisition. Rich households absorb higher commuting costs spread over larger amounts of less expensive (per unit) land farther from the city centre. In other words, rich households prefer large suburban land sites to central city sites with good access to work.

The land-use pattern is consistent with the tradition of von Thunen (Hall, 1966). The pattern consists of a series of concentric zones, beginning with a central business district. Poor households locate in the first ring, a location which provides good access and lowers commuting costs but which primarily reflects inadequate income to afford suburban land sites. Suburban land is cheaper per unit, but sites and houses are larger and more expensive. The rings farther from the centre are occupied by successively richer households because they choose to spend their money on land and housing rather than access.

Evidence of this pattern of residential location by household income can be obtained from aggregate census data or, in greater detail, from transportation surveys. Two such surveys are examined here and elsewhere in this study. One is the Greater London Transportation Survey of 41,678 households interviewed between September 1971 and June 1972. The other is the Metro Toronto Travel Survey of 3,508 households interviewed during November 1979. Each survey is a random sample of households in the urban area which identifies place of residence and place of work at a very fine level of geographical detail. In each case the urban area is divided into a large number of zones—945 in Greater London and 400 in Metropolitan Toronto. Distances between zones, in particular distances between any zone and the city centre,[3] are calculated from a grid provided for each survey. This permits us to examine residential location patterns, and later employment location patterns, in greater detail.

To examine residential location patterns, the distance of each place of residence to the city centre is calculated for each respondent in the Greater London and Toronto surveys. Three concentric zones are formed for each city: inner, middle, and outer zones. The proportion of households in each ring by household income is presented in Table 2.1. As household income rises, moving from left to right in Table 2.1, the proportion of households in the inner ring in that income category generally declines and the proportion in the outer ring generally increases. Moreover, as household income rises, average distance of the place of residence to the city centre rises. The notable exception is for the richest households in Toronto, who tend to live closer to the city centre than all but the poorest households in that city.

Table 2.1 also indicates that household income is not the sole determinant of residential location. Many rich households choose to live in the inner zone and some poor households live in the outer zone. The middle zone is a mixture of households from all income categories. This evidence serves to remind us that residential location, like most other social phenomena, is complex and *multi-faceted*. Other factors influence residential location in addition to household income.

The fact that other factors matter does not necessarily detract from this basic theory of urban residential location behaviour. The theory, while simple, is still properly considered to be an important component of urban analysis. Indeed, Evans (1985: 14) calls it 'the core theory of urban economics'. It explains the observed decline in land values from the city centre (Clark, 1966) on the basis of spatial competition for land sites differentiated by location or, more specifically, by access or transportation costs to the city centre. It emphasizes the important trade-off of land costs (space) and transportation costs (access) in the residential location decision. This trade-off provides an explanation for long commuting trips by rich households based on their preference for space rather than access. These important ideas provide a framework within which other aspects of urban residential location and spatial interaction may be incorporated.

---

[3] Central city zones contain Charing Cross Station in Greater London and Union Station in Metropolitan Toronto.

Theory of Urban Spatial Structure

TABLE 2.1

(a) *Distance of the household from the city centre by household income for Greater London, 1971–2*

| | Household income (£ '000) | | | |
	<1	1–1.75	1.75–3	>3
% Inner (0–10 km)	46.5	36.7	26.8	24.5
% Middle (10–20 km)	39.6	46.0	50.6	51.8
% Outer (>20 km)	13.9	17.3	22.6	23.7
Average distance (km)	12.0	13.1	14.7	15.1

Source: Greater London Transportation Survey, 1971.

(b) *Distance of the household from the city centre by household income for Toronto, 1979*

| | Household income ($ '000) | | | |
	<15	15–30	30–50	>50
% Inner (0–8 km)	58.6	46.7	45.3	51.4
% Middle (8–16 km)	37.4	45.3	46.7	48.6
% Outer (>16 km)	4.0	8.0	8.0	0.0
Average distance (km)	8.2	8.9	9.1	8.5

Source: Metro Toronto Travel Survey.

2.2 REFINEMENTS TO BASIC RESIDENTIAL LOCATION THEORY

The basic model can be extended in various ways to reflect differences among households. Each household in the model consists of a single worker commuting to work in the city centre at a fixed cost per mile. Family size and composition are ignored, as are social interactions. Yet modern households more often than not have more than one worker, commuting costs differ among workers, families with children prefer different living arrangements to families without children, and social interactions are often a consideration in residential location choice.

Alonso (1964) assumes the same commuting costs per mile for all households despite a great deal of evidence (Beesley, 1970, 1973; Hensher, 1976; Wales, 1978; Leigh, 1986) that commuting costs rise with earnings. The evidence is consistent with the neoclassical theory of labour supply, which argues that the value of commuting time will rise as the alternative use value, earnings from employment, rises. In that case, rich households will assess commuting time at a higher value, increasing commuting costs per mile. If preferences were the same for all households, rich households would now prefer access to cheap land because access is more valuable to them to reduce commuting costs. In order to explain the predominant land-use pattern that we observe, rich households must have a stronger appetite for land than the basic model of the previous section implies. The choice of a suburban site is more expensive in terms of commuting costs for a rich household than for a poor household.

Hoover and Vernon (1959) and Evans (1973) analyse the role of family status and social interaction in the residential location decision. Some households, particularly those with children, will prefer more land and lower density housing while other households without children will place less value on space. Hence, family status affects preferences as well as income. Rich households will be able to afford suburban land and housing, but not all rich households may prefer space over access. Single individuals and childless couples, especially young people, may prefer the accessibility provided by central city locations, particularly if they attach a high value to their commuting time.

A typical household life cycle involves changes in land preferences as family composition and income changes. A young single individual prefers a central city location with access to work and leisure activities. This is reinforced by earnings, which are typically low early in the working life. Young couples without children have similar preferences, but the arrival of children increases preferences for space at the expense of access, particularly if the slower suburban lifestyle and better suburban services such as schooling are considered to provide a superior environment in which to raise children. These preferences for space could better be satisfied at this stage because of higher earnings as the earner in the household accumulates work experience and settles into a specific career pattern. Once the children have left home, preferences may again shift to favour access over space. Thus, the distance of the household from the city centre may reflect age and the presence of children as well as income, although these factors will be related through the life cycle of earnings.

Households consider not only commuting costs to work but also social interaction costs in choosing a residential location. People prefer to live near others who have similar interests and values, providing a tendency for social agglomeration (Evans, 1973). This will increase the segregation of households on the basis of income and family status but may introduce other considerations such as ethnic group or religion. Some households may opt to locate in an area where incomes are lower and families are older because of ethnic or religious ties to that neighbourhood. These ties may have tangible expression in close association with a church or community association, or a household may simply feel more comfortable in that neighbourhood. The household is therefore willing to pay a 'neighbourhood preference premium' (Kerwin and Ball, 1974) for housing at that location. On the other hand, as families age and children move away from home, social interactions may encourage households to remain in a known neighbourhood rather than seek more accessible, less spacious surroundings. This inertia in residential relocation simply reflects a wider set of considerations than access and space.

Another important consideration in residential location may be the number of household members who are working. In particular, there are many households in which both the male and female household head choose to work. Since this situation would double commuting costs, it would tend to favour more centralized locations. Beckmann (1969) shows that residential location, in terms of distance from the central business district, will decrease as the ratio of commuters to family size increases. Oi (1976) extends Beckmann's analysis by developing a simultaneous model of residential location and labour supply for the two-adult household. A second earner in the household will pull the family toward the city centre to reduce commuting costs. The presence of young children would then push the household toward the suburbs in two ways—it would increase the demand for space and better housing and it would reduce the probability of the female head working. Hekman (1980) develops a similar model to show that higher household income has counteracting effects if it is provided by earnings from the wife, as well as husband, in a two-adult household. It increases the demand for space in the suburbs but it also increases the cost of reduced access that suburban locations imply. Thus labour supply is likely to be an important consideration in residential location decisions.

These additional factors increase the explanatory capability of the basic model. They explain, for example, why all rich households do not locate in the suburbs. Some rich households, particularly two-earner families without children, will prefer the access provided by

20   *Theory of Urban Spatial Structure*

the central city location to economize on commuting costs. Since central locations are expensive, accommodation will be restricted to small land sites, such as high-rise apartments. These apartments may in turn provide convenient social interaction with other households in similar circumstances, providing additional incentive to locate centrally until family circumstances change. As a result the central city will be likely to consist of a broader spectrum of families, rich and poor, than the suburbs.

TABLE 2.2. *Distance of the household from the city centre by various household characteristics for Greater London, 1971–2, and Toronto, 1979*

	Children		Earners		Age of head	
	None	Some	One	>1	<46 yrs	>45 yrs
Greater London						
% Inner (0–10 km)	30.2	26.1	33.6	31.0	29.6	29.8
% Middle (10–20 km)	49.1	51.3	52.7	54.0	48.9	49.4
% Outer (>20 km)	20.7	22.6	13.7	15.0	21.5	20.9
Average	14.2	14.8	13.2	13.5	14.4	14.2
Toronto						
% Inner (0–8 km)	52.6	48.0	61.8	48.0	55.2	48.7
% Middle (8–16 km)	41.4	46.0	34.1	45.0	39.0	45.2
% Outer (>16 km)	6.0	6.0	4.1	6.7	5.8	6.1
Average	8.4	8.7	7.6	8.9	8.2	8.8

Sources: Greater London Transportation Survey, 1971; Metro Toronto Travel Survey 1979.

We can see the simple effects of these additional factors in the transportation survey data used in Table 2.1. Table 2.2 presents the distribution of residents among the inner, middle, and outer zones of Greater London and Toronto and the average distance of the place of residence from the city centre for households with preschool children,[4] the number of employees in the household, and the age of the household head. The results suggest that households with preschool children tend to live farther from the city centre as expected, but the difference with other households is not large. Older household heads

[4] Only preschool children could be identified in the Greater London Transportation Survey. Thus children of preschool age were also used for the Metropolitan Toronto Travel Survey for comparison.

live farther out in Toronto but not in Greater London. Moreover, multiple-earner households are located farther from the city centre than single-earner households in both Greater London and Toronto. These unexpected results may arise because residential location involves many factors which are related. Multiple-earner households, for example, may be expected to have higher total household incomes that single-earner households. This income causes them to choose residential locations farther from the city centre. The effect of multiple earners *per se*, however, may be to pull a household toward the centre. That is, if household incomes are equal, multiple-earner households may locate closer to the city centre than single-earner households to reduce commuting costs. Household income is not controlled in Table 2.2, however, so that it is difficult to see the effect of multiple-earner households because of the related effect of household income. This is precisely Hekman's (1980) point. Similarly, household income and the number of household earners may be related to the presence of preschool children and the age of the household head. To obtain a clearer picture of the independent, or partial, effects of these factors requires a multivariate analysis of residential location. Studies using multivariate analysis will be examined in Chapter 5.

Other less easily measured factors that affect residential location decisions include geography, transportation infrastructure, the durability of housing, and public policy. Geographical features can limit urban expansion in certain directions and increase land rents in other directions by reducing the supply of sites accessible to the city centre. This may create an exclusive and socially prestigious neighbourhood commanding high rents relative to surrounding sites. Transportation networks improve access at certain locations regardless of distance from the centre. Thus freeways and subways may improve the access of certain suburban residents relative to others or to those closer to the centre. This will affect residential location preferences and thereby house and land prices and residential densities (Hartwick and Hartwick, 1972; Capozza, 1973). Housing, once built, is expensive to renovate or destroy so that most new housing is built on vacant sites. Preferences for suburban land may reflect preferences for newer housing available only in suburban locations over older housing closer to the city centre (Muth, 1969). Public policy decisions regarding zoning and the provision of local services will also have some influence on residential location decisions (Rothenberg, 1970;

Schuler, 1974). For an extensive review and critical assessment of the literature, see Richardson (1977).

No model can deal with all facets of a complex economic decision like urban residential location. The access–space trade-off model can, however, identify important elements of the decision and provide the basis to incorporate the other features discussed briefly in this section. It is a fundamental component of urban economic theory.

One important limitation that remains is the assumption of a single, central workplace. Once there are many employment centres, including a central business district, the fundamental concept of accessibility becomes more complex. Changes in employment location also become a catalyst for changes in urban spatial structure. We will turn to these issues in sections 2.3 and 2.4.

2.2.1   Residential location theory: the formal model*

Much of the theoretical research on urban spatial structure can be summarized in a basic model of residential location with reference to a predetermined workplace. The model begins with the standard economic theory of the consumer for two goods—housing and all other goods.[5] The standard model is extended to permit housing prices and household commuting costs to vary according to location. To simplify the analysis, we begin with a monocentric city—all economic activity occurs in the centre—and a featureless urban landscape. Residential location can then be simply represented by the distance, h, to the centre and the variation in housing and commuting costs by a housing price gradient $p(h)$ and a commuting cost function $c(h)$, respectively, where $\partial c / \partial h > 0$. If q is the amount of housing and x is the amount of other goods consumed, then the basic consumer problem can be written

$$\max\ u(q, x)$$

subject to

$$p(h)q + x + c(h) = y, \qquad (2.1)$$

where y is consumer income and the price of other goods x is set to 1. Then the standard first-order conditions for a maximum are

$$p(h) = \frac{\partial u / \partial q}{\partial u / \partial x} \qquad (2.2)$$

---

[5] The relative prices of all other goods are assumed constant throughout the analysis to permit aggregation. As we will see later in this section, this assumption presents some serious problems.

and

$$\frac{\partial p}{\partial h} = -\frac{\partial c/\partial h}{q} < 0 \qquad (2.3)$$

since $\partial c/\partial h > 0$. Equation (2.3) indicates that the household will incur higher commuting costs per unit of housing only if there is a compensating reduction in unit housing costs. This equation, known as the equilibrium bid-rent schedule for the consumer, provides the fundamental insight of the early residential location literature—that there must be a trade-off between unit housing costs and commuting costs.

A solution to the consumer problem can be written as

$$q = q[u(\cdot), p(\cdot), c(\cdot); y] \qquad (2.4)$$

$$x = x[u(\cdot), p(\cdot), c(\cdot); y] \qquad (2.5)$$

$$h = h[u(\cdot), p(\cdot), c(\cdot); y] , \qquad (2.6)$$

where equation (2.6) represents the location decision of the household. If households face the same price gradient $p(\cdot)$ and commuting cost function $c(\cdot)$, and if consumers have the same utility function $u(\cdot)$, then differences in location will depend only upon household income y. In particular, it can be shown (Siegel, 1975, or Simpson, 1977, ch. 2) that

$$\frac{\partial}{\partial \eta} \left(\frac{\partial h}{\partial y} \right) < 0, \qquad (2.7)$$

where

$$\eta = \left| \frac{(\partial^2 u/\partial q^2)q}{\partial u/\partial q} \right|$$

is the elasticity of the marginal utility of land (Alonso, 1964). Thus, for η sufficiently small, $\partial h/\partial y > 0$, and richer households will prefer cheaper housing and more commuting from the suburbs as observed.

Several interesting extensions mentioned above have been considered. Assume, for example, that the cost of commuting—in particular, the value of commuting time—depends upon income (Muth, 1969) so that

$$c = c(h, y), \frac{\partial c}{\partial y} > 0 \qquad (2.8)$$

and let commuting distance h enter the utility function directly (Alonso, 1964; Wheaton, 1977). Then the consumer problem is

$$\max u(q, x, h)$$

subject to

$$p(h)q + x + c(h, y) = y \qquad (2.9)$$

yielding first-order conditions

$$p(h) = \frac{\partial u/\partial q}{\partial u/\partial x} \qquad (2.10)$$

as before and

$$\frac{\partial p}{\partial h} = \frac{1}{q}\left[\frac{\partial u/\partial h}{\partial u/\partial x} - \frac{\partial c}{\partial h}\right]. \qquad (2.11)$$

In this model the bid-rent schedules are steeper than in equation (2.3) because of the monetized value of the disutility of commuting, given by $\frac{\partial u/\partial h}{\partial u/\partial x}$. In this case, the effect of income on the bid-rent schedule is

$$\frac{\partial}{\partial y}\left(\frac{\partial p}{\partial h}\right) = \frac{M}{qy}\left[\eta_{My} - \eta_{qy}\right] > 0, \qquad (2.12)$$

where $M = \frac{\partial u/\partial h}{\partial u/\partial x} - \frac{\partial c}{\partial h}$ is now the total marginal cost of travel and $\eta_{My} = \frac{\partial M/M}{\partial y/y}$ and $\eta_{qy} = \frac{\partial q/q}{\partial y/y}$ are the income elasticities of marginal travel cost and land, respectively. Thus the effect of income on residential location depends on the difference between the income elasticities of total marginal travel costs and land, $\eta_{My} - \eta_{qy}$.

Traditional analysis of residential location has concentrated on extensions to the basic theory outlined above which analyse the markets for land and housing (Strazheim, 1987, for example). Our approach is quite different. We focus on extensions to the basic theory which concern the household as a participant in the urban labour market. We argue that this focus, while generally overlooked in urban economic analysis, provides new and fruitful insights into urban economic behaviour which deserve greater consideration than heretofore.

In this section we illustrate this argument by reviewing one important aspect of this line of enquiry that has been considered in the literature—labour supply and the value of commuting time. While these two issues may appear to be unrelated, they are in fact closely related as components of the allocation of household time in the residential choice model. The development of this line of enquiry in the residential location model closely follows the analysis of labour supply and the allocation of time in consumer theory (for example

Abbott and Ashenfelter, 1976). Thus we begin with a model that considers labour supply in the residential choice problem before turning to a model in which both labour supply and the value of commuting time are considered.

Hekman (1980) argues effectively that the primary deficiency of the basic residential location model is that it ignores household labour supply behaviour. If income is an important factor in location decisions, and if earnings are an important component of income, then differences in household income imply differences in earnings which imply differences in the value of leisure and commuting time across households. Leisure and commuting time must therefore be considered in the residential location problem.

Hekman considers a single worker in the household to simplify the analysis. His focus is the labour supply behaviour of women, particularly married women as second earners in households.[6] He allocates the total time T available to the worker to work time L, leisure time l, and commuting time t. Commuting time and cost depend upon the location chosen h and upon the time spent working, which is assumed to be proportional to the number of work trips. Thus,

$$t = t(L, h), \quad \frac{\partial t}{\partial L} > 0 \qquad (2.13)$$

and

$$c = c(L, h), \quad \frac{\partial t}{\partial L} > 0. \qquad (2.14)$$

Household income is divided into earnings w per time period and unearned income y. The household maximizes a utility function which now includes leisure[7] as follows:

$$\max u(q, x, l)$$

subject to

$$p(h)q + x + c(L, h) = wL + y$$

and

$$L(h) + l + t(L, h) = T. \qquad (2.15)$$

The first-order conditions are then

$$p(h) = \frac{\partial u/\partial q}{\partial u/\partial x} \qquad (2.16)$$

[6] Other studies which consider female labour supply separately include Oi (1976) and Kohlhase (1986).
[7] See Beckmann (1974) and Henderson (1985) for similar analyses.

$$w = \frac{\partial u/\partial l}{\partial u/\partial x} \tag{2.17}$$

and

$$\frac{\partial p}{\partial h} = -\frac{\partial c/\partial h + w\partial t/\partial h + \partial c/\partial L \partial L/\partial h + w\partial t/\partial L \partial L/\partial h}{q}. \tag{2.18}$$

As in equation (2.3), the equilibrium bid-rent schedule equation (2.18) depends upon direct commuting cost $\partial c/\partial h$ but the equation now also includes commuting time $\partial t/\partial h$, labour supply behaviour $\partial L/\partial h$, and the wage rate w. The effect of household income on the bid-rent schedule is now more complex:

$$\frac{\partial}{\partial y}\left(\frac{\partial p}{\partial h}\right) = \frac{M}{qy}\left[\eta_{My} - \eta_{qy}\right] - \frac{1}{qy}\left[y\frac{\partial}{\partial y}\left(\frac{\partial c}{\partial L}\frac{\partial L}{\partial h} + w\frac{\partial t}{\partial L}\frac{\partial L}{\partial h}\right) - \eta_{qy}\right]. \tag{2.19}$$

The total marginal cost of travel is now $M = -(\partial c/\partial h + w\partial t/\partial h)$. Hekman's argument is that flatter bid-rent schedules may arise because $\partial/\partial y(\partial L/\partial h) < 0$, that is because labour supply falls for women as distance from the centre h and income y increase. This provides one explanation for the flat bid-rent schedules estimated by Wheaton (1977).

The direct effect of labour supply on residential location in this model can be seen by writing commuting time and cost as

$$t(L, h) = K(L)Dh \tag{2.20}$$

and

$$c(L, h) = K(L)Ch, \tag{2.21}$$

where $K(L)$ is the number of commuting trips, which depends on labour supplied ($\partial K/\partial L > 0$), C is the money cost per mile of a trip, and D is the time spent per mile of a trip. From (2.20) and (2.21) we can rewrite the bid-rent schedule (2.18) as

$$\frac{\partial p}{\partial h} = -\frac{K(L)C + wK(L)D + Ch(\partial K/\partial L)\partial L/\partial h + wDh(\partial K/\partial L)\partial L/\partial h}{q}. \tag{2.22}$$

Assuming that the number of commuting trips is proportional to labour supply, so that $\partial^2 K/\partial L^2 = 0$, the effect of labour supply on the bid-rent schedule is

$$\frac{\partial}{\partial L}\left(\frac{\partial p}{\partial h}\right) = -\frac{\partial K}{\partial L} + wD\frac{\partial K}{\partial L}\,q < 0. \tag{2.23}$$

Increased labour supply, and therefore increased commuting, makes the (negatively sloped) bid-rent schedule of households steeper, other factors (in particular, income) held constant. Thus households with a second earner, implying higher labour supply, will locate closer to the city centre to reduce commuting costs.

Although the household allocates time to commuting, the value of commuting time is not determined. It is assumed to be the same as the value of leisure time—namely the wage rate w. In order to treat the value of commuting time properly, commuting time must appear in the utility function of the household:

$$\max u(q, x, l, t)$$

subject to

$$p(t)q + x = wL + y$$

and

$$L + l + t = T. \tag{2.24}$$

This specification is a variant of equation (2.15) in which commuting time t, and distance h from the centre are equated. Wales (1978) formulates such a model to estimate the value of commuting time.[8] The solution to the model must satisfy

$$p(t) = \frac{\partial u/\partial q}{\partial u/\partial x} \tag{2.25}$$

$$w = \frac{\partial u/\partial l}{\partial u/\partial x} \tag{2.26}$$

and

$$w + q\frac{\partial p}{\partial t} = \frac{\partial u/\partial t}{\partial u/\partial x} \equiv v_t, \tag{2.27}$$

where v_t is the value of commuting time. The value of commuting time includes both the wage rate, as the marginal value of leisure from equation (2.26), and the reduction in housing expenditures arising from the additional time spent commuting.

Wales specifies an exponential functional form for the land rent gradient $p(t)$:

$$p(t) = \beta t^\gamma. \tag{2.28}$$

In this case,

---

[8] Wales's (1978) model incorporates taxes, but this is an unnecessary complication for our purpose.

$$v_t = w + \frac{q\gamma p(t)}{t}, \qquad (2.29)$$

where only γ is unobserved for suitable household microdata. Using the 1972 Panel Study of Income Dynamics from the University of Michigan and inserting equation (2.29) into a Generalized Cobb–Douglas demand system for q, x, l, and t Wales estimates γ to be -0.1 and v_t to be about two-thirds of the average wage rate in his sample. Thus, while there appears to be a strong positive correlation between wages and the value of commuting time in his data as predicted by economic theory, the value of commuting time appears to be different from the value of leisure and work time contrary to the assumption of models, such as Hekman's, which omit commuting time from the utility function.

The formal residential location model has proved very useful in theoretical and empirical analysis of urban structure. As we have noted, there have been many extensions involving markets other than the labour market. For a more detailed review, readers are referred to Straszheim (1987).

2.3 EMPLOYMENT DECENTRALIZATION AND THE LOCATION OF INDUSTRY

The location of industry within a city is more complex than the location of households. The location of households is explained by the access–space trade-off model suitably expanded to address other considerations mentioned in the previous section. The approach to industrial location is less unified, however. A theory which explains one type of firm will not explain the behaviour of other firms. Fortunately, our focus is not the location of industry *per se* but the spatial interaction of households and firms. Hence only a brief outline of the spatial theory of the urban firm and trends and patterns in urban employment location is required.

Trends and patterns in the location behaviour of enterprises in a city can be identified even if a comprehensive theory is elusive. In particular, the pattern of *employment decentralization* in cities has been identified in numerous empirical studies and has been the subject of considerable analysis and discussion. Employment decentralization constitutes an important stylized fact in urban studies either to be explained or as the point of departure for the analysis of other urban issues. A complete theory of urban structure must be able to explain employment decentralization and its effects on other aspects of urban structure. Thus residential location decisions must be understood when employment is decentralized.

It is useful to distinguish firms according to the effects of location on costs and revenues. Some firms are concerned about location in terms of costs. Manufacturing firms may focus on the transportation costs of inputs or outputs or a suitable site for a factory; offices may be concerned primarily with labour costs. Because the output of these firms is sold across the city or beyond, location affects costs much more than it does revenues. Other firms, such as retail outlets, are concerned about locations in terms of revenues. Inconvenient sites can deter customers regardless of the quality and price of the merchandise. A few firms may be concerned with both revenues and costs. Often, however, these firms are able to have separate locations for operations concerned with costs, such as manufacturing or warehousing, and operations concerned with revenues, such as retail outlets.

Those who analyse location as a means of reducing production costs emphasize interindustry linkages, transportation cost structures, and land prices. Vertically integrated firms—firms selling intermediate or final products to other firms—locate at the site of material inputs or of concentrated product demand, depending upon the transportation costs of inputs and outputs and the cost of land. Central city sites were initially preferred because of the transportation cost advantages of proximity to rail and water terminals. As truck transportation became viable these sites became less attractive because central sites were expensive owing to demand for the space from residential and other commercial users. Moreover, new manufacturing technology, particularly assembly lines, required more space. These factors tended to push firms out of the central city into the suburbs where new manufacturing and distribution processes could be implemented.

Other models ignore production cost but emphasize the control that a given site provides over nearby consumers by lowering the delivered price of the product. Hotelling's (1929) classic example of two ice-cream sellers on a beach may be generalized to most retail outlets and many personal and financial services. The greater the sensitivity of consumers to the delivered price, including the time and transportation costs to purchase the item, the more sellers will disperse to reduce the delivered price and increase sales. Firms view sites not in terms of their effect on production costs but their effect on revenues. Locations confer some monopoly power, since firms in convenient locations can raise prices above those of competing firms and still sell their product.

The pattern of industrial location will depend on the number of buyers and the nature of their demand for the product. Products will differ in terms of the market area required to generate sufficient sales for an adequate return to the firm. Thus small grocery stores need only a small market area, and consumers are fairly sensitive to price since they make repeated purchases. Furniture and appliance stores, on the other hand, need a larger market area and can expect less consumer sensitivity to a convenient location since consumers make these large purchases only occasionally. Hence grocery stores will be more dispersed within the urban area. A hierarchy of products will develop depending upon market area requirements with some goods being sold only in larger urban centres. Central place theory uses the concept of market thresholds to develop a hierarchy of cities; within cities it can be used to understand the pattern of location of retail industry (Berry, 1967; Kohsaka, 1986).

As population grows within a city, retail outlets will decentralize to provide consumers convenient access to products. Certain firms, such as grocery stores, will disperse widely; others, such as furniture and appliance stores, may not disperse at all until a city achieves a considerable size. A hierarchy of retail centres will emerge within a city. The largest concentration of retail activity will occur in the central business district, but other large commercial centres will emerge as a city grows. These will be accompanied by numerous smaller commercial centres dispersed throughout the city on busy traffic routes.

Not all firms are easily categorized as revenue-maximizers or cost-minimizers in terms of location behaviour. Some firms, such as head offices or regional offices of large companies, may be most concerned about locating close to the hub of business activity to enhance business contact with other firms. Much as households may be subject to social agglomeration forces, these firms may be subject to forces of agglomeration to ensure that important business information is exchanged with firms engaged in related activities (Evans, 1985, ch. 4). The forces for agglomeration in the central city of national or regional metropolises often override the forces for decentralization associated with high central city office rents.

Each of these theories provides some insight into the pervasive decentralization of employment in cities. Cost-conscious firms in manufacturing and wholesaling will often leave expensive and cramped central city sites as changes in transportation and production technology favour suburban industrial sites. Revenue-conscious firms in retail trades will often relocate in suburban commercial sites to provide shopping convenience and reduce the delivery price of goods. Even some offices will move all or part of their operations out of expensive central locations if the problem of face-to-face communications with other central firms is not serious or can be solved by splitting head-office functions (Wabe, 1966; Rhodes and Kan, 1971).

There is widespread evidence of rapid decentralization of employment in cities.[9] Mills (1972*a*, ch. 6; 1972*b*) and Kain (1968*b*) show the clear shift of employment from the central city to the suburban ring for SMSAs in the United States using census data. Population is more decentralized than employment, but retailing is almost as decentralized as population by Mills's measures. Retailing is followed closely by manufacturing as the most decentralized employment sector. Wholesaling and services are more heavily centralized. As Mills (1972*a*: 92) notes, however, his evidence is based on heavily aggregated data. In fact only the central city and suburbs are distinguished for employment data. Spatially disaggregated data would permit more careful examination of the location patterns of employment (and population) within urban areas.

Spatially disaggregated data for specific urban areas is available from transportation surveys such as the Greater London Transportation Survey and the Metropolitan Toronto Travel Survey described in section 2.1. As in section 2.1, Greater London and Toronto are divided into concentric zones, ordered in terms of distance from the city centre. The percentage of survey respondents employed and living in each zone, divided by the area of that zone, provides a measure of density independent of unit.[10] Following Mills, we can summarize the density gradient by estimating the following semilogarithmic linear model:

$$ln[D(r)] = ln[D(0)] + \delta r, \qquad (2.30)$$

where r is the distance of the concentric zone from the city centre, $D(r)$ is the density of the zone at distance r, $D(0)$ is the density at the city centre, and δ is the rate of decline of the density with increasing

---

[9] For a recent review of the literature, see Scott (1982).
[10] One could multiply each figure by the total number of respondents times the survey expansion factor to obtain actual densities per unit area.

TABLE 2.3. *Density of employment and population with distance from the city centre for Greater London, 1971–2, and Toronto, 1979*

Greater London			Toronto		
Distance (km)	Density		Distance (km)	Density	
	Empt.	Pop.		Empt.	Pop.
0–3	0.8913	0.0884	0–2	2.6579	0.4456
3–6	0.1379	0.1262	2–4	0.2387	0.3316
6–9	0.0686	0.0877	4–6	0.1576	0.2913
9–12	0.0586	0.0667	6–8	0.1251	0.1785
12–15	0.0377	0.0542	8–10	0.0831	0.0884
15–18	0.0357	0.0492	10–12	0.0709	0.0854
18–21	0.0226	0.0386	12–14	0.0392	0.0754
21–24	0.0174	0.0236	14–16	0.0334	0.0409
24–27	0.0089	0.0121	16–18	0.0159	0.0173
27–30	0.0026	0.0034	18–20	0.0038	0.0059
30–33	0.0002	0.0005	20–22	0.0015	0.0019
			22–24	0.0003	0.0014

Regression results, equation (2.30), t-values in parentheses

$l_n(D(0))$	0.3755	1.2257		0.4927	0.0455
	(0.69)	(2.44)		(1.17)	(0.15)
δ	− 0.2054	− 0.1476		− 0.3212	− 0.2648
	(7.23)	(5.59)		(10.52)	(11.77)
R^2	0.853	0.776		0.917	0.933

Sources: Greater London Transportation Survey, 1971; Metro Toronto Travel Survey, 1979.

distance from the centre. The access value of central city land implies a downward-sloping density gradient or a negative value for δ, since valuable central city land will be used most intensively. A smaller absolute value for δ implies a flatter density gradient and greater decentralization.

The results for Greater London and Metropolitan Toronto are summarized in Table 2.3. The Table provides density estimates for employment and residence or population for eleven concentric zones in Greater London and twelve concentric zones in Toronto. The concentric zone data is fitted to equation (2.30) using ordinary least squares regression to estimate δ and $ln[D(0)]$. Those results appear at the bottom of Table 2.3. A clear density gradient is observed for employment and population in each city. The coefficient δ is negative and

TABLE 2.4. *Density of employment with distance from the city centre for Greater London, 1971–2, by industrial category*

Distance (km)	Density			
	Manufacturing	Wholesale	Retail	Services
0–3	1.1601	0.5517	1.7083	0.6685
3–6	0.1981	0.1580	0.1226	0.1368
6–9	0.0722	0.0714	0.0467	0.0481
9–12	0.0500	0.0642	0.0313	0.0637
12–15	0.0299	0.0444	0.0279	0.0401
15–18	0.0228	0.0463	0.0293	0.0373
18–21	0.0174	0.0267	0.0136	0.0248
21–24	0.0120	0.0158	0.0085	0.0207
24–27	0.0073	0.0102	0.0062	0.0098
27–30	0.0011	0.0019	0.0013	0.0034
30–33	0.0000	0.0002	0.0000	0.0002

Regression results, equation (2.30), with t-*values*

$l_n(D(0))$	0.4872	0.3892	0.6766	0.5638
	(1.29)	(0.72)	(1.38)	(0.97)
δ	-0.1980	-0.2042	-0.1948	-0.1933
	(9.04)	(7.23)	(6.87)	(6.33)
R^2	0.911	0.853	0.855	0.816

Sources: Greater London Transportation Survey, 1971.

statistically significant in each case. Its value is smaller, and statistically significantly smaller, for population than employment in each city, consistent with findings that population is more decentralized than employment. The density gradient function (2.30) fits each set of data well. It explains 85 per cent of the variation in employment density and 78 per cent of the variation in population density in the Greater London data in Table 2.3. It explains 91 per cent of the variation in employment density and 93 per cent of the variation in population density in the Metropolitan Toronto data.

In each city employment density is highest in the city centre but a significant amount of employment is decentralized. In Greater London 46.6 per cent of employment is located within 9 kilometres of the city centre; in Toronto 63.3 per cent of employment is located within 8 kilometres of the city centre. Yet this leaves a substantial proportion of jobs outside the city centre, even broadly defined, many of them at or near the urban fringe.

The employment data for Greater London may be disaggregated by broad industrial category. Table 2.4 provides similar results to Table 2.3 for the four major industry groups—manufacturing, wholesale, retail, and services. The results are interesting in light of Mills's findings that retailing and manufacturing are more heavily decentralized than wholesaling and services. There is no significant difference in the rate of decline of employment density, represented by δ, among the four industry groups in Greater London. Thus no particular industrial sector appears to be leading the way in decentralizing employment in Greater London, at least at this very broad level of industrial classification.

The categorization of firms as cost-minimizers or revenue-maximizers provides a popular dynamic model of urban spatial growth and development (Hoover and Vernon, 1959; Lowry, 1964; Webster *et al.*, 1988). The model classifies firms as 'basic' if they locate independently of the intra-urban population pattern. Cost-minimizing firms in manufacturing and warehousing are therefore basic. Workers in these firms will locate according to the residential location model of the previous section based on such considerations as household income, family circumstances, and the number of workers in the household. Non-basic firms then locate to provide retail and other services to the population of workers in basic industries. The extent of decentralization of a non-basic firm will depend upon the product in accordance with the tenets of central place theory. Workers in these non-basic firms will in turn locate according to the same principles as previous workers in basic industries. These households then invite new non-basic firms to provide services to the expanded urban population. Workers in such firms will seek residential locations in the same fashion as other workers, generating new employment for non-basic industry. This iterative process continues until all urban workers are situated in terms of workplace and residential location.

Hoover and Vernon (1959) use this model to analyse the spatial development of the New York Metropolitan Area. They argue that manufacturing firms and other firms that locate independently of the spatial distribution of the population are pushed out of central locations as a result of their own growth and development. Growth and technological change result in outmoded structures on inadequate land sites in the central city as continuous material flow systems and automatic processing controls are developed which require single-storey plants on large land sites. Manufacturers are thereby forced to seek larger sites to remain competitive. Moreover, zoning restrictions in cities often inhibit industrial expansion. Nuisance industries are prevented from expanding and forced to seek an alternative site, often outside the city's current boundaries.

This decentralization of basic employment encourages workers in these industries to relocate in suburban sites nearer the workplace. The workers are provided with better access to work and cheaper suburban land. The decentralization of population will attract retail and service firms that depend upon proximity to the consumer for profitability. Thus urban growth and change involves employment decentralization, as well as population decentralization, as many firms seek larger and cheaper suburban land sites. This view is consistent with the common pattern of decentralization of employment in all four industrial groups observed for Greater London in Table 2.4.

Further insight into the process of urban employment dynamics may be provided by the theory of the central city as the incubator for new firms (Hoover and Vernon, 1959). Most new firms are small and specialized, seeking a niche in the market from which to expand. Such firms require the numerous specialized business services such as publicity and sales, information processing, financial services, and engineering and technical services. These services are available only in the central business district of large cities. Firms that succeed and grow will become more self-sufficient by incorporating many of these specialized services into the firm. They will also grow by adopting more sophisticated, capital-intensive production processes. As the attractions of the central city (its specialized services) decline, the handicaps of a central city location—expensive land, outmoded industrial sites, and congestion—grow in importance. This theory views the central city as an essential part of the economic process of wealth and employment creation but also, inevitably, as the donor of successful and growing enterprises to suburban areas. Employment decentralization is a fundamental part of the process of economic growth and change.

2.4   RESIDENTIAL LOCATION WITH DECENTRALIZED EMPLOYMENT

Decentralized employment makes residential location theory more complex because there is no unique spatial reference point. Neighbours in a suburban location may face very different trade-offs because their job locations differ. The worker whose job is decentralized can be much closer to his workplace than the neighbouring worker whose job is located in the city centre. Other factors held constant, the worker with a decentralized workplace is better off. In the extreme, if a worker is able to work from his home, he can ignore access completely and concentrate on land costs and housing.

From the standpoint of consumer theory something is missing. Every worker is better off in a decentralized workplace, and the farther from the centre the better. Firms in decentralized locations will find it easier to recruit workers, since they all prefer these jobs to central city ones. Firms in the central city will have to have higher wages than firms outside the central city to attract and maintain suitable employment levels. A wage gradient will emerge in a competitive labour market to offset the advantages of decentralized firms over centralized firms in attracting workers (Moses, 1962; Muth, 1969).

More specifically, for each worker there will exist a wage-offer gradient indicating the wage required to make the worker equally well off at each job location (White, 1988). Then, in a fashion identical to the allocation of workers to residential locations in a monocentric city, workers can be allocated to jobs by a competitive bidding process among firms. Just as land is allocated to the highest bidder, jobs are allocated to the lowest wage offer. Because transportation costs are positive, land rents decline with the distance of the residential site from the city centre. Wages also decline with the distance of the workplace from the city centre because more decentralized workplaces offer superior access–space trade-offs to all workers. The competitive bidding process in the labour market eliminates the gains to workers that decentralized workplaces would otherwise provide in the form of shorter commuting trips to work.

White (1988) draws several useful implications from this model. First, residential location depends upon workplace location as well as income and preferences. A household with low income may locate farther from the centre than a household with high income if the workplace of the low-income household is farther from the centre than the workplace of the high-income household. Residential location patterns are more complicated because of multiple determinants —not only income and factors representing household preferences, such as age of the household head and the presence of children mentioned earlier, but also workplace location. Secondly, lower wage rates in decentralized workplaces provide inducement for firms to decentralize in addition to those considerations mentioned earlier. Small firms are more likely to decentralize for this reason because 'firms which suburbanize drastically restrict the labour market area from which they hire workers' (White, 1988: 6). Firms with very skilled workers are also more likely to decentralize because very skilled workers attach a higher value (opportunity cost) to commuting time which generates a steeper wage-offer gradient and greater returns to the firm from decentralization. Thirdly, the model implies that longer commuting journeys are compensated by both lower land costs and higher wages. In this respect, the model synthesizes the views of urban and labour economists and makes an important contribution to our understanding of urban spatial structure.

Where do we go from here? What improvements are possible in the model of workplace and residential choice that has been introduced in recent years? It is the task of the remainder of this study to extend the model of workplace choice to provide a richer theoretical framework for the analysis of urban economic issues, just as the model of residential location has been enriched by Muth (1969), Evans (1973), and others. In the remainder of this chapter we look at criticisms of the standard model of urban spatial structure which suggest that extensions of the model are required. We then turn in subsequent chapters to a more complete model of workplace choice and the labour market in cities.

2.4.1 A formal model of residential location with decentralized workplaces*

Until recent years decentralized employment was accommodated in residential location models by assuming some predetermined work location for each household. Then commuting cost can simply be redefined in terms of distance or time to the work site rather than the city centre. Thus, if j is the distance of the job from the city centre and h is the distance of the home from the city centre, we may write commuting cost as

$$c = c(h, j), \quad \text{where } \frac{\partial c}{\partial h} > 0 \text{ and } \frac{\partial c}{\partial j} < 0. \tag{2.31}$$

We can then revise the basic residential location problem of equation (2.1) in a very straightforward fashion:

$$\max u(q, x)$$

subject to

$$p(h)q + x + c(h, j) = y \qquad (2.32)$$

where the land-price gradient $p(h)$ still refers to distance from the city centre, since the centre remains the preferred site. The solution to this problem satisfies the same conditions (2.2) and (2.3) as our initial problem, except for the inclusion of job location j as a parameter. In particular, the locational equilibrium condition (2.3) becomes

$$\frac{\partial p}{\partial h} = -\frac{\partial c(h, j)/\partial h}{q}. \qquad (2.33)$$

The equilibrium conditions do not change if, for example, $\partial^2 c/\partial h \partial j = 0$. Thus, in a strict model in which utility-maximizing households reside farther from the city centre than their place of work on a radial line from the city centre to obtain the lowest possible combination of commuting and land costs, commuting distance would be $h - j$ and, if commuting costs were proportional to distance, $\partial^2 c/\partial h \partial j = 0$. Equilibrium condition (2.33) is then equivalent to our original condition (2.3).

The problem is that all households prefer jobs located as far from the city centre as possible to reduce commuting costs. Thus workplace choice becomes an important decision for the household. The standard model is therefore modified again by introducing the concept of a wage gradient to leave identical workers indifferent among work locations. Workplace choice is thereby swept under the proverbial rug.

Recently, models have been developed which permit choice of both job and residential locations. Similar to equation (2.15), these models incorporate leisure in the utility function but ignore the effect of labour supply on commuting costs and earnings (Straszheim, 1984; White, 1988):

$$\max u[q(h, j), x(h, j), l(h, j)]$$

subject to

$$p(h)q(h, j) + x(h, j) + w(j)l(h, j)$$
$$= w(j)T + y - [c(h, j) + w(j)t(h, j)]. \qquad (2.34)$$

In this specification we allow all decision variables to depend upon both the residential and workplace locations, except the land-rent gradient $p(h)$ and the wage gradient $w(j)$—that is, we assume $\partial p/\partial j = 0$ and $\partial w/\partial h = 0$ as in White (1988).[11]

The model generates the usual conditions equivalent to Equations

---

[11] For justification of this specification see White (1988: 138).

(2.16) and (2.17). Using those conditions, the locational equilibrium conditions for the places of residence and work can be written as

$$\frac{\partial p}{\partial h} = -\frac{\partial c/\partial h + w\partial t/\partial h}{q} \tag{2.35}$$

and

$$\frac{\partial w}{\partial j} = \frac{\partial c/\partial j + w\partial t/\partial j}{T - t - l} = \frac{\partial c/\partial j + w\partial t/\partial j}{L}, \tag{2.36}$$

where $L(h, j) = T - t - l$ is hours worked as in equation (2.15).

Condition (2.35) appears to be equivalent to equation (2.18) when labour supply is ignored such that $\partial L/\partial h = 0$. The one important difference is that the wage rate varies by job location as indicated by equation (2.36). If $\partial c/\partial j < 0$ and $\partial t/\partial j < 0$ as expected,[12] $\partial w/\partial j < 0$ in equation (2.36), implying negatively sloped wage gradients. In fact, expressions (2.35) and (2.36) allow us to relate the wage and land-price gradients:

$$\frac{\partial w/\partial j}{w} = \frac{pq}{wL}\left(-\frac{\partial c/\partial j + w\partial t/\partial j}{\partial c/\partial h + w\partial t/\partial h}\right)\frac{\partial p/\partial h}{p}. \tag{2.37}$$

White (1988) specifies round-trip commuting cost to be $c(h, j) = 2m(h - j)$, where m is direct commuting cost per unit of distance, and round-trip commuting time to be $t(h, j) = 2s(h - j)$, where s is commuting time cost per unit of distance. One-way commuting distance is always $h - j$. In this case,

$$-(\partial c/\partial j + w\partial t/\partial j) = 2m + 2sw = \partial c/\partial h + w\partial t/\partial h \tag{2.38}$$

and the relative gradient decline is determined by the ratio of housing costs to earnings, pq/wL, or about 25 per cent. White concludes that wage-offer curves will be negatively sloped and will decline at about one-quarter of the rate that rent-offer curves decline.

This model allows us to consider the effect of job location on the bid-rent schedule of the household by differentiating equation (2.35) with respect to job location j:

$$\frac{\partial}{\partial j}\left(\frac{\partial p}{\partial h}\right) = \left[-\frac{1}{q}\left(\frac{\partial^2 c}{\partial h\partial j} + \frac{\partial w}{\partial j}\frac{\partial t}{\partial h} + w\frac{\partial^2 t}{\partial h\partial j}\right) - \left(\frac{\partial c}{\partial h} + w\frac{\partial t}{\partial h}\right)\left(-\frac{\partial q/\partial j}{q^2}\right)\right]$$

$$= \frac{1}{q}\left(\frac{\partial p}{\partial h}\frac{\partial q}{\partial j} - \frac{\partial^2 c}{\partial h\partial j} - \frac{\partial w}{\partial j}\frac{\partial t}{\partial h} - w\frac{\partial^2 t}{\partial h\partial j}\right).$$

[12] Households in this model are assumed to locate on a radial line from the origin through their job location, but farther out than their job location, which implies that $\partial c/\partial j < 0$ and $\partial t/\partial j < 0$ as required.

This expression cannot be signed with any confidence. Even with White's simple specifications for $c(\cdot)$ and $t(\cdot)$, such that $\partial^2 c/\partial h\partial j = \partial^2 t/\partial h\partial j = 0$, we have that

$$\frac{\partial}{\partial j}\left(\frac{\partial p}{\partial h}\right) = \frac{1}{q}\left(\frac{\partial p}{\partial h}\frac{\partial q}{\partial j} - \frac{\partial w}{\partial j}\frac{\partial t}{\partial h}\right) \qquad (2.39)$$

which cannot be signed without signing $\partial q/\partial j$. Since $\partial w/\partial j < 0$ and $\partial t/\partial h > 0$, the second expression is negative. If $\partial q/\partial j \leq 0$, then $\partial/\partial j(\partial p/\partial h) > 0$ and bid-rent curves become flatter as households' job locations become more decentralized. Thus otherwise identical households may have different rent offer curves solely because their job locations differ such that households with different job locations segregate into different concentric residential rings. Households with workers in the city centre outbid suburban workers for sites located closer to the centre and in-commuting predominates. White (1988: 143) concludes:

The most likely pattern (but not the only one possible) appears to be that households locate in concentric residential rings in order of the centrality of their workers' job locations. This means that, in equilibrium, households' residential and job locations will be nonnegatively related to each other.

Under the circumstances, the effect of job location on commuting distance is unclear. The greater the number of workers in the city centre relative to suburban employment locations, the farther out workers at the suburban work sites are forced to live, so that commuting distance may be positively or negatively related to job location, other factors equal.[13]

This model provides a good starting-point for analysis of workplace choice. Once decentralized employment is admitted to the standard model of urban spatial structure, workplace choice must be introduced. In the model in this section, residential and workplace location are determined simultaneously so that the locational equilibrium (h^*, j^*) may be written as a solution to equations (2.35) and (2.36) in terms of the parameters of the system, namely

$$h^* = h\left[q(\cdot), l(\cdot), p(\cdot), w(\cdot), c(\cdot), t(\cdot); y, j^*\right] \qquad (2.40)$$

$$j^* = j\left[q(\cdot), l(\cdot), p(\cdot), w(\cdot), c(\cdot), t(\cdot); y, h^*\right]. \qquad (2.41)$$

Note that it is not possible to distinguish these two equations in terms

---

[13] i.e. this proposition would hold for all workers regardless of skill level and all households regardless of income.

of explanatory factors, since the two equations contain the same list of determinants. This result is not surprising—we cannot obtain two distinct solutions from the same consumer problem without further restrictions. In econometric terms, the equations above are not identified. This clearly complicates empirical work and invites further specification of the behavioural relationships for residential and workplace location. In Chapters 3 and 4 we address this problem by developing a more complete treatment of the urban labour market and its role in the analysis of urban spatial structure. We then return to empirical analysis of location decisions in Chapter 5.

White (1988) draws some interesting implications from her model. She argues that households with more income will commute farther, as in the monocentric city, but that residential location will be segregated on the basis of workplace location. As a result, the ring of households in any particular income group commuting to a particular ring of workplace locations may be 'thin' and households may only be indifferent to residential location within this narrow ring. If we introduce dimensions of household heterogeneity—such as family composition, age of the household head, and the presence of a second earner as discussed earlier—then these rings will become considerably thinner. White argues that more skilled workers will have higher wages and attach a higher value to commuting time as in expression (2.29). This in turn raises the wage-offer curve of skilled workers in expression (2.36)—they demand higher wages as compensation for longer in-commuting. Firms therefore have a stronger incentive to locate in the suburbs the larger is the skilled workforce as a proportion of total costs. Hence wage-offer curves, and therefore wage gradients, will be steeper for skilled workers.

2.5 CRITICS OF URBAN SPATIAL THEORY

It is easy to criticize any theory. A theory is an admittedly simplified view of the world designed to focus on specific important aspects of an issue and the focus precludes consideration of many other less important factors. The omitted factors provide an easy target for critics to argue that the theory is incomplete, unrealistic, or concentrating on the wrong factors. It is more difficult, but also more useful, to demonstrate that the predictions of a theory are false and that extensions of the theory, or alternative theories, can be formulated to provide predictions which are not false.

Several implied criticisms of the basic access–space trade-off theory of Alonso (1964) have already been mentioned in this chapter. We have also seen, however, that the basic model can be extended with some added complexity to address much of the criticism. In particular, decentralized workplaces and labour supply and demographic considerations have been incorporated into the basic model. The consideration of other factors, such as the durability of housing, social agglomeration, and the influence of local government policy, may also be warranted. Such extensions emphasize the value of the basic theory as a good starting-point for the analysis of urban structure.

Researchers have found some evidence which appears to be inconsistent with the basic model. Wheaton (1977), for example, finds that the demand for land and the opportunity cost of travel appear to increase at a similar rate with income in San Francisco. Under these conditions other factors, such as housing market externalities and the fiscal incentives of municipal fragmentation, may be more important than consumer choice in explaining residential location, although Hekman (1980) provides an explanation of Wheaton's results based on a model of residential choice and labour supply as discussed earlier. Other authors have argued that the urban land-rent gradient does not decline with distance from the city centre, as the Alonso model predicts (Kain, 1975; Jackson, 1979).

Such criticism is not a primary concern for our purposes, however. Our primary concern is the interaction between workplace and place of residence, not the residential location decision *per se* or its ramifications. We are therefore particularly interested in the adequacy of the basic model with regard to the explanation of commuting patterns. The basic model argues that commuting patterns are primarily determined by income, land rent, and commuting costs for a predetermined workplace location. Yet actual patterns of commuting analysed in a number of studies appear to be incompatible with this prediction.

Kain (1975) divided Detroit into six concentric rings. He found that workers in better-paid occupations were less likely to live in the ring in which they work regardless of workplace location. This is consistent with the trade-off theory for inner rings but not for outer rings. Workers who work in the outermost ring are expected to live in the outermost ring since it provides both cheap land and access to work. This is particularly true for workers in better-paid occupations since they are assumed to have stronger preferences for cheap land in the outermost ring and stronger preferences for short commuting trips because they place higher value on commuting time (Wales, 1978; White, 1988). Yet, in Kain's results, workers in better-paid occupations are as likely to settle in the ring in which they work whether they work in the innermost or outermost ring of Detroit.[14] Similarly, Duncan (1956) found earlier that manual workers in Chicago travelled shorter distances to work than non-manual workers regardless of workplace location despite the fact that manual workers are paid less than non-manual workers. Manual workers with workplaces in the city centre travelled 22 per cent less distance on average than non-manual workers with workplaces in the centre, but 26 per cent less distance when manual and non-manual workers with workplaces outside the city centre were compared. Outside the city centre where the land-rent gradient is less steep, gains from greater commuting in terms of cheaper land are smaller. Hence, higher-paid non-manual workers should reduce their commuting relative to manual workers but the opposite is found.

This pattern of commuting is not confined to cities in the United States. Simpson (1977, ch. 3) found similar results for Greater London and the South-East Lancashire Conurbation in the United Kingdom. Workers in better-paid occupations are still less likely to live in the same borough as they work whether the workplace is in the city centre or the farthest suburbs. Mean commuting distance is estimated to be relatively greater for better-paid occupations in the outermost boroughs as Duncan found for Chicago. These tests use aggregate data and very simple statistical techniques. Complicating factors are largely ignored. The tests do, however, suggest that other important factors may be involved in determining urban spatial structure.

Hamilton (1982) examines the basic trade-off theory in a different manner. Decentralization of employment in cities reduces the required commuting distance, but commuting distance is minimized only if each worker lives on the suburban portion of the ray connecting the city centre, the workplace, and the residential location. Otherwise a job exchange or housing exchange can improve the welfare of those involved in the exchange. Suppose that a worker lives closer to the city centre than his workplace. Then he can improve his welfare by finding any house on the ray from the city centre through his

---

[14] One possible criticism is that Kain's study really does not cover suburban Detroit. Higher-paid workers who work in the outermost ring are living farther from the city centre as predicted in 'bedroom suburbs' outside the Detroit SMSA and the purview of Kain's study.

workplace which is farther out and closer to his workplace. If the house he finds is occupied by a worker in the city centre, both workers are better off if they exchange houses, since each worker will be closer to his workplace. Ideally, these exchanges should continue until they are no longer mutually advantageous. At that point each worker will live on the opposite side of the radial line connecting the city centre, his workplace, and his place of residence.

Although decentralization of employment reduces required commuting distance for urban workers it also can lead to 'wasteful commuting', which is not possible in a monocentric city. Hamilton calculates the minimum average commuting distance required in cities in the United States and Japan from estimated population and employment-density gradients. He compares this distance to the actual average commuting distance from survey data. Commuters in the United States require a minimum average commuting trip of 1.1 miles, but actually commute an average of 8.7 miles. The minimum commuting trip in Japan is 1.8 miles compared to an observed average trip of at least 6 miles. Hamilton concludes that the basic theory predicts location patterns and consequent commuting distances very poorly. Commuters in the United States travel about eight times as far as necessary and commuters in Japan travel about three times as far as necessary. The difference in the degree of wasteful commuting may be attributed to the greater population density in Japanese cities.

Hamilton's assumptions may be questioned even in terms of the basic trade-off theory of residential location decisions. Consumers are concerned with space (land and housing) as well as access (commuting costs) and their preferences for land and housing are an important element of the basic model. Rich households may choose long commuting trips, regardless of workplace location, in return for the benefits of suburban housing. Thus long commuting trips are not wasteful but an expression of housing preferences despite commuting costs (White, 1986). Hamilton does not argue, however, that income and preferences do not matter. He argues that the theory implies that each worker will live on the opposite side of his workplace from the city centre. This clearly permits rich workers to live farther from a given workplace than poor workers, but it does not permit rich workers working in the city centre to live as far out as rich workers working in decentralized employment locations. Yet if a rich worker receives a wage premium because he works in the centre, he may decide to spend that income on space rather than access if his preferences for space are strong. Hamilton's calculations may thereby overstate wasteful commuting arising from the choice of residential location, but this is unlikely to account fully for the wasteful commuting observed.

Hamilton acknowledges other problems. Housing and jobs are heterogeneous and similar individuals and jobs may locate close together, reflecting social and commercial agglomeration effects discussed earlier. Central cities may primarily contain high-income jobs and low-income housing while suburbs may primarily contain low-income jobs and high-income housing. Rich workers will be unwilling to move into low-income housing areas and unable to find suburban jobs.[15] Poor workers will be unable to find central city jobs or suburban housing that they can afford (Kain, 1968a).[16] Hamilton concedes that this problem is relevant, but denies that it could explain wasteful commuting. He notes that central city and suburban incomes differ, but only by a modest 15 per cent in the United States. The spatial segregation of workers and jobs required to explain wasteful commuting is much larger than this.

Two-worker households have been ignored. Hamilton notes, however, that there are opposing effects in the model. The second worker in a household is unable to minimize commuting distance. The two workers could, of course, minimize collective commuting costs but this would still lead to longer commuting than predicted by the model for two one-worker households unless both household members worked at the same location. Thus wasteful commuting is overstated. The offsetting effect, however, is that two-worker households are likely to locate closer to the city centre. This means that the density gradient of workers is steeper than the density gradient for the population used to determine the average minimum commuting trip required. Thus Hamilton's calculations overstate the average minimum commuting trip and understate wasteful commuting as well. The implication is that the net effect is unlikely to be large enough to affect his conclusions.

The criticism of the basic trade-off model of urban spatial structure is weak in two respects. First, the empirical evidence is rudimentary.

[15] Why do high-income jobs not relocate in the suburbs? In some cases, such as the financial service industry, there may be other factors affecting location that override labour costs as discussed earlier. Firms are willing to pay a wage premium, as well as a land rent premium, to locate centrally.

[16] This requires some argument that poor workers are prohibited from purchasing small amounts of suburban land and erecting affordable housing. Zoning laws are not an answer in themselves. Why are such zoning laws enacted throughout suburban areas?

Commuting patterns ignore important factors such as two-worker households and household income. The individual travel patterns are examined by aggregate data, inviting aggregation bias and making it difficult to assess the influence of other factors. Multivariate empirical analysis using disaggregated data would provide more compelling evidence. Nevertheless, the extensive empirical evidence contradicting the basic model, however rudimentary, invites further investigation of the theory of urban spatial structure. Secondly, no alternative theory is provided. The critics do not even offer, never mind test, an alternative model of commuting travel. Can a simple alternative model, or a simple extension of the basic model, overcome many of the suggested deficiencies? If so, what are the crucial weaknesses or omissions of the theory that must be addressed?

2.6   WORKPLACE CHOICE AND URBAN STRUCTURE

Effective criticism of a model often leads to extensions and new insights. For example, the basic model of residential location and urban structure has been extended to consider the supply of housing in the Muth–Mills model (Brueckner, 1987) to provide a more complete treatment of urban land-use in a monocentric city. Extensions to consider markets other than land and housing may also provide useful insights. We argue that it is time to shift the focus to crucial aspects of labour market behaviour that have been ignored by the basic model and by urban scholars in general—in particular, the *choice of workplace* by urban workers. In the basic model with centralized employment workplace choice cannot occur but, once the basic model is extended to include decentralized employment, workplace choice must be considered. Models to date, however, have only considered labour supply behaviour arising from the consumer choice problem in a rudimentary fashion. Further examination of workplace choice behaviour and the role of the labour market in the analysis of urban structure and urban issues is required.

Emphasis to date on the choice of residential location rather than workplace choice to analyse urban structure could well be misplaced. Consider, for example, the frequency with which residential and workplace choice decisions are made. Workers are likely to be faced with workplace choice decisions more often than residential location decisions because rates of employment separation exceed rates of residential relocation. Simpson (1980) finds that 21.1 per cent of workers in Greater London in 1971 changed jobs in the previous year while only 10.6 per cent changed place of residence. This is not surprising, since the cost of a residential move is considerably higher than the cost of a change in employment. What is surprising is that such a prominent phenomenon as workplace choice has received little or no attention.

Authors have acknowledged this gap in the theory of urban spatial structure. Hamilton (1982: 1046), for example, is quite explicit in suggesting reasons for the poor performance of the basic model:

Some people may have found it in their interest to change jobs . . . and found new jobs which did not conform to the optimization rules. Then, if moving cost exceeds the present value of the wasteful commute, the optimum behavior is to endure the wasteful commute. According to this model, the mean commute should be a weighted average of the optimum and random commutes . . . Empirically the weights seem to be .75 and .25, which suggests that a disequilibrium model would be much more useful than the available equilibrium model.

Other authors have emphasized circumstances in which workplace choice decisions are likely to dominate residential location decisions because of high residential moving costs. Home-owners face greater moving costs than renters and may be less residentially mobile because of the costs of selling and purchasing a house (Hughes and McCormick, 1981). The second worker in a household[17] faces greater moving costs than does a worker in a single-worker household because of the commuting cost implications of a move for the primary worker (Beesley and Dalvi, 1974). These circumstances, home-ownership and multi-earner families, are sufficiently common in modern market-orientated economies to be concerned about their implications.

Still other authors have emphasized the need for a dynamic model of urban structure. Vickerman (1984) argues that a crucial component of a dynamic model is migration decisions, both inter-urban and intra-urban. Such migration models adapt labour supply theory, especially human capital and job search theory, to explain spatial choices (Gordon and Lamont, 1982; Gordon and Vickerman, 1982; Linneman and Graves, 1983). The task then is to understand both workplace and

---

[17] The second worker earns less money and/or works less steadily than the primary worker in the household. In this sense the second worker's impact on the residential location decision is smaller. The second worker is likely to be a wife or, in some cases, a young adult living with parents.

residential location behaviour and their interrelationship within and between cities (Weinberg, 1979; Linneman and Graves, 1983). This is clearly a call for a theory of workplace choice.

A gap exists in the theory of urban structure which requires a theory of workplace choice to be integrated with the theory of residential and employment location in a city with decentralized employment. The gap has been widely acknowledged but also widely ignored. Hamilton's argument above recognizes the important role of workplace choice decisions but regards them as generating 'random commutes' in a 'disequilibrium model'. Siegel (1975) finds that workplace location is, if anything, more responsive to residential location than residential location is to workplace location from household interview data in the San Francisco Bay Area. His reasoning, however, is weak: 'the household is induced to separate its home and job location in favour of a job location closer to the relevant geographic employment center' (p. 34).

We have seen in this chapter that the introduction of residential location models with decentralized employment necessitates some analysis of workplace choice. White's (1988) model provides the basis for a synthesis between the views of urban economists, who focus on the trade-off between commuting and land costs, and labour economists, who focus on the compensation for time spent commuting. A simple mental experiment suggests that the synthesis is far from complete, however. Picture two cities of equal size, each with a central business district and a suburban employment centre. Now suppose that most of the employment in one city is contained in the city centre but that the other city's employment is much more decentralized; its suburban employment centre is almost as large as its central business district. Ask yourself whether residential and workplace location, commuting patterns, and wage and land-rent gradients would be the same in these two cities. If your answer, like mine, is no then we both recognize that the *spatial distribution of labour demand* is a crucial issue in understanding many aspects of urban structure. Existing models such as White's cannot deal with this issue satisfactorily because they only consider consumer behaviour and labour supply. Thus White's model determines the wage at which a worker is willing to work at any workplace location, given his residential location. Whether the worker accepts a job at that location then depends on a matching offer from a firm at that location, which can only be considered by introducing labour demand in a meaningful way. Moreover, as we shall see, the rudimentary treatment of labour supply and workplace choice in the residential location model ignores an important body of recent research on information, job search, and job matching in labour economics.

3

INFORMATION, SEARCH, AND MATCHING: A SURVEY

WE have argued that urban spatial economics requires a theory explaining how workers find jobs in cities. How can such a theory be formulated? Fortunately, the job search behaviour of workers has been studied extensively in recent years, permitting us to begin by drawing upon a large and powerful body of economic theory—the economics of information in general and theories of job search and job matching in particular.

Conventional job search analysis must be extended, however. Standard theory gives very little attention to spatial issues despite the implicit importance of spatial considerations in search behaviour. Has job search theory dealt adequately with spatial issues? Do we understand the 'where' as well as the 'how' of job search? Can analysis of where workers find jobs give us new insights into how workers find jobs? These largely forgotten issues in the job search literature are the focus of this survey chapter and subsequent chapters.

Chapter 3 selectively surveys the literature, restricting the survey to developments which help us to formulate a theory in Chapters 4 and 5 explaining how workers find jobs in urban space. This selection includes the model of job search that is now well established in economics textbooks, as well as more recent research on job matching. It also includes the so-called 'island economy' which can provide our theory with an explicit spatial dimension for further development and empirical testing. The selection excludes more recent developments in the economics of information which do not contribute to this study such as the literature on screening (Blaug, 1976) and signalling (Spence, 1974), on person-specific information and agency (MacDonald, 1984), on implicit contracts (Rosen, 1985), and on job search and consumption (Seater, 1977), and other contributions to microeconomic theory (McKenna, 1985, ch. 6). These exclusions render the survey manageable in a single chapter.

3.1 INFORMATION AND THE LABOUR MARKET

A primary concern of economics is the study of the process by which markets allocate scarce resources among competing wants. A central issue is the capability of the market to convey signals, usually prices, which eliminate excess demand or supply of the product in question when there is no government interference and when buyers and sellers are numerous. This naturally leads to the study of the manner in which these signals (that is, information) are gathered and used.

Arrow (1959) pointed out the inconsistencies in an economic theory which ignores the problem of market coordination. If each buyer and seller takes prices as given to determine consumption and production decisions, then who determines the equilibrium prices? That is, who determines the prices which eliminate excess supply and demand in all markets? All or a subset of buyers and sellers must be price-setters operating under imperfect information about the equilibrium price and about market responses to the range of prices from which they might choose. Actual markets involve price setting and price bargaining or what Arrow refers to as 'a shifting set of bilateral monopolies' (p. 47) which involve some degree of price indeterminacy.

The important question is not whether economic theory has ignored elements of reality, but whether and how these omissions matter. This obviously is a much more difficult question but one to which considerable attention has been devoted in recent years. The economics of information and search examines the manner in which market signals are generated and how they affect economic behaviour. It is therefore at the heart of the study of market coordination and the analysis of economic problems associated with market performance.

Arrow (1974) subsequently speculated that economic behaviour under imperfect information might be particularly relevant to the analysis of the labour market. Two considerations account for this prediction. First, labour is non-standardized or heterogeneous. Workers vary with regard to many relevant characteristics including schooling, experience, on-the-job training, physical ability, mental ability, employment preferences, attitudes, determination, and leadership. Jobs differ according to their requirements of these factors as well as working conditions, wages and fringe benefits, location, and other elements of that elusive objective known as job satisfaction. As a result, more than in most other markets, the identification of appropriate transactions by sellers (workers) and buyers (firms) is complex and prone to error. Information costs are high because of the many dimensions of a job–worker match to be considered, but this also raises the potential gains from acquiring information that improves the job match. The enormous information industry in the labour market—including public and private employment agencies, newspapers, and trade magazines—provides testimony for this argument.

Secondly, the nature of labour services dictates that the technology of information transfer is primitive with regard to many non-pecuniary aspects of the job–worker match. The information industry can rapidly transmit data on starting salaries, qualifications (such as schooling and previous work experience), and job responsibilities. Information on remaining important aspects of the job environment cannot easily be conveyed other than by person-to-person contact, necessitating employment interviews and accounting for their continuing importance as a source of information about jobs and workers. In an era when financial and other markets are making extensive use of technological advances in communications to provide the latest information on prices, product availability, and product characteristics from around the world, the labour market continues to rely on relatively expensive employee interviews in much more localized markets. Since information that can only be obtained by interviews will apparently continue to be valuable in the job–worker match, the labour market will be unable to take full advantage of cost-reducing developments in communications technology available to many other markets. It is the nature of the labour market that makes the costs of search, related to the *spatial* barriers between buyers and sellers in the market, important and ensures that decisions will be made without the prohibitive cost of full information even in narrowly defined local markets.

3.2 BASIC THEORY OF JOB SEARCH

Stigler (1961, 1962) began formal analysis of information in the economy.[1] He considered the simple, but still informative, case of an economic agent faced with a known probability distribution of wage offers for labour services. The agent knows the wage distribution but does not know which offer will be made when any particular employer is contacted. In effect, he is viewed as making a random draw

---

[1] For a discussion of the analysis of job search prior to Stigler, see Feinberg (1978*b*).

from the distribution of wage offers, which permits basic statistical theory to be applied.

From an economic standpoint, the crucial notion is that the distribution of available wage offers provides a benefit to information acquisition, or job search, in the form of an expected increase in the wage offer as each offer is received. A wage offer, as a unit of information, can be viewed as a good whose primary cost is the cost of the time spent searching for it. Regardless of the form of the distribution of wage offers, each additional search can be expected to yield a smaller marginal benefit in the form of an expected improvement in the highest wage offer received (Simpson, 1977, ch. 2). When the benefits from additional search no longer exceed the costs from additional search, information acquisition should stop if the objective is to maximize the net returns from search. Thus knowing the distribution of wage offers and the personal costs of search, a job-seeker may determine the number of searches—or offers—which will be expected to achieve maximum net returns.

The analysis by Stigler was only an instructive first step. Stigler's job-seeker can formulate not only a search period associated with the maximum expected net return but also an expected best wage offer. Suppose, then, that a wage offer at least as good as the expected best offer is received before the search period is over. Further search would be inappropriate since a better offer is unlikely and the expected net return to continued search would be negative. Thus a superior strategy is to formulate an acceptable, or reservation, wage offer and adopt an optimal-stopping rule (McCall, 1965). If the reservation wage offer is matched or exceeded, accept it and stop the search. The rule is optimal because, given the distribution of future offers, the gain from another search does not justify the cost.

Subsequent research has concentrated on the optimal-stopping rule, or sequential search. Although the model can be extended to situations in which the assumed distribution of wage offers is unknown (McCall, 1970), some have argued that the model is suboptimal when even modest errors between the expected and actual wage distribution are realized (Gastwirth, 1976). Moreover, Burdett and Judd (1983) find sequential search to be incompatible with search equilibrium when all individuals face search costs. Such considerations may give rise to more complex rules. Gastwirth's 'truncation rule' is a hybrid of sequential search and Stigler's optimal-search-length rule: Search until a predetermined reservation wage is offered or, if a predetermined search length has been reached, choose the maximum offer received. Alternatively, Gal *et al.* (1981) and Morgan (1983) specify a 'simultaneous search model' in which each individual chooses a reservation wage as in sequential search and the number of job applications to send out. This model receives empirical support for young workers in the United States (Stern, 1989). While more complex search models may reflect actual search behaviour, however, the sequential search model constitutes a useful basis for analysis of economic behaviour.

Several interesting and testable predictions arise from the basic sequential job search model, focusing on the marginal benefits and costs of search. Factors which increase the expected variation in wage offers raise the benefits to search, leading to higher reservation wages and longer searches. Feinberg (1978*a*), for example, found that individuals facing wage distributions with larger means and standard deviations, defined in terms of the individual's occupation and urban area of residence, did indeed have larger reservation wages and increased search duration. Factors which lower search costs also lead to higher reservation wages and longer searches (Feinberg, 1977, 1978*a*; Mellow, 1978).

The role of search costs is particularly interesting for our purposes. In Feinberg (1977), for example, higher travel costs to work raise the reservation wage and reduce search duration. The other major factor in Feinberg's study is unemployment benefits which reduce search costs and lengthen search. The positive correlation between unemployment benefits and search duration has been widely explored (Mortensen, 1986: 866) but travel costs and the spatial aspects of search have been largely ignored.

3.2.1 Basic model of sequential search[*]

The basic model assumes that a job-seeker faces a known distribution of wage offers given by the density function $f(w)$ and the distribution function $F(w)$, where w is the wage offer. For a single time-period, the job-seeker chooses a reservation wage, w^*, such that

$$\int_{w^*}^{\infty} [w - w^*] f(w) \, dw = c, \qquad (3.1)$$

where c is the marginal cost of search. The left-hand side of equation (3.1) is the marginal benefit of search, which is simply the marginal expected gain from search when the first offer above w^* is accepted. As c rises, w^* must fall to maintain equality in equation (3.1). This in turn increases the probability of finding an acceptable wage, $1 - F(w^*)$, and shortens the search.

Simple extensions include allowance for a specified offer arrival rate λ, which may vary according to economic conditions and individual characteristics, and replacement of the wage offer by a value function $V(w)$ to incorporate expected future benefits from search. Thus in a short period of length Δt the probability of an offer arriving is approximately $\lambda \Delta t$ and the value of that offer is $V(w)$. For an infinite horizon with fixed interest rate ι, $V(w) = w/\iota$. Then equation (3.1) becomes

$$\frac{\lambda}{\iota} \int_{w^*}^{\infty} [w - w^*] f(w) \, dw = c. \tag{3.2}$$

The solution to equation (3.2) gives the reservation wage w^* as before, provided that the individual chooses to search. If w^* does not exceed the value of non-search activity ('leisure'), b, then an individual may withdraw from job search. If, for example, the offer arrival rate, λ, declines such that w^* must also decline given c, then job-seekers may be discouraged from job search. Similarly, an increase in social assistance payments will raise b and may discourage search.[2]

As in equation (3.1), changes in search costs, c, will directly affect job search. Higher search costs will lower the reservation wage and reduce the duration of search, and vice versa. Search costs are often given very little attention, but they will be a central issue in our analysis of search behaviour for the simple reason that an important component of search costs is spatial, or transportation, costs. We can immediately associate search costs with the direct spatial costs of attracting an offer, which may include one or more trips to a prospective job site, and the implied commuting costs of the job or the implied residential moving costs should the job be chosen. In Chapter 2 we specified travel costs to be a function of distance to the job, h, and earnings $y = w^*$. Thus, we may now write

$$c = c(h, w^*), \frac{\partial c}{\partial h} > 0, \frac{\partial c}{\partial w^*} > 0 \tag{3.3}$$

[2] Such increases may arise under current programmes that raise social assistance when an additional child is born to a single mother. It may then no longer be profitable to work given the high tax-back rates under social assistance in most jurisdictions, i.e. $w^* < b$. Other factors, such as child-care costs, may also reduce the effective return from work.

to indicate that more distant jobs imply higher search costs. The specification of spatial costs has two immediate implications. First, individuals will seek closer jobs, other factors equal.[3] Secondly, as individuals seek more distant jobs as search progresses, the reservation wage must decline to raise marginal search benefits and reduce the implied time costs of travel. Mortensen (1986: 859–60) notes that evidence indicates that the reservation wage declines as search proceeds. He explains this phenomenon by assuming that workers are liquidity-constrained, but another explanation arises directly from the consideration of the spatial nature of search costs. Job-seekers sample nearby jobs first and, if they are unsuccessful, more distant and costly searches are conducted which imply a lower reservation wage. Thus we see that spatial considerations can immediately extend our understanding of the job search process.

In Chapter 4, we focus directly on the spatial issues in job search. For now, however, we turn to other useful extensions of the conventional economics of information and job search—namely job matching and the island economy.

3.3 JOB MATCHING

Job matching extends the search for information about employment beyond the acceptance of a wage offer. Since labour is heterogeneous, finding a suitable match of workers and jobs is complex and subject to error. A worker continues to learn about a job's conditions and requirements while performing its tasks and an employer continues to learn about a worker's abilities and motivation from his performance of those tasks. As new information is accumulated, the suitability of the match is reassessed. If the worker is dissatisfied, he quits; if the employer is dissatisfied, the worker is discharged. Either form of job turnover will lead to renewed job search. A worker's employment history can therefore be viewed as a series of job searches and job matches.

Consistent with models of job search, information acquisition is viewed as a random draw from a known probability distribution (Johnson, 1978; Jovanovic, 1979; Flinn, 1986). In the case of job matching, wage offers are replaced by a factor informing the worker and employer of the value of the job match. The factor provides only

---

[3] In particular, this assumes that the probability distribution of wage offers is the same at all locations, i.e. $Prob\ [w > w^*] = 1 - F(w^*)$ does not vary spatially.

imperfect information, since the true value of the match can only be estimated, but the true value of the match is more accurately estimated as more information is received. One draw is made each period of employment so that more information (more draws) requires a longer period of employment. In this fashion the worker and employer learn over time by obtaining more information to assess the value of the job match more accurately. In each period the accumulated information is used to decide whether a separation (quit or discharge) is warranted. If a separation is not warranted, employment and accumulation of information about the job continues.[4]

The job-matching literature captures an important feature of information acquisition in the labour market. Information acquisition does not stop once a job has been accepted because the terms and conditions of employment and the worker's suitability for the job are uncertain. Much of this uncertainty can be alleviated only by experiencing the job and reassessing the situation as expectations are confirmed or rejected. In this sense workers must try out jobs and employers must try out workers. Job search is only part of the story because it is limited to information acquisition prior to actually experiencing the job.

The job-matching model explains a number of important labour market phenomena. It provides an explanation for turnover resulting from inappropriate job matches at all stages of the business cycle. This turnover, which occurs in good as well as bad business conditions, reflects the process by which the market may allocate labour to its best available use. Turnover related to the business cycle is ignored only for analytical convenience and can be appended or integrated to provide a complete theory. It also explains the high degree of turnover and unemployment among young workers at all stages of the business cycle. Young workers have the most to learn about employment and the most to gain by trying out jobs or 'job shopping' (Johnson, 1978). Moreover, mismatches are likely to be detected early in a job so that turnover will decline with job tenure (Jovanovic, 1979). Thus young workers can expect a period of job shopping followed by a more stable career once a suitable match is identified. Mobility tends to reduce wage dispersion among young males in the United States (Borjas and Rosen, 1980; Flinn, 1986) as unsuitable matches are rejected. Job matching explains wage growth over the life cycle,

---

[4] For further discussions and defence of the basic assumptions of job-matching models, see Dagsvik *et al.* (1985).

regardless of on-the-job training, by the fact that job stability, or job tenure, arising from suitable matches increases with work experience and age (Jovanovic, 1979). Suitably matched (older) workers produce more, and are paid better, than unsuitably matched (younger) workers. This view challenges the traditional human capital view that earnings improvement arises from investment in education and work-related training.[5]

Since worker heterogeneity is at the heart of the job-matching problem, it is useful to consider how heterogeneity might be explicitly introduced. Johnson (1978), for example, considers the role of education in job matching. The value of a job match is assumed to depend upon information about a worker's general ability and about a worker's preferences and aptitude for a specific job. Education is viewed as a means of reducing a worker's uncertainty about his general ability while employment experience reduces uncertainty about preferences and aptitude for a specific job as well as general ability. Education reduces the likelihood of a mismatch and thereby reduces turnover and earnings dispersion just as employment experience does. In other words, education changes the way in which workers assess various jobs to reduce errors and mismatches. Jovanovic (1979) agrees that education—as well as ability, sex, and race—may affect the matching process.

A complete theory of information acquisition in the labour market includes both job search and job matching. Every successful job search leads to a job match; every unsuccessful job match leads to a job search. Because our concern is with the spatial outcome of job search, we shall refer to that outcome as a job–worker match. Job search is then the process by which a job–worker match is realized.

3.4 SPATIAL CONSIDERATIONS—THE ISLAND ECONOMY

Job search theory also provided a badly needed foundation for observed wage inflexibility in the market economy. In particular, Phelps *et al.* (1970) fostered the study of individual behaviour under imperfect information in the labour market as the basis for the observed behaviour of aggregate employment, unemployment, wage rates, and prices. This approach remains an important part of modern macroeconomic reasoning. The approach is also interesting because it con-

[5] For a review of this controversy and some recent evidence on the issue see Barron *et al.* (1989).

tains an important, although usually ignored, spatial element.

We are not directly concerned here with the microeconomic foundations of macroeconomics provided by search theory. These foundations are, in any case, quite controversial.[6] We are interested instead in the spatial implications of the search model which help us to understand the effect of job–worker matching on urban spatial structure and related urban labour market problems. These implications are quite clear in the search literature as we will show in the following pages. In this chapter, the relevant literature will be reviewed. The implications of this literature will then be developed in subsequent chapters.

Phelps (1970*a*) provides the starting-point. Although previous search models had referred briefly to the time and direct money costs of travel as the major costs of search, Phelps introduces an explicit spatial dimension to the search model with this passage:

> I have found it instructive to picture the economy as a group of islands between which information flows are costly: To learn the wage paid on an adjacent island, the worker must spend the day travelling to that island to sample its wage instead of spending the day at work. (p. 6)

Spatial costs arise only in the event that a worker must leave his island to gather information on another island. Islands thereby correspond to the concept of local labour markets of unspecified dimension, within which search costs are ignored. For convenient reference we will call this framework the 'island economy'.

Lucas and Prescott (1974) extended the island economy to develop a rigorous model of the 'natural rate' of unemployment arising from competitive equilibrium. They argue that the model requires differing wage rates for a given type of labour to induce job search, which in turn requires the assumption of spatially distinct markets or islands in the tradition of Phelps *et al.* (1970). In Lucas and Prescott's framework wages clear the labour market on each island in each period in response to labour demand shocks. These shocks are independently distributed over all islands such that the aggregate change in demand is zero. Workers decide to remain on the same island and work or to leave the island and search while temporarily unemployed. Unemployed workers are allocated over islands to equate the expected marginal costs and marginal benefits of search on each island receiving workers.

---

[6] Some aspects of this controversy are discussed in Ch. 6.

Workers are induced to search by adverse demand shocks that reduce local wage rates because they know that demand shocks are autocorrelated within a given island—an adverse shock now increases the probability of an adverse shock next time as well. This autocorrelation of shocks raises the expected benefits of search to find an island enjoying favourable labour demand shocks and rising real wages. This search for jobs on other islands is costly in Phelps's sense that it requires a period of unemployment. Lucas and Prescott's objective is to demonstrate that their island economy will have some positive level of search unemployment, or natural rate of unemployment, over the long run.

Lucas and Prescott provide a very useful basic model of an economy. They describe a stochastic stationary state in which wages differ across islands and workers move between islands generating some unemployment. Policies which reduce the costs of search on other islands, such as more generous unemployment insurance programmes, will increase this level of unemployment. Unanticipated changes in aggregate demand will move the unemployment rate and the rate of increase in aggregate wages in opposite directions, generating the well-known Phillips's curve trade-off (Santomero and Seater, 1978). Jovanovic (1987) shows that the model can explain procyclical job search and labour productivity combined with countercyclical unemployment, as is actually observed in aggregate time-series data. Rowe (1987) shows that the model can even be used to generate extreme Keynesian macroeconomic predictions when kinked demand curves are introduced.

In the Lucas and Prescott model dissatisfied workers are informed about markets where demand conditions are favourable by the usual channels—that is, formal ones such as advertising and informal ones such as personal contacts. Search is uncoordinated, however. A worker does not know where other job-seekers are going so that actual shortages and new arrivals on an island will differ by a random amount. It is this lack of coordination, coupled with persistent random demand shocks, which accounts for continued unemployment in the economy.

This characterization of search invites many interesting questions, particularly from a spatial perspective. Search, like other economic behaviour, may be uncoordinated to some extent. It is unlikely, however, to be entirely unsystematic. Will job-seekers choose a favourable island at random? Will they always choose the nearest favourable island? What accounts for the island they choose? From this ignored spatial perspective we take up the search problem in the context of the island economy of an urban labour market in the next chapter.

3.4.1 Sequential search on the island economy[*]

Lucas and Prescott's (1974) formulation is primarily concerned with the aggregate search unemployment implications of the island economy. Here we focus simply on the individual search decision as in Mortensen (1986: 889–91) as a basis for analysis of the spatial implications of the model. Let λ continue to represent the offer-arrival rate during search on other islands where c is the cost of search. Now, however, the worker has to choose between search on another island and remaining on the current island, where a wage w is offered at the beginning and where offers arrive at some rate α that is generally different from λ. The returns to search, given a minimum reservation wage of w, are

$$\frac{\lambda}{\iota} \int_{w}^{\infty} [z - w] f(w) \, dz - c \tag{3.4}$$

which must exceed the returns to remaining on the current island, which are

$$\frac{\alpha}{\iota} \int_{w}^{\infty} [z - w] f(w) \, dz. \tag{3.5}$$

Thus, workers will search only if

$$\frac{\lambda - \alpha}{\iota} \int_{w}^{\infty} [z - w] f(w) \, dz - c \geqslant 0 \tag{3.6}$$

and will choose reservation wage w^* to satisfy

$$\frac{\alpha}{\iota} \int_{w^*}^{\infty} [z - w^*] f(w) \, dz = c \tag{3.7}$$

as in equation (3.2). Equation (3.6) implies that workers will search only if offers arrive more quickly elsewhere.

Despite the explicitly spatial setting of the island economy, spatial considerations are minimized. A natural extension of the model is to consider differential search costs based on travel distance as in equation (3.3). This implies that workers will prefer to search nearby islands first unless the offer-arrival rates differ across islands. Thus search may involve a series of short moves in successive periods as workers choose to search a nearby island in each period, but may also involve longer moves to islands where offers are expected to arrive at a faster rate than on nearby islands. In an urban context, for example, workers might opt for a local search or for search at a large employment centre, such as the central business district, where more offers are likely to be received. We will return to such questions in subsequent chapters.

3.5 ENTERPRISE SEARCH FOR WORKERS AND JOB MATCHING

Job search by workers will continue only as long as there are benefits to search, associated with a distribution of wage offers by enterprises. Why do enterprises generate different offers and why do those offers not collapse to some 'going wage'? These are difficult and unresolved issues in the search literature, but certain important ideas have emerged which will be useful to us later.

Part of the answer to this question is that enterprises have some monopsony power to determine wage rates because of the costs of job search. They can raise wage offers to increase their share of hires among job-seekers contacting them and to decrease their share of quits by employees seeking and finding better offers elsewhere. Similarly, enterprises can lower their wage offers to reduce their labour force without an immediate and massive departure of workers because most workers will want to assess employment opportunities and wage rates elsewhere before quitting. This does not preclude enterprises from laying off workers instead of lowering wage rates, owing to contractual obligations that are either explicit (collective agreements) or implicit.[7]

Mortensen (1970) and Phelps (1970*b*) developed two of the earliest models of enterprises as monopsonists owing to employment information costs. Firms can adjust their level of vacancies by adjusting their wage rate relative to the wage rates offered by rivals, although rivals' wage scales may not be known with certainty. Some enterprises will eliminate their vacancies more rapidly by outbidding rivals, forcing rivals to retaliate with wage offers that are more realistic in relation to competing firms and their labour-force requirements. In this sense the monopsony power from job search is dynamic—it depends critically on the short-run rigidities or inertia of rival firms

---

[7] For a review of the extensive recent literature on implicit contracts see Rosen (1985).

and workers associated with employment information costs. Firms can only reduce vacancies by attracting workers from the unemployment pool or by making what Mortensen (1970) calls 'net transfers'— attracting workers from other firms by making better offers.

Imperfect knowledge of rivals' wage offers will generate an unpredictable turnover history, although other factors may be involved as well. In particular, jobs and workers are heterogeneous so that job search is important as discussed earlier. Firms seek to maximize the returns from each vacancy filled by choosing the right worker in terms of skills, motivation, personality, and other criteria. Workers, in turn, respond to a job offer on the basis of such factors as its interest, challenge, and career prospects as well as the initial wage offer. Once a job offer is accepted, however, the employment relationship or job match will continue only if both the worker and employer remain satisfied as each discovers more information about the other. In the job-matching models, more information is conceived to be a random draw so that job matches can generate an unpredictable turnover history for firms as a matter of chance. If a firm is unlucky in its job matches, vacancies will rise, requiring an aggressive recruitment policy. One element of this policy is attractive wage offers to lure new workers. Thus unlucky firms at any point in time have higher wage offers than their counterparts who are more fortunate in job matching, leading to a sustained distribution of wage offers as the element of luck shifts across firms.

Once the concept of job matching is introduced, further explanation for worker immobility is apparent. Suppose that an enterprise makes low wage offers to its workers. They begin to search elsewhere, seeking a better offer. Wages are not the only factor in a satisfactory job match, however, and workers may refuse marginally better wage offers because they fear a less satisfactory job match in non-monetary terms. As a result competing firms may have to pay a substantial risk premium to induce workers to move from a certain match to a risky, uncertain match.

Further heterogeneity of firms may also be introduced. MacMinn (1980) shows, for example, that if workers differ in their search costs and firms differ in their production costs, then an equilibrium wage distribution is produced and job search is sustained. In general, however, the behaviour of firms in the job search literature requires extensive further research and it does not serve our purpose to pursue this literature further.

It serves our purpose to turn to the island economy depicted in the previous section. Each island has a number of firms, typically spatially concentrated in commercial districts. These firms adjust their wage offers in accordance with their recruiting needs, which in turn depend on the product demand shocks they receive and on their fortune or misfortune in job matching reflected in employee turnover. While job matches are random, demand shocks are not; there are growing islands, experiencing a series of positive demand shocks, and declining islands experiencing a series of negative demand shocks. Such autocorrelated demand shocks reflect the unbalanced growth along spatial and industrial lines of a typical market economy, ignoring cyclical fluctuations.

Baily (1975) has investigated the behaviour of profit-maximizing firms in such circumstances. Each group of identical firms represents an industry in Baily's system, but may equally well represent identical firms on a particular island in a spatial economy. Each island will choose an optimal wage pattern in which the long-run equilibrium level of wages falls short of the value of the marginal product of labour by an amount equal to the return on investment in hiring and training workers. This provides an entry fee to new firms. Islands on which product demand is growing will pay higher wages than islands on which demand is declining. These equilibrium wage differentials will persist in response to variation in growth rates and employment opportunities between islands. The resulting distribution of wage differentials across islands will sustain job search behaviour of the sort described by Lucas and Prescott in addition to search behaviour arising from random job matching.

In reality, firms are spatially concentrated and the distribution of firms is uneven across islands. Where there are many firms on an island, competition for local workers will be more intense and wage rates will rise as they will on islands experiencing demand growth in Baily's model. The effect of higher wages will be to attract workers from other islands to relocate or, given the intense competition for land and high land prices locally, commute to work from other islands. The higher wage rate will serve as compensation for the costs of commuting. Islands on which firms are spatially concentrated in large employment centres can expect to have higher wage rates relative to other islands in order to recruit workers from a greater area around them. The result will be wage gradients which decline with distance from employment centres (Moses, 1962) as compensation to workers for commuting. Nelson (1973) uses the same logic to explain why larger establishments pay higher wages than smaller establishments to recruit over longer distances.

3.5.1 A model of labour recruitment under dynamic monopsony*

Baily (1975) provides a model of the behaviour of firms in the labour market when they have dynamic monopsony power. He justifies this power with the argument that workers face mobility costs which restrict the rate of change (growth or decline) in the workforce available to a firm as the attractiveness of its jobs changes relative to jobs elsewhere. Baily summarizes the relative attractiveness of the jobs in a firm by its wage relative to the average wage offered elsewhere in the economy, w. Thus, he specifies

$$\frac{\dot{L}}{L} = g(w), \quad \frac{\partial g}{\partial w} \equiv g_w > 0, \quad \frac{\partial^2 g}{\partial w^2} \equiv g_{ww} < 0 \qquad (3.8)$$

where $\dot{L} \equiv \partial L/\partial t$ is the rate of change of the workforce, assumed to be homogeneous, available to the firm over time. In a perfectly competitive environment with no mobility costs, $g_w \to \infty$ since workers will flock to the firm (leave it *en masse*) as its wage rises above (falls below) the rate offered by other firms. In the presence of mobility costs, however, changes in the workforce are more modest. Thus the wage rate may differ among firms, at least temporarily, as they try to adjust the size of their workforces.

The wage rate becomes a decision variable for the dynamic monopsonist, since it affects the supply of labour to the firm over time. Thus the firm must choose levels of capital, labour, and the wage rate over time to maximize the present value of profits:

$$\max_{K, L, w} \int_w^\infty e^{-tt} [\, p(t)X - wL - \rho K \,]\, dt$$

subject to

$$X = F(K, L) = Lf\left(\frac{K}{L}\right), \quad \frac{\partial F}{\partial L} > 0, \quad \frac{\partial F}{\partial K} > 0$$

$$L \geq 0$$

$$\dot{L} = g(w)\, L \text{ from (3.8)}$$

$$K \geq 0$$

given $L(0) > 0$,   (3.9)

where output X is produced under constant returns to scale for inputs capital K and labour L, where p is the product price, where ι is the discount rate as before, where ρ is the cost of capital, and where $L(0)$ is the initial allocation of labour to the firm.

This problem yields the maximizing conditions that

$$p(t)\frac{\partial F}{\partial K} = \rho \qquad (3.10)$$

$$-L + \lambda g_w\, L = 0 \ \text{ or } \ \lambda = \frac{1}{g_w} \qquad (3.11)$$

and

$$\frac{\partial \lambda}{\partial t} = \iota\lambda - p(t)\frac{\partial F}{\partial L} + w - \lambda g(w). \qquad (3.12)$$

Equations (3.11) and (3.12) describe the optimal wage path of the firm given the standard conditions for the optimal utilization of capital in equation (3.10) and the labour supply condition (3.8). Substituting equations (3.10) and (3.11) into equation (3.12) then gives us the optimal wage path $\dot{w} \equiv \partial w/\partial t$:

$$w + \frac{\iota - g(w)}{g_w} + \frac{g_{ww}\dot{w}}{[g_w]^2} - p(t)\frac{\partial F}{\partial L} = 0. \qquad (3.13)$$

Baily then proves that, for a constant price $\tilde{p}$, there exists a unique optimal wage path given by the constant wage $\tilde{w}$ that satisfies equation (3.13) for $\dot{w} = 0$, or

$$\tilde{w} + \frac{\iota - g(\tilde{w})}{g_w(\tilde{w})} - \tilde{p}\frac{\partial F}{\partial L} = 0. \qquad (3.14)$$

This stationary solution corresponds to a static monopsonist ($\dot{L} = 0$) when $g(\tilde{w}) = 0$, since then

$$\tilde{w} + \frac{\iota}{g_w} = \tilde{w}\left(1 + \frac{1}{\eta_L}\right) = \tilde{p}\frac{\partial F}{\partial L}, \qquad (3.15)$$

where $\eta L = \tilde{w}g_w/\iota$ is the elasticity of labour supply. The difference is that, in the dynamic monopsony case, differences in labour force growth as a result of differences in product demand across firms will yield differences in wage paths. In particular, firms with growing labour forces will pay higher wages to recruit workers.

If mobility costs generate dynamic monopsony behaviour, then there is an explicitly spatial element to these costs that has been ignored. In particular, workers will be less likely to join a firm and more likely to leave it the greater the distance they have to travel to work there, other factors equal. Thus, we could introduce spatial costs by respecifying equation (3.8) as

$$\dot{L} = g(w, r)L, \, g_w > 0, \, g_{ww} < 0, \, g_r < 0, \quad (3.16)$$

where r is the distance marginal workers must travel to work in the firm and $g_r \equiv \partial g/\partial r$ denotes the effect of increasing distance on the recruitment of workers—as r increases, workers are less likely to join the firm unless the wage w is raised to compensate for travel costs.

If search is spatially systematic then marginal workers will be the most distant members of the firm's workforce, assuming all workers are paid the same wage.[8] Then r denotes the 'catchment area' of the firm, since it is the greatest distance workers in the firm must travel.

Nelson (1973) takes a similar approach to the analysis of labour supply under monopsony. He assumes that the wage firms must pay rises as the catchment area increases—specifically, the greater the distance the marginal worker must travel relative to the closest firm. He is then able to show that the wage rate offered by a firm will depend upon its size—that is, its labour-force requirements—relative to the surrounding population density.

The model represented by equation (3.16) has interesting new implications for the urban economy.[9] We can immediately see that larger firms will pay higher wages to attract a larger workforce from a greater distance, other factors equal.[10] Moreover, both large and small firms in areas where employment is concentrated will have to pay higher wages to collectively attract more distant workers. Thus, for example, central city firms will require a larger catchment area and must pay higher wages to achieve it, emphasizing that the urban wage gradient arises from the interaction of the producer's interests as well as the consumer's interests in the urban economy. Unlike the analysis in Chapter 2, producers are active agents in urban economic activity.

---

[8] Marginal workers are the first to leave if the relative wage of the firm declines because there are very few employment contracts in which firms compensate more-distant commuters.

[9] In addition to earlier implications noted by Baily (1975), e.g. that wage rates will be positively correlated with the growth rate of the firm.

[10] In particular, as Nelson points out, the density of available workers in the area surrounding the firms would be assumed to be the same. We will return to this issue in Ch. 4.

3.6   CONCLUDING REMARKS

Despite many problems the search literature represents a valuable addition to our understanding of economic behaviour. Applications of the economics of information and search abound.[11] Yet its application to urban economics and spatial analysis has received little attention. This unexplored area offers a new and potentially fertile horizon for urban labour market analysis to which we now turn.

[11] Further general discussion of the search model is unnecessary for our purposes and could only duplicate other work. For an excellent general discussion of the economics of search at a technical level see Lippman and McCall (1976). McKenna (1985) and Mortensen (1986) provide good surveys of the literature pertaining to the labour market.

4

JOB–WORKER MATCHING IN
URBAN SPACE

THE previous chapter identified two crucial aspects of search in the labour market. First, labour is a heterogeneous commodity. This implies that job matching is complex and prone to error. Face-to-face contact between the prospective employer and employee—the personal interview in hiring—can reduce the probability of an unsatisfactory match, although it can by no means eliminate it. The omnipresence of such screening attests to its value to the job-matching process despite the fact that it adds substantially to the cost of job search. Secondly, the cost of job search is primarily spatial in character, consisting of the time and direct cost of transporting job applicants from one place of employment to another. Other marginal job search costs such as reading newspapers and magazines, checking employment agencies, and telephoning friends and relatives to obtain information on job vacancies would seem to be less important. They also appear to be declining relative to screening costs because of technological developments in communications.

This chapter extends the theory of job search by examining these two aspects. Although the spatial character of search is often mentioned, no general theory of spatial search is available. This chapter seeks to provide this theory for job-seekers and employers. In doing so, it identifies a specific aspect of labour heterogeneity that is crucial to spatial search. That aspect is skill, defined in conventional terms as general training. With a spatial model of job–worker matching we are able to extend the theory of urban structure and solve some of the problems identified in Chapter 2.

4.1 BEHAVIOUR OF WORKERS

We consider a worker seeking employment in a spatial economy. Search costs arise from travel costs associated with the optimal search strategy, which normally involves direct contact with employers at the place of employment to assess the prospective job match. Our concern is the spatial pattern of search and job matching, which has been ignored in previous work. This section sets out the general model that will guide subsequent analysis, including various extensions and refinements.

The island economy described in Chapter 3 is useful to consider the spatial mobility of workers. Travel costs within islands—or local labour markets—are assumed to be negligible, but travel costs between islands are significant. The problem is to predict the island or islands on which any worker is likely to search and to predict the island on which a job match is likely to occur. This viewpoint will be particularly useful later in interpreting the empirical evidence, in which islands must correspond to intra-urban areas for which data is available.

The general model consists of two principles. The first principle is that *search is spatially systematic* from a seeker's place of residence. Suppose that a job-seeker is considering two prospective job offers, believed to be alike in all respects except workplace location. Which job is sought first? It will be the job that involves the smaller spatial cost, other factors equal. That cost has two components. The first component is the spatial cost of screening, including interview(s). A job-seeker may begin from his place of residence or, since some job-seekers are employed, his place of work. The second component of spatial cost is daily commuting. This component will favour the job that is located closer to his place of residence. The job that is farther from his place of residence implies either larger commuting costs or residential relocation costs which render it less attractive.[1]

Consider a job-seeker living on one island. He will prefer a job offer on that island to any offer elsewhere, other factors the same, because of the travel cost advantages. Moreover, he will prefer a job offer on a nearby island to one that is farther away in terms of travel time. Induced to leave his island of residence to seek opportunities elsewhere, a job-seeker will not choose an island at random but will systematically seek out job locations that economize on immediate travel costs and ultimate commuting or relocation costs.

---

[1] Spatially systematic search is similar to the 'nearest neighbour' approach to routing spatial search discussed by Maier (1990). In Maier's paper the nearest neighbour approach proves to be a useful heuristic rule to the routing problem because the optimal rule is prohibitively complex to determine in all but the simplest cases. In our model we add commuting cost considerations which enhance the attractiveness of the nearest neighbour rule even more.

This principle is entirely consistent with the standard human capital model of migration (Greenwood, 1975, 1981) in which information costs are ignored. Migration costs, both direct and psychic, are proportional to distance. Therefore, workers prefer shorter moves, other factors equal. The job search perspective extends this reasoning to non-migrants and the general problem of mobility within, as well as between, urban areas. This extension permits a broader examination of urban and labour market questions concerning mobility.

The second principle, however, moves us beyond human capital theory to consider imperfect information and job search. We argue that *skill acquisition broadens the spatial extent of job search*. If the individuals undertaking job search are alike in all respects except skill level, then the individual with the higher level of skill will conduct the broader search in spatial terms. The key element of job and worker heterogeneity is skill level, which must be defined carefully before the argument can be made.

It is conventional to distinguish between general and specific training (Becker, 1964). General training enhances the productivity of a worker in many firms while specific training enhances productivity only in one firm. Since general training involves skills that are portable, the worker will be required to pay for it. Specific training costs, on the other hand, will be borne by the firm that benefits, at least partially (Hashimoto, 1981). Most of the skills that we identify are general skills arising from institutional training in schools, universities, and other post-secondary institutions plus industrial training arising from formal apprenticeship programmes. Indeed, it is quite difficult to identify specific training components of jobs, other than to infer their importance from wage growth and on-the-job experience (Mincer, 1970). Hence our focus is on identifiable general training to determine skill level. These differences in skills are the focus of earnings differences among workers in the human capital model.

The concept of specific training developed by Becker is quite restrictive in order to examine job mobility decisions and their consequences for career wage development among workers. For our purposes an additional distinction is useful. Becker's specific training may be called enterprise-specific training. Becker's general training may continue to be identified as general if it enhances the productivity of a worker equally in *all* firms. If the training increases productivity only in a subset of the total job population, such as an occupation or industry with more than one employer, then it may be called non-enterprise-specific.

More training is non-enterprise-specific than general. Moreover, the non-enterprise-specific component of training rises with skill level (the total amount of general and non-enterprise-specific training). Much early schooling is broadly applicable and therefore general. Technical and academic streams begin to narrow the applicability of training in high school. Further specialization occurs in post-secondary education, particularly in professional and graduate programmes which often follow an initial degree. Specialization entails an increase in the non-enterprise-specific component of training in the sense that the training excludes the individual from more and more jobs requiring a comparable amount of training of a different nature. A high-school degree permits a variety of manual, clerical, sales, service, and even some managerial opportunities for employment. A university degree in Economics or Geography, for example, will eliminate most of these jobs in favour of a more limited number of sales, managerial, and professional positions. High-school degrees are largely interchangeable, at least where course options are limited, while university degrees are not. The Economics or Geography graduate who goes on to a higher degree in city planning will find job choice even more restricted if non-enterprise-specific skills are to be applied.

Rising non-enterprise-specific content in skill acquisition has important job search implications. Simpson (1980) considers a worker switching jobs in anticipation of better wages elsewhere.[2] The cost of job mobility is the forgone wages during the search and during the time that the worker is retrained in the new job. The retraining costs will in turn depend directly on the new skills that must be acquired. Enterprise-specific skills from the previous employer will be lost and new enterprise-specific skills must be acquired, but these will be at least partially financed by the employer. Non-enterprise-specific skills, however, are financed by the worker since the skills are transferable to other firms. A worker who makes a 'radical' job change—

---

[2] These expectations may not be realized. The job search model with adaptive expectations (Phelps, 1970*a*, 1970*b*) predicts that workers do not anticipate cyclical downturns and leave jobs which, in retrospect, are superior to anything available. Workers are then forced to take an inferior job (or no job) until general economic conditions improve. The job search model is essentially an equilibrium model in which workers choose among various activities, including search unemployment. Lay-offs and skill obsolescence are ignored. Yet even laid-off workers are likely to begin their job search by seeking jobs which utilize their skills fully. This is the argument used by Lilien (1982) to explain the effect of employment variation by industry on the aggregate level of unemployment.

one involving the loss of a large proportion of the non-enterprise-specific training previously acquired in another occupation or industry—will probably 'start at the bottom' at a low wage. His wage will only rise as non-enterprise-specific skills are acquired either formally in schooling or apprenticeship programmes or on the job. It is for this reason that downward skill movement is rare (Hunter and Reid, 1968, ch. 4).[3]

Workers try to minimize the loss of non-enterprise-specific skills by restricting the range of jobs they seek. The range of jobs is restricted to those that require the non-enterprise-specific skills previously acquired, which will define normal career paths for workers. Since more skilled workers have more non-enterprise-specific skills, they will be more restricted in their search and less likely to make radical job changes. This argument explains the decline in occupational mobility as skill level rises (Hunter and Reid, 1968, ch. 4; MacKay *et al.*, 1971, ch. 10). For example, MacKay's own study of engineering plants in the United Kingdom found that skilled workers were less likely to change occupation or industry than semi-skilled or unskilled workers, and more likely to choose employers within the occupation and industry of previous employment, regardless of labour market conditions.

This relationship between skill acquisition and job mobility is examined in very general terms by Weiss (1971) and Schaeffer (1985). They show that, if education leads to specialization, then a more educated worker is less likely to switch careers. A new career will not employ previously acquired skills to the full extent, imposing costs on a career switch. These costs are smaller the less educated, and therefore the less specialized, the worker. Weiss and Schaeffer are clearly referring to what we have called the non-enterprise-specific component of training in their analysis.

The spatial implications of this argument are also important. The retention of non-enterprise-specific skills from previous employment or schooling implies a restriction in the range of jobs sought that is equivalent to a reduction in the expected density of suitable job vacancies. Since more-skilled workers have more non-enterprise-specific skills, they will be more restricted in their search. That is, they will expect a lower density of suitable job vacancies. Thus skill

---

[3] This observation may vary to some extent with the business cycle, since workers who do not anticipate a cyclical downturn may be forced into inferior jobs temporarily.

acquisition broadens the spatial extent of job search—an equivalent number of offers can normally be obtained only by a more spatially extensive search for less dense job vacancies.

The analysis assumes that workers with different skill levels will adopt search strategies that imply the same expected number of offers. This assumption may be questioned because conventional models (Stigler, 1962, or McCall, 1970) imply that more-skilled workers earning a higher wage will have higher search costs because they value their time spent searching at a higher rate. More-skilled workers will therefore sample fewer job offers offsetting the spatial implications of skill level on search extent. This argument ignores the job-matching problem and the benefits to job-seekers provided by information about employment that cannot be monetized or otherwise quantified. As discussed in Chapter 3, the importance of these benefits can be judged by the widespread adoption of informal information networks to supplement formal information networks in job search (Rees, 1966). Job-seekers can choose between more extensive and less time-consuming formal search methods and more intensive and time-consuming informal search methods. Search strategy concerns both search duration (the reservation wage) and choice of search technique. The higher valuation of time by more-skilled workers may be expected to be reflected in the adoption of formal search techniques which will permit more searches per unit time *and* more spatially extensive search. Skilled workers do not have to choose fewer offers so much as a different search strategy that is more suitable to their broader spatial search.[4]

There is evidence that more-skilled workers do choose formal search techniques to a greater extent and that their search is more extensive. Sheppard and Belitsky (1966) found that informal sources of job information, especially references from friends and relatives, were more important for unskilled and semi-skilled workers than for skilled workers. Macredie (1972) found that the use of formal information networks increased with the level of education and the occupational status of the job-seeker. Rees (1966) and Parnes (1954) found that informal information networks predominated in the search behaviour of manual, but not non-manual, workers. Holzer (1988) found that unemployed youth in the United States with generally low skills

---

[4] For a more formal argument see Simpson (1977, ch. 2). Some of this argument is outlined in sect. 4.1.1 below.

used informal information networks because they provide the best employment opportunities. Hence education and other aspects of general and non-enterprise-specific training are related to changes in search method.

Corroborating evidence also appears in the literature on migration. Studies have shown that the deterrent effect of distance on job search and interregional migration declines with education level. Schwartz (1973, 1976) argues that more-educated workers adopt a greater search radius because the information costs of distant job opportunities are lower for them than for less-educated workers. Inoki and Suruga (1981) find corroborating evidence for Japan. Denslow and Eaton (1984) argue that more-educated workers have fewer intervening opportunities. The argument in this section is compatible with both explanations but more comprehensive than either one. Fewer intervening opportunities (smaller job-vacancy density) encourage the adoption of formal search techniques which broaden the search radius and increase the probability of receiving and accepting more-distant job offers, other factors equal. Thus there will be smaller spatial variation in earnings for more educated workers, as found by Hanushek (1981) for the United States. There is no reason, however, to restrict the argument to interregional or inter-urban migration since it applies equally well to intra-urban job search and mobility whether the consequences are altered commuting patterns or residential relocation.

Becker (1964) rejuvenated Adam Smith's observation that the degree of specialization is determined by the extent of the market into which those services are sold. Skill acquisition means greater specialization in labour services. This specialization is limited by the size of the market. An alternative interpretation of this principle has been articulated in this section: If the size of the total market implies no effective limit to the degree of specialization, then specialization through skill acquisition can proceed as long as the worker increases the proportion of the market into which he sells his services by broadening the spatial extent of his search. In this way skill acquisition, job search, and job mobility are interrelated as suggested by Schaeffer (1985). In the island economy, less-skilled workers have a higher probability of sampling job offers from their island of residence than more-skilled workers. This probability gap declines as distance to other islands increases and the gap becomes negative as, for more distant islands, more-skilled workers have a higher probability of job offers. This pattern of search arises as a consequence of skill acquisition decisions.

4.1.1   *Spatial aspects of search strategy on the island economy**

Some progress has been made in understanding the spatial search strategy of workers, as outlined in the previous section. From equations (3.4) and (3.5) in section 3.4.1 we have the returns from search in the island economy to be

$$\frac{\gamma}{\iota} \int_{w'}^{\infty} [z - w] f(z) \, dz - c_\gamma, \tag{4.1}$$

where $\gamma = \alpha$, λ is the arrival rate for local offers (α) and offers from some other island or islands (λ), w is the wage offer prior to search, ι is the discount rate, and c is the cost of search where $c_\lambda = c > c_\alpha = 0$ in equations (3.4) and (3.5). We may generalize for more than two locations by considering search costs to vary according to distance to the island, h, as in equation (3.3):

$$c = c(h), \quad \frac{\partial c}{\partial h} > 0. \tag{4.2}$$

Assuming search costs increase sufficiently rapidly, there is a distance H such that

$$\frac{\gamma}{r} \int_{w'}^{\infty} [z - w] f(z) \, dz - c(H) \leq 0. \tag{4.3}$$

Then the individual will search only on islands within distance H and the island at distance H will constitute the spatial boundary of search for the individual. Search is spatially systematic because workers will search the jobs within the spatial boundary in increasing order of search costs, other factors equal (Maier, 1987: 195).

The model may be extended in several interesting ways. First, offer-arrival rates, γ, may differ among islands. In this case, islands with higher γ will have higher net returns for given distance (search cost). Thus search by workers, although spatially systematic in the sense defined above, may not simply proceed in order of increasing distance and search costs. Workers may choose locations with higher arrival rates—the central business district and other large employment centres in urban areas[5]—as well as nearby locations. This result is streng-

---

[5] And, correspondingly, large and rapidly growing urban centres in the context of regional job search.

thened if it is assumed that workers know that wages differ across islands (for example McCall and McCall, 1987) since better labour market conditions for workers normally imply both higher arrival rates and higher wages. The perception of an urban wage gradient by job-seekers, for example, favours centralized search, other factors including travel distance being equal.

Secondly, we may introduce worker heterogeneity in the form of general training. If G is the amount of general training—and hence the skill level—of workers then the reservation wage will depend directly upon G, other factors held constant. Thus, $w^* = w^*(G)$, $\partial w^*/\partial G > 0$ and we can rewrite equation (3.3) as

$$c = c(h, G), \quad \frac{\partial c}{\partial h} > 0, \quad \frac{\partial c}{\partial G} \left(= \frac{\partial c}{\partial w^*} \frac{\partial w^*}{\partial G} \right) > 0, \qquad (4.4)$$

where $\partial c/\partial G > 0$ represents the rising value of search and commuting time with earnings and skill level, consistent with the literature and empirical evidence reviewed in Chapter 2. The immediate implication is that more-skilled workers search over a shorter distance for jobs, other factors equal, since

$$\mathrm{d}c = \frac{\partial c}{\partial h} \mathrm{d}h + \frac{\partial c}{\partial G} \mathrm{d}G = 0 \quad \Rightarrow \quad \frac{\partial h}{\partial G} = - \frac{\partial c/\partial G}{\partial c/\partial h} < 0. \qquad (4.5)$$

We have seen from the evidence in the previous section, however, that it is just the opposite—that skill acquisition broadens the extent of search. Our explanation is that rising non-enterprise-specific skills reduce the expected density of suitable job vacancies, requiring broader search for an equivalent number of offers and more formal, spatially extensive search techniques. Thus we may once again re-specify search costs to include a measure of the 'mix', m, or proportion of informal search procedures used relative to formal procedures (Simpson, 1977: 54–5):

$$c = c(h, G, m), \quad \frac{\partial c}{\partial h} > 0, \quad \frac{\partial c}{\partial G} > 0, \quad \frac{\partial c}{\partial m} > 0. \qquad (4.6)$$

Since informal procedures are more time-intensive, $\partial c/\partial m > 0$ is assumed. Hence, again examining the total differential

$$\mathrm{d}c = \frac{\partial c}{\partial h} \mathrm{d}h + \frac{\partial c}{\partial G} \mathrm{d}G + \frac{\partial c}{\partial m} \mathrm{d}m = 0 \quad \Rightarrow \quad \frac{\partial h}{\partial G} < 0, \quad \frac{\partial h}{\partial m} < 0. \qquad (4.7)$$

We see that workers can offset the effect of skill acquisition on search costs by reducing m, that is, by adopting a search strategy involving a greater mix of formal search procedures. Indeed, evidence suggests that changing the mix permits more spatially extensive search by skilled workers to enhance job choice.

Search strategy in a spatial economy is complex. Our analysis has identified several important considerations—distance, offer-arrival rates, spatial wage variation, general training, and the mix of formal and informal search strategies—in the search decision. A more complex model of search behaviour is clearly possible, but it is not necessary for our purposes as we turn to the spatial equilibrium implied by workplace choice behaviour in our model.

4.2   BEHAVIOUR OF EMPLOYERS

Information scarcity compels firms to recruit workers actively because they cannot rely on a common 'competitive wage' to fill vacancies as they arise. Firms with higher vacancy rates will have to raise wage offers to reduce quits and to encourage job-seekers to accept their employment offers; firms with low vacancy rates can maintain or lower their wage offers. As dynamic monopsonists, firms can regulate the net inflow of labour by their wage offers. Wages are not the only factor in employee recruitment, however, and other aspects of the firm's recruitment strategy will be examined as well.

The problem of worker heterogeneity and job matching is important. Cost-minimizing employers must consider applicants with different backgrounds, abilities, and personalities to select the most productive worker for the job in question.[6] Firms that raise their wage offers to attract applicants and induce them to accept offers of employment must still decide which applicant should receive an offer. Any information that will assist the firm in 'screening' applicants to find the most productive worker will be valuable, so that the economic problem of screening can be quite important (Arrow, 1973; Spence, 1974; Blaug, 1976; Aigner and Cain, 1977). Formal information networks, including job advertisement and employment agencies, will be supplemented by informal information about the applicants. Such information will be obtained not only by personal contact

---

[6] In fact, the problem may be more complex if the employer has in mind a long relationship with the employee in which many jobs in a variety of career paths must be considered.

through job interviews but also by referrals from other employers, employees, and friends, relatives, or acquaintances outside the workplace.

Employers, like individuals seeking jobs, have to decide on a search or recruitment strategy which blends formal and informal information sources. For jobs requiring a high degree of skill, the density of suitable applicants will likely be relatively small in the vicinity of the employer because of the non-enterprise-specific content of accumulated skills, as argued in the previous section. If an employer seeks to attract a given number of applicants at each skill level, applicants for jobs requiring a high degree of skill must be attracted from greater distances. The use of informal information networks is likely to involve greater cost and risk in general because of its random nature and reliance on personal contacts. This cost and risk is likely to rise with distance, however, because most personal contacts will be local. Thus formal information networks will be more attractive to locate distant applicants and employers will substitute formal information networks for informal ones as skill requirements and the extent of search increase.

Shultz (1962) provides a complementary argument and corroborating evidence. Employers do not go to the labour market regularly for any particular type of specialized labour. There is less tendency to keep informed about labour market conditions in these circumstances. When skilled labour is needed formal channels are used, such as national or regional press advertising, specialized trade or professional journals, and national or regional employment services. Unskilled labour, on the other hand, is being recruited fairly regularly from the local market. Employers keep better informed about local labour market conditions for these occupations. This knowledge permits more informal methods of recruitment to be undertaken.

It is not clear from Shultz's argument, however, why employers necessarily recruit locally for unskilled workers but regionally or nationally for skilled workers. It is also not clear why employers choose to be informed about local labour market conditions for unskilled workers, but not about those conditions for skilled workers. The answer provided here is the non-enterprise-specific content of skills and its consequences for spatial search strategy and the choice of information sources. Shultz's argument adds the idea that the choice of recruitment strategy may also be influenced by job turnover. Turnover (quits, lay-offs, and discharges) tends to be higher for unskilled workers. The job-matching literature would explain this phenomenon in terms of age, since unskilled workers tend to be younger (Johnson, 1978; Flinn, 1986). The human capital literature would cite the complementarity of skill (general and non-enterprise-specific training) and specific training, which creates incentives for stable employment (Becker, 1964; Hashimoto, 1981; Rosen, 1985). The segmented labour market literature would add institutional and attitudinal factors (Cain, 1976; Harrison and Sum, 1979). Employers would therefore have more recent experience with the labour market for unskilled workers because of higher turnover. This would reduce the costs of informal information by eliminating many of the 'start-up' costs associated with reactivating the network. Employers would therefore find informal information networks, resulting in less extensive spatial search, to be more attractive for unskilled workers.

Rees (1966) found that Chicago employers preferred informal information networks to provide applicants from the neighbourhood of the firm to reduce turnover, absenteeism, and tardiness owing to transportation problems, particularly among female employees. They also preferred neighbourhood rather that metropolitan newspapers for the same reasons. Such recruitment techniques were unable to produce sufficient applicants for jobs with high skill requirements, however, and could be used much less frequently.

An older survey of employers in the San Francisco–Oakland area by Malm (1954) provides further evidence of the influence of skill requirements on search strategy. Malm found that about one-third of respondents would recruit throughout California or even nationally to find candidates for managerial and professional jobs. This proportion declined for sales people and declined even further for clerical and production employees, who were 'commonly sought rather close at hand' (p. 516). Larger firms recruited more widely, especially for managerial and professional employees, because of their substantial labour requirements. Local hiring, in the 'immediate vicinity' or 'part of the metropolitan area', tended to rely on informal networks—direct hiring at the gate or referrals from unions, friends, and relatives (p. 518). Metropolitan-wide, regional, or national hiring relied heavily on formal networks—advertising, employment agencies, and labour scouting. The recruiting area varied not only by skill level but, to some extent, by the employer's view of labour market conditions. Wider recruiting and more extensive, formal techniques were adopted in a tighter labour market at skill levels which would normally recruit locally using informal information networks.

4.3 SKILL, SEARCH, AND SPATIAL MATCHING

The previous two sections indicate how the economics of job search and job matching can be extended to include spatial considerations and the choice of search technique. The extensions follow from the examination of skill acquisition and its effect on job vacancy density. Density declines as skills are acquired because skills are largely non-enterprise-specific—that is, they raise the productivity of the worker in a subset of the jobs to which previous skills were applicable. Jobs requiring higher skills require more extensive spatial search, including greater reliance on formal information networks. We observe more extensive, and formal, search behaviour as skill level rises in surveys of the search behaviour of workers and the recruitment behaviour of firms.

It is useful to think about the market equilibrium which arises from these extensions. Equilibrium, in which wages eliminate any anticipated excess demand or supply in all markets (Hicks, 1939; see also Phelps, 1985), provides a useful point of reference for further labour market analysis, such as incorporating insufficient wage adjustment as an additional source of underemployment and other problems. We shall have more to say about these issues when underemployment is discussed in Chapter 6. For now, equilibrium is a convenient concept with which to focus on the extensions in this chapter to standard models of human capital and worker mobility.

There is a constant flow of workers into and out of employment in any urban market economy. Workers decide to enter the labour market or to quit existing jobs. Firms may lay off or discharge workers. Vacancies arise as new jobs are created and departing workers are replaced. This worker mobility is an important component of economic growth and change in any urban area.

Workers begin their search by formulating a strategy. This strategy is captured by the adoption of a reservation wage in the search literature. The reservation wage represents the worker's assessment of the job he can expect to obtain that will render further search unprofitable. Expectations can adjust as search proceeds and the job-seeker accumulates labour market information which causes him to reassess his reservation wage. Thus an unanticipated series of low offers will cause the seeker to lower his reservation wage as he learns the sad truth about market conditions (Phelps, 1970*a*). Once his lowered expectations are realized and an acceptable offer is found within a reasonable period of time, equilibrium will be restored. In equilibrium, search will proceed without significant revision of workers' expectations and unemployment will be as low as is consistent with the normal transfer of workers into new jobs.

Search for an acceptable offer will involve two crucial considerations. First, workers will seek jobs as close as possible to their place of residence to economize on search and commuting costs. Secondly, workers will seek jobs that require the skills that they have acquired. Skilled workers will adopt a different strategy from unskilled workers, one that permits more spatially extensive search by relying on formal information networks more heavily. Simpson (1980) captures these spatial considerations by allowing the probability of a worker accepting a job offer to depend upon the distance of the worker's residence from the job location as well as the wage offer. Unskilled workers are less likely to find and accept distant job offers than skilled workers; hence, the effect of distance in reducing the probability of accepting an offer is larger as skill level declines.

In this model the urban economy consists of clusters of firms at various locations or islands. Workers reside on each island with specified population density. Labour demand is predetermined. Firms must satisfy this demand by recruiting sufficient workers. In equilibrium, the maximum distance over which workers are recruited to satisfy demand will depend upon three factors—the ratio of labour demand to the population density of the workers considered (which represents a measure of the spatial structure of the relevant portion of the urban area), the wage rates offered, and the skill level of the workers being recruited. A higher demand-to-density ratio will increase the maximum recruiting distance, or labour catchment area; higher wage offers will reduce the catchment area by increasing the probability of workers accepting the offers made; and more-skilled workers will have to be recruited over a wider area because non-enterprise-specific training implies fewer suitable job opportunities at their skill level.

Information and mobility costs give firms dynamic monopsony power. This means that firms can control their net inflow of workers by the wage (and non-wage) offers made to workers. The inflow of workers will also depend upon the catchment area required and thus upon the demand-to-density ratio and the skill level under consideration. The optimal wage offers will therefore vary according to these factors. Any wage offer will recruit fewer workers in a poorer local labour market environment, represented by a higher demand-to-density ratio on the island in which the firm is located, because of greater competition for local workers. A poor local labour market environment will be less important for skilled workers, however. Fewer suitable opportunities among jobs offered at their skill level will cause skilled workers to engage in more extensive search and firms to engage in more extensive recruitment for skilled workers regardless of local labour market conditions. Hence the effect of local labour market conditions will be less important for skilled than unskilled workers.

A firm's optimal wage policy in equilibrium will vary by local labour market conditions for recruitment and by skill level. Poor local conditions will raise wages to increase the rate of job acceptance by local residents and to increase the catchment area, particularly for less-skilled workers whose search is more spatially confined. The urban wage gradient generated by this behaviour will be consistent with earlier predictions based solely on compensation for commuting costs (Moses, 1962). Wages will be higher for firms in the central business district because local labour market conditions are tight— there are many jobs per local resident. Higher wages recruit workers by compensating them for increased commuting to the city centre. As distance from the city centre increases, local labour market conditions improve and wage rates fall. Similar, but less elevated, peaks in the wage gradient will appear around suburban employment centres such as major industrial parks.

The wage gradient generated by the basic model clearly incorporates the spatial distribution of labour demand within the city. Cities with very centralized employment demand will have steeper wage gradients than cities in which employment is more decentralized. Thus the criticism in Chapter 2 of the wage gradients generated by residential location theory with decentralized employment is addressed in our approach. The urban wage gradient is determined within the model by the interaction of labour supply and labour demand in a spatial context.

There is a major and testable distinction between this approach and the conventional residential location model, involving the role of skill. In the conventional model more-skilled workers have a higher value of commuting time. This causes them to be more responsive to wage offers by local firms to reduce commuting costs, other factors equal. The factor which causes long commuting is a preference by

highly paid skilled workers for suburban locations where job opportunities are poor as discussed in Chapter 2. From suburban locations,
however, skilled workers are *more responsive* to local employment
offers and local labour market conditions. The crucial consideration
ignored in this argument is search and matching in the labour market
and the role of non-enterprise-specific training in altering spatial
search behaviour. This consideration implies the opposite conclusion—that skilled workers are *less responsive* to local conditions.
Given an appropriate model that encompasses both approaches, the
relative importance of these considerations may be assessed empirically. This is one objective of the next chapter.

4.3.1   A spatial model of job–worker matching*

Despite the dynamic nature of the job-search and job-matching literature and the island economy, we can consider a static model of
job–worker matching in the island economy which will provide us
with important and testable implications regarding urban structure
and labour market behaviour. The static model is particularly useful
because of its compatibility with the static model of urban spatial
structure outlined in Chapter 2 and with available cross-sectional data
on urban spatial structure from transportation surveys. A complete
dynamic model is beyond the scope of this study and beyond the
scope of currently available data, although there are some clear dynamic implications from the study. These dynamic considerations are
considered in subsequent chapters.

   We may begin with a very simple, but instructive, preliminary
analysis involving two employment centres—a central business district and a suburban employment centre. Suppose that a suburban
household with a single worker is located a distance h from the central
business district and a distance l from the suburban, or local, employment centre. Assume, as dictated by residential location theory, that
the household residence and the suburban employment centre are
located on a radial line from the central business district with the
residential location farther from the city centre than the suburban
employment centre so that $l < h$. Divide the city into two districts or
'islands' consisting of L_c workers living in the district that includes
the city centre and L_l workers living in the district that includes the
suburban employment centre. Suppose that there are N_c jobs in the
city centre and N_l jobs at the suburban employment centre, where

$N_c > N_l$. Then labour market equilibrium requires that

$$N_c + N_l = L_c + L_l. \tag{4.8}$$

We now need to introduce a simple model of spatial job search behaviour consistent with the precepts discussed in this chapter. As a first step, we assume that workers are homogeneous and that they adopt spatially systematic search. Let $f(w, x)$ be the probability that a worker will accept a job involving commuting distance x and offering wage w. Then we expect from job search theory that $\partial f/\partial w > 0$ and from spatially systematic search that $\partial f/\partial x < 0$. Equilibrium in the suburban employment centre requires that the worker be offered a wage w_l such that all vacancies are filled or

$$f(w_l, l) = \frac{N_l}{L_l} \equiv s, \tag{4.9}$$

where s is jobs per worker in the suburban district. Since most of the jobs are in the centre, $s < 1$ and all suburban employment requirements are filled by suburban residents.

Some suburban residents must be attracted to work in the central business district, however, by firms paying a wage $w_c > w_l$ to attract them. Hence equilibrium also requires that

$$f(w_c, h) = \frac{N_c - L_c}{L_l} = 1 - s \tag{4.10}$$

in order to attract the remaining suburban workers to the central city.

The expected commuting distance of a worker, given probability density $f(w, x)$, is

$$E(x) = \int_0^\infty x f(w, x) dx \tag{4.11}$$

for a given wage, w. In the simple case here, the expected commuting distance of the worker at distance h from the centre and l from the suburban employment centre is

$$r = h - j = f(w_l, l) . l + f(w_c, h) . h = s . l + (1 - s) . h, \tag{4.12}$$

where j is the distance from the workplace to the city centre as in Chapter 2. Equation (4.12) indicates that, given h and l, commuting distance varies with s, the ratio of local jobs to local workers. In particular,

$$\frac{\partial r}{\partial s} = l - h < 0$$

so that the higher is the ratio of local jobs to local workers, the more local commuting is done and the lower is r. Thus, by rearrangement of equation (4.12), job location, j, depends directly upon local employment opportunities, s, given household location, h, as follows:

$$j = h - [h - s . (h - l)] = s . (h - l) \qquad (4.13)$$

such that $\partial j/\partial s = h - l > 0$ and $0 < \partial j/\partial h = s < 1$.

The urban wage gradient in this simple model arises because suburban workers must be compensated for the additional time they must spend to commute to the city centre. Note, however, that the wage gradient will vary depending upon the spatial distribution of jobs and workers between the two islands, captured by the variable s. That is, from equations (4.9) and (4.10) and the condition that $\partial f/\partial w > 0$ we can write

$$\frac{\partial w_l}{\partial s} > 0 \quad \text{and} \quad \frac{\partial w_c}{\partial s} < 0.$$

Hence, a city with a smaller suburban employment centre in relative terms (smaller s) will have a steeper wage gradient because central city firms will have to pay a larger premium to attract a larger proportion of suburban residents to central city jobs. This is a potentially testable feature of wage gradients that is not captured by conventional theory of urban spatial structure.[7]

This simple model is generalized in Simpson (1980). Consider now a multiplicity of islands or employment centres available to a worker. If there are N jobs on an island and the local density of potential workers is D then labour market equilibrium implies

$$\int_0^r D f(w, x) \, dx = N \qquad (4.14)$$

or

$$\int_0^r f(w, x) \, dx = F(w, r) = \frac{N}{D} \equiv s, \qquad (4.15)$$

where r is the maximum commuting distance, or catchment area, required by firms on the island in question. This definition of r is consistent with its use in equation (3.16) earlier for spatially systematic search because the marginal workers at the firm—those workers who would leave first if wages began to decline—will be those commuting the greatest distance. We can now write

---

[7] Testing would require labour market activity data at a detailed spatial level which, to my knowledge, is not readily available.

$$r = R(w, s), \quad \frac{\partial R}{\partial w} < 0, \quad \frac{\partial R}{\partial s} > 0. \tag{4.16}$$

The catchment area increases with increases in local employment demand relative to local labour supply, s, and with decreases in local wage offers, w.

Simpson (1980) relaxes the assumption of worker homogeneity to introduce the effects of different levels of skill acquisition on search. If G is the level of general training acquired by a worker and $f_x \equiv \partial f/\partial x$ is the effect of distance on the probability of seeking and accepting a job offering a given wage, then the effect of skill level on spatial search extent is given by $\partial f_x/\partial G$. This effect may be positive or negative depending upon the importance of the job search model developed in this chapter. Since the value of commuting time increases with skill level G, we would expect a greater reluctance to search for jobs as distance increases among more-skilled workers, or $\partial f_x/\partial G < 0$ from this effect alone. Analysis of job search behaviour implies, however, that skill acquisition broadens the spatial extent of search because skills acquired are partly non-enterprise-specific. Hence we would expect $\partial f_x/\partial G > 0$ from job search. This provides us with a very clear test of the importance of job search behaviour *vis-à-vis* the value of commuting time often used in conventional analysis — namely that $\partial f_x/\partial G > 0$ only if job search behaviour dominates the value of commuting time.

From equation (4.11) we see that the expected commuting distance depends directly on the effect of skill on the extent of spatial search, that is

$$sign\left[\frac{\partial E}{\partial G}\right] = sign\left[\frac{\partial f_x}{\partial G}\right], \tag{4.17}$$

other factors equal. In particular, however, we are concerned about the effect of variations in local labour market conditions and wage rates. For firms we can see from equation (4.15) that

$$sign\,[\partial F_r/\partial G] = sign\,[\,\partial f_x/\partial G\,]$$

and from equations (4.15) and (4.16) that $R_s = 1/F_r$ so that

$$sign\,[\partial R_s/\partial G\,] = -\,sign\,[\partial f_x/\partial G\,].$$

If job search is sufficiently important that $\partial f_x/\partial G > 0$ then we would expect $\partial R_s/\partial G < 0$ so that the effect of local labour market conditions on recruiting distance or catchment area would decline as skill level rises, other factors equal. Thus the recruitment of more-skilled workers is less sensitive to local labour market conditions.

The behaviour of wages will reinforce this conclusion. To see this, consider again Baily's model of firms with dynamic monopsony power represented by equation (3.16) where spatial costs of recruitment have been introduced:

$$\dot{L} = g(w, r)\,L, \quad g_w > 0, \quad g_{ww} < 0, \quad g_r < 0.$$

From equation (4.16) this implies that

$$\dot{L} = g(w, s)\,L, \quad g_w > 0, \quad g_{ww} < 0, \quad g_s < 0 \tag{4.18}$$

because $\partial r/\partial s > 0$. Since $sign\,[\partial R_s/\partial G] = -\,sign\,[\partial f_x/\partial G]$, we have

$$sign\left[\frac{\partial g_s}{\partial G}\right] = sign\left[\frac{\partial f_x}{\partial G}\right]. \tag{4.19}$$

The optimal constant-wage path equation (3.14) can now be written to incorporate differences in labour market conditions, represented by s:

$$\tilde{w} + \frac{1 - g(\tilde{w}, s)}{g_w(\tilde{w}, s)} - \tilde{p}\,\frac{\partial F}{\partial L} \equiv A(\tilde{w}, \tilde{p}) = 0. \tag{4.20}$$

We can now ask how wages will behave as labour market conditions, s, vary across the island economy. From equation (4.20), $g_s < 0$ implies $A_s > 0$ and $sign\,[\partial g_s/\partial G] = sign\,[\partial f_x/\partial G]$ implies that $sign\,[\partial A_s/\partial G] = -\,sign\,[\partial f_x/\partial G]$. Since

$$\frac{A + g_{ww}\dot{w}}{g_w^2} = 0 \tag{4.21}$$

from equation (3.13) for the optimal wage path for the firm and since $g_{ww} < 0$,

$$\dot{w}_s > 0 \tag{4.22}$$

and

$$sign\left[\frac{\partial \dot{w}_s}{\partial G}\right] = -\,sign\left[\frac{\partial f_x}{\partial G}\right]. \tag{4.23}$$

Thus the optimal path of wages is responsive to changes in the labour market environment across islands, s, and the skill level of workers, G. Wage rates rise faster as competition for local workers, represented by s, increases and wage rates rise to a lesser extent as skill level rises only if job search considerations dominate the value of commuting time, such that $\partial f_x/\partial G > 0$.

The behaviour of wages in the island economy depicted above is to reinforce the behaviour described in the very simple model at the beginning of this section. As local competition for workers, s, increases workers are more likely to accept local jobs because of attractive local wage rates, since

$$\frac{\partial f}{\partial s} = \frac{\partial f}{\partial w} \frac{\partial w}{\partial s} > 0. \qquad (4.24)$$

This effect will diminish with skill level, however, if skill acquisition broadens the spatial extent of job search. Wage rates will not respond as much to local labour market conditions, s, for skilled workers, since

$$\frac{\partial f_s}{\partial G} = \frac{\partial f}{\partial w} \frac{\partial w_s}{\partial G} < 0 \text{ if } \frac{\partial f_x}{\partial G} > 0. \qquad (4.25)$$

On the other hand, if search behaviour is sufficiently unimportant and the value of commuting time is the dominant consideration then the effect of s on the acceptance rate of local jobs by skilled workers will be greater, since

$$\frac{\partial f_s}{\partial G} = \frac{\partial f}{\partial w} \frac{\partial w_s}{\partial G} > 0 \text{ if } \frac{\partial f_x}{\partial G} < 0. \qquad (4.26)$$

Thus we have some clear propositions concerning the effect of local labour market conditions, the value of commuting time, and job search on commuting behaviour in an urban area. We have that

$$\frac{\partial E}{\partial s} \equiv E_s < 0 \qquad (4.27)$$

from equation (4.11), or that expected commuting distance declines as local labour market conditions, represented by the ratio of local jobs to local workers, increases. We also have from equation (4.25) that

$$\frac{\partial E_s}{\partial G} > 0 \text{ if } \frac{\partial f_x}{\partial G} > 0, \qquad (4.28)$$

or that this responsiveness to local labour market conditions declines when search considerations dominate, and from equation (4.26) that

$$\frac{\partial E_s}{\partial G} < 0 \text{ if } \frac{\partial f_x}{\partial G} > 0, \qquad (4.29)$$

or that this responsiveness increases when the value of commuting time is the dominant consideration as in conventional urban location models. The clear difference in prediction about commuting behaviour in equations (4.28) and (4.29) provides a test of the empirical relevance of job search behaviour in workplace choice decisions.

5

JOB–WORKER MATCHING AND URBAN COMMUTING

THE first two chapters review the standard economic theory of urban spatial structure and criticize it because it ignores the choice of workplace which arises when employment is decentralized. The third chapter reviews the theory of labour markets as a basis for a theory of workplace choice. The fourth chapter provides a theory of workplace choice in which workers formulate spatial job search strategies that depend upon skill acquisition decisions. Successful search results in a workplace choice or spatial job–worker match.

What does this job–worker matching model imply about commuting patterns and other aspects of urban activity? Chapter 2 has already presented some evidence on commuting behaviour that is apparently inconsistent with the standard theory in which only residential location, not workplace choice, is considered. Can these inconsistencies be explained by incorporating our model into the analysis? In this chapter a more complete examination of commuting behaviour is undertaken to assess the predictive capability of the matching model *vis-à-vis* the standard theory. In the next chapter other aspects of urban labour market behaviour are considered in a similar fashion.

The job–worker matching model provides an extension to the standard theory rather than a direct alternative. The model addresses workplace choice behaviour, which is ignored by the standard theory. Hence we are not testing an alternative theory; we are assessing the value of the job–worker matching model as part of an extended theory of urban spatial structure. This assessment involves both the identification of limitations or falsified predictions of the standard theory without workplace choice and demonstration that these limitations can be overcome by incorporating job–worker matching into the standard theory.

The first section of the chapter briefly considers the data and methodology used to assess the model we have developed. The second section develops a basic model of residential location and workplace choice to explain commuting decisions. The model is tested both directly and indirectly in the third section. The basic model is assessed further with regard to commuting patterns by race and sex in the fourth section, followed by some concluding remarks.

5.1 EXPLAINING RESIDENTIAL LOCATION AND WORKPLACE CHOICE

The model of workplace choice in Chapter 4 is a static model. Although the ultimate goal may be a fully specified dynamic model of urban spatial structure and the urban economy, the static model is a useful intermediate step for several reasons. First, a static model allows us to focus on the essential, long-run features of workplace choice, allowing us to see clearly the distinctive predictions of the model. In particular, we can see how it interacts with the standard theory of residential location, which is also a static model. The static theories of workplace choice and residential location should be compatible to permit integration. Secondly, this static integrated model is appropriate for empirical analysis using available cross-sectional data from urban transportation surveys and geographical subdivisions of national censuses. Dynamic models require longitudinal data on individual units (households) or spatial aggregates through time, but data on individual households is not yet available through time at a suitably disaggregated geographical level. Aggregate data, linking geographical subdivisions of cities through time, are available but present serious problems of aggregation bias.[1] Thus cross-sectional data on households appear to represent the best evidence currently available to examine workplace choice and residential location decisions and a static model is appropriate for such analysis. Thirdly, as mentioned earlier, dynamic models are often built from an originally static framework. Once some corroborating evidence is available to support the workplace choice model, dynamic analysis can be investigated. We will return to this question in the final chapter.

Although the model is static, the process we seek to understand is a dynamic one. Over time individual circumstances and the structure of the urban economy change. A typical individual life cycle involves

---

[1] When testing models of individual behaviour with aggregate data, one must make certain assumptions about the functional form of the equations describing individual behaviour in order to aggregate. The assumptions may be incorrect and bias the tests of individual behaviour.

some or all of the following: leaving the parents' home, marriage, children, separation/divorce, remarriage, children leaving the home, and retirement. These changes in individual circumstances, along with improvements in real household income and net worth, can trigger residential relocation within the city even if workplace location does not change. Workplace location does change, however, and at a rate far in excess of the rate of residential relocation according to evidence in Chapter 2. An individual, especially early in his career, may try out various jobs to assess career opportunities and his own interests and capabilities. Even later in life, career advancement may require new employment. Unintended job changes may arise through lay-off or discharge. Job search, while most common early in the working life, occurs until retirement. Commuting patterns of individuals change frequently because of residential and workplace relocation decisions.

At any point in time, then, individuals may be engaged in residential location decisions, workplace choice decisions, or both. There is no way to know which decisions have been made most recently in the absence of retrospective, or longitudinal, data. Lacking more information, we can conceive of individuals making *interdependent* residential location and workplace location decisions. In some cases, these decisions may actually be made together. New urban residents will often find a job and a place of residence at the same time, with each decision having some influence on the other. In other cases, one of these decisions will clearly be made prior to the other. As discussed in Chapter 2 (section 2.6), home-owners and second earners in households are less residentially mobile and more likely to make workplace choice decisions as if their place of residence were fixed. Yet there will be cases when these groups do change place of residence with or without a change of workplace. Without more information we must model residential and workplace location as interdependent or simultaneous in a static framework.

5.2 DETERMINANTS OF RESIDENTIAL LOCATION

The standard model of residential location outlined in Chapter 2 has a rich theoretical and empirical tradition. In that literature certain features are essential. Any empirical study must begin from a variant of the basic model in which employment is decentralized. The model then predicts that workers will locate on the opposite side of the city centre from their workplace where land is cheaper. As the workplace is located farther from the centre, the workers may commute shorter or longer distances depending upon the degree of employment decentralization in the urban area. If we use the city centre as our point of spatial reference, we may locate the workplace and place of residence according to distance from that point. We would then expect that the residential location (distance from the centre) would increase as the workplace location (distance from the centre) increased, other factors equal.[2]

Other factors are also essential, however. First and foremost is household income. The standard model assumes that as income increases, the demand for space increases more than proportionately. Workers therefore locate further from their workplace the greater is their household income. Critics of this theory who emphasize social agglomeration and other housing externalities or the effects of local government finance would still emphasize the role of household income in increasing the distance of the place of residence from the place of work. Thus household income is a crucial factor to be included in almost any model of residential location. A second essential factor is the number of workers in the household. Additional earners in the household increase commuting costs and tilt the trade-off between access and space toward access. Since employment density is greater toward the city centre, greater access for more than one worker in a household is generally achieved by a residential location closer to the city centre. A third essential factor in the residential location decision is the stage of the household life cycle. In particular, Siegel (1975) argues that older households and households with children have stronger preferences for suburban locations regardless of workplace location.

We have seen the effects of these factors individually in Tables 2.1 and 2.2. In some cases, such as household income, the expected pattern of increasing suburbanization of households with increasing income was quite clear from the cross-tabulated data. In other cases, such as the number of workers in the household or the stage of the household life cycle, the pattern was unclear. The problem is that these factors are closely related. Thus we would have to examine the relationship between residential location and the number of workers

---

[2] i.e. the coefficient on job locations as a determinant of residential location in a multiple regression model should be positive, other factors equal. For more discussion of this point, see sect. 5.2.1.

in the household by household income category and stage of the life cycle. Complex and numerous cross-tabulations could be used but multivariate analysis, and in particular linear regression analysis, is more appropriate for this task.

Siegel (1975) captures these essential features of the standard model of residential location in a basic linear regression model that explains residential location in terms of the four factors mentioned above—namely job location, household income, the number of employed household members, and household life cycle characteristics represented by the age of the household head and the presence of young children. In his model we would expect greater household income to increase residential location (distance from the city centre), additional workers in the household to have the opposite effect and decrease residential location to improve access, and the presence of young children and an ageing household to increase demand for more distant residential locations.

Siegel's model of residential location is quite simple, but this should not be seen in a negative light. It captures the essential features of the standard model discussed in Chapter 2. Its data requirements are not insurmountable. Indeed, Siegel uses the model quite successfully to study intrametropolitan migration in the San Francisco Metropolitan Area. Moreover, the model can be integrated with the model of workplace choice in Chapter 4 to assess the importance of workplace choice to the analysis of urban spatial structure. This regression model for residential location is specified in equation (5.3) in the next section.

5.2.1   An econometric model of residential location*

Following conventional urban location analysis in Chapter 2, we define residential location as the distance, h, of the home from the city centre and workplace location, j, as the distance of the job from the city centre. Using the model of residential location from a decentralized workplace in section 2.4.1, we obtain expressions for residential and workplace location as in equations (2.39) and (2.40):

$$h^* = h[q(\cdot), l(\cdot), p(\cdot), w(\cdot), c(\cdot), t(\cdot); y, j^*] \qquad (5.1)$$

$$j^* = j[q(\cdot), l(\cdot), p(\cdot), w(\cdot), c(\cdot), t(\cdot); y, h^*]. \qquad (5.2)$$

These equations, however, are not distinguishable empirically—that is, they are not identified in econometric terms—because they contain the same list of determinants. Hence, we cannot investigate the residential location behaviour and the workplace choice behaviour specified in these equations as distinct and separate elements of behaviour.

The problem that we have identified is that more analysis of workplace location behaviour is required. Our analysis in Chapters 3 and 4 enables us to specify a proper structural equation for workplace location to extend the model and replace equation (5.2). We are therefore able to take equation (5.1) as a structural equation for residential location, given a workplace location equation to be specified below.

Most empirical work has considered workplace choice to be exogenous, or determined independently from household location. Then equation (5.1) states that h depends upon j and upon household income y [3] and other parameters of the location problem. In particular, we are concerned about factors which vary across individuals. For example, we may assume that the urban land-price and wage gradients facing individuals are the same, allowing us to concentrate on factors which affect commuting costs $c(\cdot)$ and time $t(\cdot)$ in equation (5.1)—namely the number of employed workers in the household, *nemp*—and factors which affect individual preferences and hence consumption of housing $q(\cdot)$ and leisure $l(\cdot)$—namely the age of the household head, *age*, and the presence of young children, *chldn*. We can therefore specify a model of the form

$$h = \alpha_0 + \alpha_1 j + \alpha_2 y + \alpha_3\, nemp + \alpha_4\, age + \alpha_5\, chldn + \varepsilon_h, \qquad (5.3)$$

where ε_h is the error term. We would expect that $\alpha_1 > 0$ since in-commuting is expected to predominate, other factors equal. Commuting distance may then increase or decrease, depending upon the degree of employment decentralization. [4] Thus, if commuting distance is

$$h - j = \alpha_0 + (\alpha_1 - 1)j + \alpha_2 y + \alpha_3\, nemp + \alpha_4\, age + \alpha_5\, chldn + \varepsilon_h$$

---

[3] Variable y represents unearned income in sect. 2.4.1. As in the empirical literature on labour supply, however, we assume that the effect of a \$1 change in earned household income is equivalent to a \$1 change in unearned household income. In effect, this allows us to ignore more complex interactions of residential location and labour supply in this model. The effect of second earners on residential location and household labour supply identified by Hekman (1980) is, however, captured by the inclusion of the number of employed workers, *nemp*, in the model. Additional discussion of the labour supply effects in this model is left until Ch. 6.

[4] Sect. 2.4.1 presents the argument for in-commuting with decentralized employment, based on White (1988).

from equation (5.3), then

$$\frac{\partial\,[h-j]}{\partial j} = \alpha_1 - 1 > 0\ (<0)\ \ as\ \ \alpha_1 > 1\ (<1).$$

From previous discussion we would also expect that $\alpha_2 > 0$, $\alpha_3 < 0$, $\alpha_4 > 0$, and $\alpha_5 > 0$. This is precisely the specification estimated by Siegel (1975) in his study of residential location behaviour in the San Francisco Bay Area.

5.3   DETERMINANTS OF WORKPLACE CHOICE

The model of workplace choice rests on two fundamental propositions that link job search and skill-acquisition decisions. The model extends the human capital framework to the spatial dimension. In that sense we have what might be termed an expanded human capital framework.

The first proposition is that job search is spatially systematic. Other factors equal, a worker prefers a job closer to his place of residence to reduce search and commuting costs. Local jobs have priority over comparable jobs involving greater travel. This proposition is essential to the idea of an urban wage gradient and to the human capital model of migration decisions. Spatially systematic search means that workplace choice depends upon residential location. Individuals in suburban locations are more likely to seek jobs in their own, or surrounding, suburbs while individuals living in the centre of the city will seek jobs in or near the centre.

Convention, in particular the standard residential location model of the previous section, dictates that our spatial reference point should be the city centre. As before the residential and workplace locations can be represented by the distance of the home and workplace from the city centre. We can then express household location as a determinant of job location because of spatially systematic search. As residential location increases, spatially systematic search implies that job location should also increase. Moreover, employment density decreases with distance from the city centre. Even a random search about the place of residence would be expected to yield more offers where employment density is greater toward the city centre as discussed in section 4.1.1. Job-seekers, aware of the higher employment density toward the city centre, are likely to spend more time searching in that direction. Spatially systematic search will be orientated locally and toward the city centre, implying that as residential location increases, job location should increase but at a smaller rate.[5]

The model, as it stands, cannot be distinguished empirically from the standard residential location model, which says that residential location depends upon workplace location. Indeed, authors have gone this far before, notably Siegel (1975: 34) who argued that 'the household is induced to separate its home and job location in favour of a job location closer to the relevant geographic employment center'. More analysis of workplace choice behaviour is needed to provide a distinctive model.

Our analysis in Chapter 4 satisfies this requirement. Given the urban structure—specifically, the spatial distribution of employment and working population—the labour market equilibrium conditions in a market where job search is spatially systematic will imply that, from a particular residential location, a worker will respond to local labour market conditions. Specifically, workplace choice is more likely to be local—and commuting commensurately reduced—the greater the ratio of jobs to workers in the local market. The introduction of urban structure, or labour market conditions, in this manner provides us with a distinctive workplace choice model based upon the proposition of spatially systematic search.

The second fundamental proposition introduced in Chapter 4 adds considerable predictive content to the model, distinguishes the model from a conventional model based solely on the value of commuting time, and, as we shall see, provides some new perspectives on urban behaviour and policy prescription. This proposition is that skill acquisition broadens the spatial extent of job search. The proposition is consistent with the hypothesis in human capital theory that the degree of specialization of a worker is determined by the extent of the market into which his services are sold. Skill acquisition requires a larger market and, in terms of workplace choice, a more spatially extensive search. It is also consistent with migration evidence that education increases mobility, since a more spatially extensive search for employment is more likely to imply inter-urban or interregional migration.

The second proposition implies that the response to opportunities for employment in the local labour market will differ according to skill level. As a worker becomes more skilled and adopts a more

---

[5] For more formal discussion of this point, see sect. 5.3.1.

spatially extensive search strategy, he becomes less responsive to local opportunities. A skilled worker, by the very nature of his specialized training, must look beyond the local labour market to cover the entire city, region, or nation. An unskilled worker, on the other hand, can be expected to concentrate on local employment opportunities initially. The outcome of the search, in terms of its duration and location and the quality of the job found, will then depend upon local labour market conditions to a much greater degree.

We can now think of the urban area as a series of local labour markets or islands. In Chapter 4 we have argued that an appropriate measure of local labour market conditions in a spatial search model involving workers and enterprises is the ratio of jobs to workers on the island.[6] If this ratio, measuring local excess demand for labour, is high then local employment opportunities are good. Enterprises will have greater difficulty recruiting workers in these circumstances, particularly at lower skill levels where search is more likely to be confined to the local area. They will need to adopt more aggressive recruitment techniques including more attractive offers of employment. This will increase the likelihood of a favourable local job–worker match for all workers but to a greater degree the lower the skill level of the worker involved. In a multiple regression equation this ratio may be introduced as an additional determinant of job location to distinguish job and household location behaviour.

As it stands, the job location model could be justified on commuting considerations alone, regardless of the spatial job search behaviour postulated in Chapters 3 and 4. Both considerations of the value of commuting time and spatial job search behaviour lead us to expect, however, that the effect of local employment opportunities will differ by skill level. To capture this aspect of behaviour, we may introduce skill-specific ratios of jobs to workers to assess the differential effects of local employment conditions by skill level. As skill level increases we would expect *greater* sensitivity of job location to local employment conditions if the value of commuting time dominates and *less* sensitivity if spatial job search considerations—that skill acquisition broadens search extent—dominate.

---

[6] Ellwood (1986) calls this the 'import ratio' in his study of the spatial mismatch problem for young blacks in the United States. His measure lacks the theoretical justification provided by Simpson (1980) but performs better than any other measure of local labour market conditions in his study. Lewin-Epstein (1985) also uses the ratio of youth to jobs as a measure of neighbourhood employment opportunities in his analysis of Chicago. These studies are considered further in Ch. 6.

A regression model incorporating these features provides us with a static general model of workplace choice to interact with the standard model of residential location. The model simultaneously determines workplace and residential location. In the absence of some clear indicator of the dynamic sequence, either workplace location or residential location or both locations may have changed according to the residential and workplace location behaviour we have specified. In particular, the model no longer ignores workplace choice decisions in determining urban spatial structure.

The model allows us to examine the effect of skill level on commuting decisions. The residential location model alone predicts that more-skilled workers attach, if anything, a higher value to their commuting time. Hence they should be more responsive to local employment offers and local labour market conditions. If the standard theory is correct, and our model of job–worker matching can be ignored, then the effect of skill level on workplace choice should be reversed. That is, given residential location considerations captured in our model, the only effect of skill level should be to increase sensitivity to local job opportunities. But the matching model from Chapter 4 predicts that this effect is far less important than spatial search behaviour which causes more-skilled workers to be less responsive to local conditions. The simultaneous model of residential and workplace location we have specified permits us to test the predictions of the two models. The workplace location regression model is specified in equation (5.7) in the next section. Combined with the residential location model given by equation (5.3), it provides us with an estimable simultaneous model of residential and workplace location to test our predictions.

5.3.1 An econometric model of workplace location*

The model of workplace choice may begin from equation (4.12) or equation (4.27) to specify

$$j = \beta_0 + \beta_1 h + \beta_2 s, \qquad (5.4)$$

where j and h are job and home location defined in terms of distance from the city centre and where s is the ratio of jobs to workers on the island or residence, as defined earlier. The model predicts that job seeking will be locally and centrally orientated, or that $\partial j/\partial h = \beta_1 > 0$, and that commuting distance declines (or j increases, given h)

as local employment conditions improve, or that $\partial j/\partial s = \beta_2 > 0$.[7]

The effect of skill level is ambiguous, depending on the relative importance of job search and the value of commuting time. We may introduce the effect of skill level by specifying skill-specific local labour market conditions and assessing their effects on workplace location. Thus, we want to expand equation (5.4) in the form

$$j = \beta_0 + \beta_1 h + \beta_2(G)s, \qquad (5.5)$$

where s is skill-specific and where the effect of s on j, $\beta_2(G)$, depends on skill level. Let i be an index ranking skill level in ascending order and let s_i be the corresponding ratio of jobs to workers at that skill level on the island of residence. Then a linear version of equation (5.5) is

$$j = \beta_0 + \beta_1 h + \beta_{2i} s_i, \qquad (5.6)$$

if the worker is in skill group i, where we define

$$\beta_{2i} \equiv \beta_2 \text{ if skill group 1}$$

and

$$\beta_{2i} \equiv \beta_2 + \beta_{3i} \text{ if skill group } i > 1.$$

If there are Γ skill groups then we may write the regression model for workplace choice as

$$j = \beta_0 + \beta_1 h + \left(\beta_2 + \sum_{i=2}^{\Gamma} \beta_{3i} G_i \right) s_i + \varepsilon_j, \qquad (5.7)$$

$$\text{where } G_i = 1 \text{ if in skill group } i > 1$$

$$= 0 \text{ otherwise}$$

and ε_j is the error term. As before, we expect that $\beta_1 > 0$ and $\beta_2 > 0$. The effect of skill level on the relationship between local labour market conditions, s, and job location, j, will vary, however, depending upon the relative importance of job search considerations and the value of commuting time. Specifically, we expect that, if job search considerations predominate as in equation (4.28) and more-skilled workers are less sensitive to local labour market conditions, then

$$\beta_{3i} < 0 \; \forall \, i$$

and

$$\beta_{3i} > \beta_{3i+1} \left(\text{or } \left| \beta_{3i} \right| < \left| \beta_{3i+1} \right| \right). \qquad (5.8)$$

---

[7] See equation (4.13) in sect. 4.3.1 for a simple and direct derivation of these predictions.

On the other hand, we would expect that, if the value of commuting time predominates as in equation (4.29) and more-skilled workers are more sensitive to local labour market conditions, then

$$\beta_{3i} > 0 \ \forall \ i$$

and

$$\beta_{3i} > \beta_{3i+1}. \qquad (5.9)$$

The predictions contained in equations (5.8) and (5.9) offer a clear test of the importance of the job–worker matching model specified in Chapter 4 *vis-à-vis* conventional analysis concentrating on the value of commuting. This test should be carried out in the model of the joint determination of residential and workplace location represented by the econometric model of equations (5.3) and (5.7).

5.4 EVIDENCE ON WORKPLACE CHOICE, RESIDENTIAL LOCATION, AND COMMUTING

Evidence on commuting by skill level provides some support for the workplace choice model. Rees and Shultz (1970) provide information on distances travelled to work in Chicago for carefully defined categories of occupation. The categories can be arranged in groups in order of increasing skill,[8] based on Rees and Shultz's own rankings: janitors and material handlers; fork-lift truckers, punch-press operators and truck-drivers; tab' operators; maintenance electricians and tool- and die-makers; and accountants. The data indicate that workers are more likely to travel long distances (more than 15 miles) to work, and less likely to travel short distances (less than 2.5 miles) to work, the higher their skill level. This pattern is more easily identified for males than females. Indeed female commuting behaviour appeared to be different from male commuting behaviour, an issue that we will consider further in the next section.

These results are corroborated by Duncan's (1956) earlier study of the Occupational Mobility Survey for Chicago. The commuting distance of workers varied directly and significantly with socioeconomic level and, to a lesser extent, workplace centralization. More-skilled

---

[8] Skill level generally means the normal level of formal education and vocational training required for the job. Informal on-the-job training may also be important to a lesser extent, but it is rarely considered. In a human capital framework, skill-level rankings can be based on wages at some specified point in each worker's career, such as his peak earnings.

workers commuted longer distances to work on average whether their workplace was located in the central business district or not. The problem with such evidence is that skill level, individual earnings, and household income are likely to be closely related. A skilled worker with high earnings is likely to live in a household with high income, since earnings are the major source of household income. Since the residential location model predicts that a household with high income will locate further from the workplace, even if the household members value commuting time more, greater commuting by skilled workers *per se* is not inconsistent with the residential location model. We need to account for the effects of residential location decisions, in particular the effect of household income on residential location, to isolate the effect of workplace choice.

Other evidence, discussed in Chapter 2, is more difficult to dismiss in this fashion. Kain's (1975) evidence that workers in better-paid occupations commute further in Detroit is more difficult to reconcile with residential location theory because is applies regardless of workplace and residential location. All workers who work in the outermost ring would be expected to live there, but better-paid workers are less likely to do so. Residential location theory would predict that they would be more likely to do so because of higher household income and the greater value they place on commuting time. Simpson (1977) found similar evidence for Greater London and the South-East Lancashire Conurbation in the UK.

More convincing evidence requires us to take account of residential location decisions before examining workplace location and commuting patterns. The direct way to do this is by regression analysis based on equations (5.3) for residential location and (5.7) for workplace location. Simpson (1980) uses this approach with the 1971–2 Greater London Transportation Survey and Simpson (1987) and Simpson (1989) replicate the analysis with the 1979 Metropolitan Toronto Travel Survey. In each case the survey provided information on all the required variables for 30,759 commuters in Greater London and 2,245 commuters in Toronto except the ratio of jobs to residents in each skill group in the local area surrounding the place of residence. This variable can be calculated for Greater London from the 1971 Census of England and Wales Workplace and Transport Tables and for Metropolitan Toronto from unpublished data from the 1981 Census of Canada.

This procedure requires us to accept census boundaries as local labour market areas, namely the thirty-two boroughs of the Greater

London Council and the six boroughs and outlying census subdivisions of the Toronto Metropolitan area. Whether these boundaries are appropriate is debatable and, given more disaggregated data, one could experiment with the boundaries. The boundaries are, however, generally recognized local boundaries of fairly large submetropolitan areas, averaging about one-quarter of a million people. The areas appear to be large enough to provide local employment opportunities and to impose significant costs on search and commuting outside the area. In this sense they correspond to the islands parable used in the last two chapters. At the same time the areas are small enough, and hence numerous enough in a large city like London or Toronto, to provide substantial variation in local employment opportunities faced by residents across the city. In this respect the boundaries for the variable imposed by census data seem about right.

In order to estimate the residential location equation (5.3) and the workplace location equation (5.7) directly and without bias, one must take account of the simultaneous determination of residential and workplace location decisions in the model. If the model is correctly specified, this requires the use of two-stage least-squares regression or a similar procedure.[9] Simpson (1989) tests the null hypothesis of no interaction between residential and workplace location for Toronto using Hausman's (1978) specification test and rejects it convincingly in favour of the alternative hypothesis that residential and workplace location are simultaneously determined. In fact, the residential location equation provides very poor regression results when it is estimated by ordinary least squares under the null hypothesis of no interaction but it provides quite reasonable results when two-stage least-squares estimation is used on the model specified by equations (5.3) and (5.7).

Simpson (1980, 1987) provides various estimates of the model using two-stage least squares for Greater London and Toronto. The results of these studies are summarized in Table 5.1. The results for the residential location equation indicate that a one-kilometre increase in the distance of the workplace from the city centre increases the distance of the residence from the centre by an average of 0.7 kilometres in Greater London and 1.65 kilometres in Toronto. These results are consistent with conventional residential location theory as

---

[9] Since the equations are over-identified the obvious single-equation regression procedures to obtain consistent estimates are two-stage least squares or limited-information maximum-likelihood estimation.

TABLE 5.1. *Full sample regression estimates of residential and workplace location for Greater London and Toronto* (method is 2SLS; *t*-values in parentheses; commuting distance in km)

	Greater London		Toronto	
Residential location equation (5.3) to explain h				
Constant	5.71		− 0.17	
j	0.67	(102.2)	1.65	(16.6)
y	0.75	(34.5)	0.037	(2.8)
nemp	− 0.63	(16.6)	− 0.59	(2.6)
chldn	0.17	(2.8)	− 0.14	(2.1)
age	0.17	(2.8)	0.37	(0.99)
Workplace location equation (5.7) to explain j				
Constant	− 0.40		− 0.15	
h	0.68	(85.2)	0.71	(3.7)
s_1	2.89	(32.3)	3.40	(2.4)
$s_2.G_2$	− 0.71	(7.4)	− 0.24	(1.1)
$s_3.G_3$	− 2.31	(27.9)	− 1.05	(6.1)
$s_4.G_4$	− 2.89	(31.8)	− 2.31	(6.4)

Notes: *j* = distance of the job from the city centre; *y* = household income (£'000 or $'000); *nemp* = no. of employed persons; *chldn* = no. of preschool children present; *age* indicates household head > 45 yrs.; *h* = distance of the household from the city centre; s_1 = local ratio of jobs to workers for the lowest skill group; s_i = local ratio of jobs to workers for skill group *i*(*i* = 1, . . . , 4); G_i is a dummy variable indicating skill group *i*.

Source: Simpson (1980, 1987).

presented in Chapter 2, which predicts a positive correlation between household and workplace location to reflect commuting toward the city centre. That the effect is larger for Toronto is consistent with the discussion in Chapter 2 and the evidence in Table 2.3 that employment is more centralized in Toronto than in Greater London.[10] An increase of £1,000 in household income increases the distance of the residence from the city centre by an average of 0.75 kilometres in Greater London in 1971; a comparable increase of $5,000 in household income in Toronto in 1979 increases average residential distance by 0.19 kilometres.[11] The presence of a second earner in the house-

[10] The greenbelt around Greater London may also have some effect since it distorts the rent gradient and residential location decisions (Evans, 1985: 200–4).
[11] Using an exchange rate of £1.00 = $Can.2.50 and a doubling of prices between 1971 and 1979, £1,000 in 1971 and $Can.5,000 in 1979 are roughly comparable.

hold reduces the distance of the residence from the city centre by an average of 0.6 kilometres in both Greater London and Toronto. Household heads over 45 years of age locate 0.17 kilometres farther out in Greater London than household heads 45 years of age or younger, and 0.37 kilometres farther out in Toronto. Households with preschool children locate 0.17 kilometres farther out in Greater London than households without preschool children. Anomalously, they locate 0.14 kilometres closer to the centre than their counterparts without preschool children in Toronto.[12]

The results of the two studies for the residential location model are generally consistent with the predictions of the basic theory. Location of the workplace, household income, and family circumstances (number of workers, age of the head, and the presence of children) affect residential location decisions. Both regressions are statistically significant and all the coefficients are individually significant[13] with the exception of age of the household head in Toronto. Our main interest, in any case, is not in residential location *per se* but in accounting for the major socioeconomic factors that influence residential location so that we may examine the workplace location decision in equation (5.7). In this respect, the fact that the residential location model conforms to expectations is a reassuring start.

The results for the workplace location model in Table 5.1 support the job–worker matching model. A one-kilometre increase in the distance of the residence from the city centre increases the distance of the job from the city centre by 0.68 kilometres in Greater London and 0.71 kilometres in Toronto. That is, given the residential location decision explained by equation (5.3), workplace location is not random but is geared to local job opportunities. Since employment density is greater toward the city centre, jobs are found primarily in that direction, but residential location in the suburbs pulls the search locus in the same direction.

This pull varies by skill level, however, in a manner consistent with the job–worker matching model and contrary to predictions that rely on the value of commuting time.[14] Consider, for example, a household

---

[12] Alternative measures of family structure, such as the presence of children 16 years of age or younger, are not the answer to this anomaly. Simpson (1987) reports that this measure was used in the analysis of the Toronto data but it gave the same anomalous result.

[13] A 5%-level of significance is used for all statistical tests in this chapter and in Ch. 6.

[14] See, in particular, the coefficient sign predictions of equations (5.8) and (5.9) in sect. 5.3.1.

located 10 kilometres from the city centre and consider the average case in which the number of local jobs equals the number of local workers.[15] The results in Table 5.1 imply that unskilled and semi-skilled workers find jobs 9.3 kilometres from the centre on average in Greater London and 9.0 kilometres from the centre in Toronto. This implies a very local employment search and short commuting trips. As skill level increases, the distance to the workplace increases despite the higher valuation of commuting time by more-skilled workers. Skilled manual workers find jobs 8.6 kilometres from the centre on average in Greater London and 8.8 kilometres from the centre in Toronto. Junior and intermediate non-manual workers find jobs 7.0 kilometres from the centre in Greater London and 8.0 kilometres from the centre in Toronto. Professional employees find jobs 6.4 kilometres from the centre in Greater London and 6.7 kilometres from the centre in Toronto. These results are not explained by residential location decisions, in so far as they have been captured by equation (5.3). In particular, the argument that skilled workers commute farther solely because they use their higher earnings to purchase residential sites further from the city centre is not supported by the evidence, since household income has been included in equation (5.3) to explain residential location. In high-income households workers choose workplaces farther from home the higher their skill level, consistent with the spatial job search behaviour described in Chapter 4 and the implied criticism of residential location theory from aggregate commuting evidence reviewed earlier in this section. If the only consideration were commuting costs, workers would locate closer to their place of residence the greater their skill level because commuting costs rise with earnings. Thus these results are not predicted by the basic theory of urban spatial structure unless it is extended to consider the job–worker matching model of workplace choice. The workplace location equations and the differences in response to local labour market conditions by skill level are all statistically significant in these results.[16]

Further indirect tests of the model of residential and workplace location choice from these studies are summarized in Table 5.2. Population groups can be distinguished in each survey that have different degrees of residential and workplace mobility. Simpson (1980) distin-

[15] That is, $s_i = 1$ for all i.

[16] Standard F-tests are used to test the explanatory significance of all regressions and the patterns of job location by skill level.

TABLE 5.2. *Subsample regression estimates of residential and workplace location for Greater London and Toronto* (method is 2SLS; *t*-values in parentheses; commuting distance in km)

Regressors	Greater London		Toronto			
	J c , 2 e*	Movers	Heads	Non-heads	Owners	Renters
Residential location equation (5.3): dependent variable is h						
Constant	4.63	7.21	− 0.17	− 0.17	− 0.18	− 0.05
j	0.72	0.53	1.47	1.81	1.75	1.34
	(80.5)	(12.9)	(12.4)	(11.3)	(10.9)	(13.8)
y	0.62	0.62	0.052	0.020	0.037	0.018
	(20.1)	(5.0)	(2.9)	(1.1)	(2.1)	(0.9)
nemp	− 0.33	− 0.28	− 0.16	− 0.82	− 0.72	− 0.15
	(6.3)	(1.0)	(0.5)	(2.3)	(2.3)	(0.4)
chldn	− 0.08	− 0.33	− 0.10	− 0.15	− 0.12	− 0.13
	(0.8)	(1.3)	(1.3)	(1.5)	(1.4)	(1.4)
age	0.36	− 0.10	0.66	− 0.03	0.22	0.45
	(4.1)	(0.2)	(1.4)	(0.1)	(0.4)	(1.0)
Workplace location equation (5.7): dependent variable is j						
Constant	− 1.07	1.84	0.57	− 0.85	− 0.60	− 0.16
h	0.78	0.46	0.26	1.10	0.92	0.84
	(69.9)	(10.0)	(1.1)	(2.8)	(2.7)	(3.5)
s_1	2.66	2.81	0.79	6.53	5.75	2.46
	(21.7)	(4.9)	(0.5)	(2.0)	(2.2)	(1.5)
$s_2.G_2$	− 0.58	− 0.31	− 0.37	− 0.34	− 0.04	− 0.54
	(4.0)	(0.5)	(1.5)	(0.6)	(0.1)	(1.8)
$s_3.G_3$	− 2.11	− 2.83	− 1.19	− 1.15	− 1.14	− 0.95
	(19.4)	(5.2)	(5.3)	(3.5)	(4.6)	(4.0)
$s_4.G_4$	− 2.58	− 2.69	− 2.58	− 2.36	− 2.81	− 1.60
	(17.9)	(4.9)	(5.8)	(3.2)	(5.1)	(3.3)
no. obs.	14,020	1,079	1,133	1,112	1,324	921

Note: variable definitions as Table 5.1.
* job-changers and second earners.
Source: Simpson (1980, 1987).

guishes between workers who changed only their workplace and workers who changed only their place of residence in the previous year in Greater London. The behaviour of the former group should be explained by the workplace choice model. Earners other than the household head are included in this group based on the argument that their residential location decision is predetermined by the household head (Beesley and Dalvi, 1974). As expected, the workplace choice model performs better for this group. In particular, the location of the job is more responsive to the location of the residence in the workplace choice model,[17] while the pattern of responsiveness by skill level is maintained. For workers who changed only their place of residence, on the other hand, the residential location model performs better as expected. In this case residential location is more responsive to workplace location.

Simpson (1987) is unable to distinguish residential moves and job relocation for Toronto. Household heads are instead compared with non-heads and home-owners are compared with renters. Workplace location decisions should be more important for non-heads than heads (Beesley and Dalvi, 1974) and should also be more important for home-owners than renters because of the transaction costs of buying and selling a house (Hughes and McCormick, 1981). This prediction is confirmed by the Toronto data. The workplace location of non-heads and home-owners is more sensitive to local labour market conditions at all skill levels and more responsive to residential location than that of household heads and renters. These empirical studies suggest that the workplace choice model advanced in Chapter 4 adds to our understanding of urban spatial structure. More than just clearing up a theoretical loose end, it provides an explanation for several empirical anomalies in the pattern of workplace and residential location and commuting.

Simpson (1987) adapts the model of residential and workplace location represented by equations (5.3) and (5.7) to explain urban commuting distances. This requires the assumption that residential and workplace locations are aligned with respect to the city centre. This is a prediction of residential location theory since alignment offers the cheapest combination of commuting and land costs. It is also a plausible working assumption in the workplace choice model if job search is directed where employment density is greatest toward the city centre. There is also some evidence to support this assumption in Simpson (1980), who reports that 70 per cent of workers in Greater London lived beyond their workplace and were more or less directly aligned with their workplace and the city centre.[18] This assumption

---

[17] That is, the estimate $\partial j/\partial h = \beta_1$ from equation (5.7) is larger for job-changers and second earners than for the entire sample (Table 5.1) or for movers, as we would expect. For more discussion of this result see Simpson (1980: 344).

[18] Specifically, the angle formed at the city centre by the location of the residence and the workplace was less than 45°.

permits us to represent commuting distance simply by the difference between residential and workplace location from three possible models —the residential location model (5.3) alone, the workplace location model (5.7) alone, and the simultaneous residential and workplace location model consisting of equations (5.3) and (5.7). The explanatory power of these three models of commuting distance can then be compared.

The results of this model comparison, while hardly definitive, are quite interesting. The workplace location model provides a better explanation of commuting distance than the residential location model in several respects. The workplace location model explains a much larger proportion of the variation in commuting distance. As Hamilton's (1982) results would suggest, the residential location model— that is, job location, household income, the number of employees in the household, the age of the household head, and the presence of children from equation (5.3)—explains very little of the variation in commuting distance, only 1.4 per cent for the Toronto survey. The workplace location model—residential location and local jobs per worker by skill group from equation (5.7)—explains 15.3 per cent of the variation. Given the large variation in individual behaviour in such data, the latter level of explanatory power is usually considered to be quite respectable. Moreover, when the residential and workplace location models are combined, only the variables from the workplace location model are significant as a group with the signs predicted by the theory.

5.5 FURTHER EVIDENCE—COMMUTING DIFFERENCES BY SEX AND RACE

Other studies of commuting patterns have examined differences in commuting between women and men and between workers in racial majority and minority groups. These studies have generally been based upon the traditional access–space trade-off model of residential location and urban structure, although there are some interesting exceptions. Examination of this literature at this point reinforces earlier criticism of the traditional approach and allows us to evaluate the need for the job–worker matching model to understand commuting behaviour.

Analysis of commuting behaviour by sex and race is often motivated by concern for equality of social opportunity. Opportunities can be unequal through outright discrimination in employment or housing or through more subtle social pressures which restrict certain groups. In particular, female workers may suffer discrimination in the workplace or social pressures in the home which limit their choice of employment relative to comparable male workers. Workers in racial minorities may also encounter discrimination in employment and housing which affects their welfare relative to other comparable workers in society. Such inequity may then be addressed by various forms of anti-discrimination legislation where it is deemed to be a social problem.

Studies have found that married female workers commute shorter distances than married male workers. White (1977) argues that the traditional access–space trade-off model can account for this difference. Her model begins with the assumption that married women work only in suburban firms while men work in the city centre. She bases this assumption on evidence that married women are more likely to work in the suburbs than men. Under this assumption White shows that two-earner families outbid other households for residential sites near the workplace location of married women, resulting in shorter commuting trips for married women than married men.

White's argument is correct, given her assumptions, but her assumption of predetermined workplace locations for men and women is restrictive. We can relax this assumption by allowing both workplace and residential choices to be made. In fact, this is what other scholars have done. Kain (1962), for example, argues that married women are predominantly secondary earners in families who adopt more casual job search methods than their husbands. This leads to restricted job search and shorter commuting. Rees and Shultz (1970) argue that married females prefer nearby jobs more than married males because of domestic responsibilities. Beesley and Dalvi (1974) argue that married women are restricted because residential location decisions are made by the husband with reference to his workplace. Married women only make job location decisions. Singell and Lillydahl (1986) find that commuting distance is reduced when males move but increased for females who move, which supports Beesley and Dalvi's argument. Other indirect evidence on the difference in residential and workplace location for household heads and other household workers in Simpson (1987) also supports this view. The evidence on male and female commuting behaviour has, by and large, been rudimentary and unconvincing, based on aggregate data. Only

Rees and Shultz (1970) use household data, but they focus on wages and employment rather than commuting behaviour *per se*.

Notice that in Beesley and Dalvi's argument married women work in suburban firms because they live in nearby suburban locations, quite the opposite of White's (1977) argument. While White's argument is plausible, it is not the only possible one. Using the access–space trade-off model of residential location from a predetermined workplace, White's approach ignores other arguments based on workplace choice. This study argues that this approach is unduly restrictive. The study provides a model of workplace choice which can expand the conventional approach to urban structure to include the arguments provided by Kain and by Beesley and Dalvi. It provides a more general model in which the relative importance of residential choice and workplace choice can be assessed empirically.

Simpson (1989) takes a direct approach to the issue by estimating the residential and workplace location equations (5.3) and (5.7) separately for men and women for the Toronto household microdata. These results are summarized in Table 5.3. As before, Hausman's (1978) test rejects the hypothesis that residential location can be estimated independently of workplace location—that is, as if workplace location were predetermined. Estimating the two equations simultaneously using two-stage least squares, the study finds remarkably similar residential location behaviour for men and women,[19] contrary to Beesley and Dalvi's hypothesis that males dominate residential location decisions. Moreover, the presence of a second earner has a similarly weak centralizing effect for both male and female residential location decisions, contrary to White's thesis that residential location choice in two-earner households is significantly different from residential location choice in one-earner households.

The interesting differences in male and female behaviour in Table 5.3 arise for workplace location decisions. Male workplace location behaviour is much more centralized, generating longer commuting as observed in other studies cited at the beginning of this section. The coefficient on household location is very close to 1 for females, indicating that workplace location is very close to residential location, while it is only 0.39 for males. Favourable local labour market conditions (variable s_1 in Table 5.3) reduce commuting from the local

---

[19] In fact, the explanatory power of the residential location equation is stronger for working females, the majority of whom are married, than for males.

TABLE 5.3. *Regression estimates of residential and workplace location for females and males in Toronto* (method is 2SLS; *t*-values in parentheses; commuting distance in km)

Regressors	Females		Males	
Residential location equation (5.3)				
Constant	– 0.04		– 0.24	
j	1.48	(12.3)	1.61	(12.2)
y	0.020	(1.1)	0.044	(2.6)
nemp	– 0.32	(1.0)	– 0.40	(1.3)
chldn	– 0.03	(0.3)	– 0.12	(1.4)
age	– 0.26	(0.5)	0.80	(1.7)
Workplace location equation (5.7)				
Constant	– 0.53		0.34	
h	0.98	(2.0)	0.39	(1.6)
s_1	4.82	(1.4)	1.62	(1.0)
$s_2.G_2$	9.85	(2.0)	– 0.96	(1.3)
$s_3.G_3$	– 2.63	(4.0)	– 1.96	(4.7)
$s_4.G_4$	– 2.28	(3.4)	– 2.42	(5.9)
no. obs.	996		1,249	

Note: variable definitions as Table 5.1.
Source: Simpson (1989).

area, but the statistically significant skill-specific pattern observed in Tables 5.1 and 5.2 is only apparent for males. This may simply reflect the fact that almost all female jobs are white-collar jobs[20] and that the remaining two-skill categories in the study offer insufficient variation in skills to observe any clear pattern in workplace location. The study suggests that the secret to better understanding of male and female commuting differences lies in more careful theoretical and empirical analysis of differences in workplace location behaviour and its causes, not conventional analysis of differences in residential location behaviour. Hence, the analysis and empirical work in this study to this point provide a basis for better understanding of differences in commuting behaviour by sex.

A similar argument can be made with respect to commuting by racial groups. The conventional approach concentrates on residential choice and argues that discrimination in housing restricts the residen-

---

[20] Only 0.4% of the sample of females fell into the second skill category, skilled manual workers, where the coefficient is large and has the wrong sign.

tial choice of minorities. This restriction creates a spatial mismatch between some workers in racial minorities and their jobs, which increases their commuting trips (Kain, 1968*a*). This argument has led many urban policy-makers to concentrate on housing discrimination despite questionable supporting evidence (Lapham, 1971). McCormick (1986) challenges this viewpoint. He finds that West Indians in Birmingham, UK are more mobile in terms of residential location than Asians but suffer equally long commuting trips relative to whites. Moreover, very few of these long commuting trips by West Indian and Asian workers are to white suburbs. Most of them are to a single industrial area where there is a substantial residential community of these minorities. Housing discrimination does not appear to be the major problem.

McCormick argues that we must look at the labour market and discrimination in employment. He considers a city with two districts. Individuals who live in one district find it costly to search in the other district. Local search, or search in one's own district, increases as the probability of local job offers increases. McCormick argues, however, that racial discrimination introduces differential job rejection rates between the minority group, the Asians and West Indians, and the majority group. This reduces the probability of local offers for Asians and West Indians and increases commuting. Higher job rejection rates may also result in greater unemployment and lower wages for Asians and West Indians, although the evidence is restricted to commuting.

McCormick's model is consistent with our job–worker matching model. His districts introduce the spatial search costs of an island economy. Job search depends upon the probability of local job offers, which differs by race. In our model, the probability of local job offers depends more generally upon urban spatial structure, represented by the ratio of jobs to workers by skill group. Racial discrimination, or higher job rejection rates, are equivalent to fewer local jobs per worker which leads to greater commuting. McCormick also argues that skilled workers may 'bump down' (Reder, 1955) and accept unskilled jobs to increase their probability of finding local jobs to reduce commuting. This argument is consistent with our hypothesis that skill acquisition broadens the spatial extent of job search.

Because McCormick's focus is limited to discrimination and commuting, however, his analysis of workplace choice is less general. The role of urban structure is ignored in the formal model where local employment opportunities differ by race but not by location. In our model the role of urban structure in workplace choice and commuting is explicitly incorporated. McCormick's treatment of skill is similarly restricted to the argument that workers facing poor local employment prospects may seek local jobs for which they are overqualified.[21] In our model skill is an integral part of workplace choice and commuting behaviour, since more-skilled workers are less responsive to local employment conditions. Evidence in the previous section indicates that skill is an important factor determining workplace choice and commuting behaviour. Fortunately, McCormick accounts for skill differences in his empirical work.

The literature on commuting differences by sex and race reinforces the argument that the traditional approach to residential location and urban spatial structure is deficient. Many scholars, in analysing commuting differences by race and sex, have naturally turned to workplace location decisions of one form or another to incorporate discrimination in the labour market. McCormick (1986, 377) notes, however, that 'Perhaps surprisingly, there have been no attempts to model formally how job search and journey to work differs among residents of a given neighbourhood.'

This has been precisely the task of this study. The expanded model of spatial structure, involving both workplace and residential location, can accommodate the approaches to commuting behaviour by race and sex in the literature. The traditional model, on the other hand, can accommodate only a few of the approaches to this problem and may have pointed many scholars in the wrong direction.

5.6 CONCLUDING REMARKS

A lot of theory may not be very compelling without at least a little supporting evidence. This chapter has assembled and summarized a growing body of evidence on commuting behaviour in support of the workplace choice model developed in Chapter 4. Much of the evidence simply questions the adequacy of the traditional theory of urban spatial structure to predict commuting patterns by itself. Some of the evidence tests the workplace choice model directly with a model of residential choice and finds strong empirical support from transport-

---

[21] This possibility is discussed in Ch. 4 but dismissed as relatively unimportant for the population as a whole. This does not mean that it may not be important for certain minority groups, such as those facing discrimination. Such underemployment is considered further in Ch. 6.

ation survey data in the United Kingdom and Canada. Still other evidence assesses commuting behaviour by race and sex by adopting, implicitly or explicitly, a workplace choice model consistent with the general model developed in Chapter 4. This evidence, while not conclusive, certainly encourages further investigation of workplace choice and the urban economic issues that it raises.

Workplace choice, once recognized, raises many new issues. It links urban economic issues directly to the labour market. At the same time it provides a new, spatial perspective on traditional issues in labour economics. Up to now we have dealt mainly with such conventional urban economic issues as commuting. It is now appropriate to examine new issues that link urban and labour economics. Many of these issues have been addressed by urban scholars in the past without the benefit of an explicit analytical framework.

The foremost issues are underemployment and poverty, issues that are rarely ignored by textbooks in urban or labour economics. If job search and workplace choice affect commuting decisions then they may also affect individual success in finding and keeping a job and in sustaining sufficient employment income to escape poverty. Our model of the urban economy which includes workplace choice leads us naturally to consider these issues and to assess the impact of spatial structure on urban labour market performance.

6

JOB–WORKER MATCHING AND UNDEREMPLOYMENT

MOST economic activity and economic problems occur in and around cities in a developed economy. Underemployment—including unemployment, part-time employment, and poverty arising from inadequate earnings—is no exception. Moreover, underemployment tends to be spatially concentrated in older inner-city areas (Kain, 1968a; Mooney, 1969; Mills, 1972a; Metcalf and Richardson, 1980; Vipond, 1980, 1983; Evans and Richardson, 1981; Evans, 1984).[1] Most urban economics textbooks devote considerable attention to underemployment because it is an important urban problem with a distinct spatial character, although its origins are seen to lie primarily outside the scope of urban economic analysis in the nature of a market economy (Mills, 1972a; Evans, 1984). The distinct spatial pattern of unemployment in cities is viewed as arising from residential location behaviour which confines low-income households to older, inner-city housing.

Some prominent urban scholars have attempted to link urban spatial structure, commuting problems, and urban underemployment. Kain (1968a) argues that the decentralization of employment in cities and the confinement of minority workers to the inner cities creates a 'spatial mismatch' of jobs and workers in the United States. The spatial mismatch penalizes black Americans in particular in the form of unemployment, underemployment, and jobs involving expensive commuting. Other prominent studies of urban underemployment by Forrester (1969) and Banfield (1970) agree, citing the lack of local jobs for the underemployed in the central cities of the United States, combined with the rapid in-migration of the underemployed to low-cost housing in the central cities, as crucial elements of the urban problem.

[1] Spatial concentration of poverty is apparently less characteristic of rural areas, at least in the United States. Auletta (1982: 197) e.g. reports that 'In rural areas it's not uncommon . . . to find the rural poor living next door to more affluent families.' Thus the poor are less prone to spatially segregated neighbourhoods in rural areas than in urban areas.

Spatial mismatch remains a significant and controversial issue in urban and labour market studies (Smith and Welch, 1987). Recent controversy concerns the role of spatial mismatch in black youth underemployment in the United States. Ellwood (1986) carefully assesses the spatial mismatch problem. He uses, among other measures, our preferred measure of local labour market conditions, jobs per worker in the local area, which he calls the import ratio. He finds that a high import ratio significantly increases the employment rate for young blacks in Chicago but the effect is small. He concludes that spatial mismatch is not the crucial problem. Leonard (1987) reports evidence from Chicago and Los Angeles, however, which disputes Ellwood's conclusion. He finds that the proportion of blacks in a firm is significantly influenced by the distance of the firm from the main ghetto, especially in Chicago where residential segregation is more pronounced. He also cites considerable evidence from other studies that local labour market conditions affect earnings for black workers—specifically, that blacks in the inner city earn less than comparably qualified blacks in the suburbs. He concludes that

In contrast to some recent studies emphasizing the fluid and mobile nature of urban labor markets where distance between job and home counts for little, this study finds evidence of very differently colored labor markets within a few miles of each other, demonstrating the importance of detailed analyses of localized labor markets within a city. (Leonard, 1987: 324)

Analysis of the spatial mismatch hypothesis suffers not from lack of empirical support but from lack of an explicit model linking urban spatial structure and the labour market. Kain and others argue informally or implicitly that workplace choice affects not only urban commuting behaviour, as discussed in the previous chapter, but also employment prospects. Leonard (1987) develops a more formal model in which the spatial mismatch problem arises simply from a model in which workers face fixed residential location and commuting costs. Ellwood (1986) observes correctly, however, that commuting costs alone cannot provide a persuasive argument because they are too small to explain the enormous level of underemployment observed. He sees job search behaviour as the crucial theoretical issue in the spatial mismatch debate.[2] Yet no one has provided an explicit model of urban structure that incorporates workplace choice, com-

---

[2] We might repeat here that Leonard's model also does not provide an explanation of commuting behaviour by skill level observed in Ch. 5. It therefore cannot serve as a general model of worker mobility in cities.

muting costs, and job search behaviour until now. Now that we have developed a model of this nature and found empirical support for its predictions regarding urban commuting behaviour, we can consider the effects of urban structure on underemployment more carefully.

Underemployment is a complex economic issue with a history of controversy too long to review here. Nevertheless some discussion of the issue is necessary. The conventional approach to urban economics can ignore the causes of underemployment and focus upon its spatial consequences through residential location theory. This approach is adequate for urban studies *only if* urban structure has no effect on underemployment. If we wish to investigate urban structure as a potential factor causing underemployment, then we must consider the nature of the underemployment problem and the role that urban spatial structure may play. This requires attention to the underemployment problem *per se* in analysis of the urban economy.

The next section considers the underemployment problem with particular reference to its consequences for the urban economy. Although the underemployment problem may arise in the broader context of macroeconomic stabilization, we focus here on the labour market. This focus is necessary to render the survey manageable; it also provides us with the literature most relevant to consider the effect of workplace choice behaviour on underemployment. We restrict ourselves to the general underemployment problem and its effects on urban structure through residential location in the next section. We then turn in the following section to the issue of spatial mismatch and the potential effect of urban structure on underemployment through our model of workplace choice. This is followed by a review of the empirical evidence on urban structure and underemployment and some concluding remarks to summarize the relevant issues for the examination of urban employment policy in Chapter 7.

6.1   UNDEREMPLOYMENT AND LABOUR MARKET THEORY

Underemployment is one of the major issues that has divided economists from Adam Smith to Karl Marx to John Maynard Keynes to the present. This section can only hope to summarize the modern debate as it pertains to the labour market and, ultimately, to the spatial distribution of underemployment in urban areas.

An important aspect of the modern debate is the issue of equilibrium in the market for labour services. As discussed in Chapter 3, an important recent development is the economics of information, examining the effect of information on market adjustment. Equilibrium is defined not in terms of exact market clearing (demand always equals supply) but in terms of correct expectations such that 'the outcomes of the participants' attempts to carry out their individual plans are going to be consistent with participants' expectations' (Phelps, 1985: 60). Disequilibrium arises in the labour market when workers and employers base their decisions on incorrect expectations of wages and other market conditions. Disequilibrium (excess demand or supply of labour in the usual sense) then generates signals which will guide market participants toward expectations and, where permitted, actions which correspond more closely to the equilibrium outcome.

The job–worker matching model developed in Chapter 4 is based on this information-orientated approach to labour market equilibrium. The model is based on the island economy of Phelps (1970*a*, 1970*b*) and Lucas and Prescott (1974). In these models local wage rates adjust to clear each island in each period. Job search, and hence unemployment, arises because workers receive local wage offers which they expect to be able to improve upon elsewhere. In Phelps's model workers receive low offers because of adverse general demand shocks arising from the business cycle. Because the shock is general, workers' expectations of better prospects elsewhere are not realized. Cyclical unemployment arises from resistance by workers to wage reductions leading to search for alternative jobs. The unemployment, while cyclical in nature, arises from incorrect expectations not wage inflexibility. Disequilibrium arises from imperfect information not other barriers to employment. In Lucas and Prescott's model, on the other hand, there is no cyclical unemployment. Adverse demand shocks on some islands are matched by favourable demand shocks on other islands to leave aggregate demand unchanged. Adverse demand shocks lead to (correct and rational) expectations of further adverse shocks to come, generating search for better offers elsewhere. Lucas and Prescott show that continual demand shocks of this sort, affecting different islands at different times, generate a significant level of equilibrium, or frictional, unemployment. Lilien (1982) and Samson (1985) show that changes in employment variation across industries, arising from such demand shocks and generating job search, can account for rising unemployment during the 1970s in the United States and Canada, although their interpretation of the evidence remains controversial (Abraham and Katz, 1986).

These and other attempts to provide a rigorous microfoundations for the behaviour of underemployment in a market economy have provided a challenge to Keynesian macroeconomics which, at least in North America, has been closely associated with wage and price inflexibility and labour market disequilibrium. This challenge has forced Keynesians to re-examine the microfoundations of their model. Much of this re-examination has concentrated on the labour market, where Keynesians cite transaction costs and/or institutions as impediments to the wage flexibility required for rapid market clearing (Okun, 1981, for example). More recently, a number of models have identified problems in managing the workforce under imperfect information as the basis for efficiency wages that are rigid and often lie above equilibrium levels to prevent market clearing over much of the business cycle (Akerlof and Yellen, 1986; Bulow and Summers, 1986; Stiglitz, 1987).[3]

The debate over labour market clearing in the macroeconomy is of more than scientific curiosity. On the one hand, if the market does not clear during business recessions, then there is an excess supply of workers and job rationing. Some workers are involuntarily underemployed because they are unable to supply all the labour they want to supply at current wage levels regardless of search effort.[4] To prevent loss of production and provide equal opportunities for employment, aggregate demand must be increased by monetary and fiscal expansion during recessions. On the other hand, underemployment may arise in the process of workers' response to market-clearing wage adjustments arising from demand shocks which may or may not be cyclical. In this case further demand shocks from government are unnecessary and potentially destabilizing. This is not to say that underemployment is a pleasant experience for workers and unworthy of social assistance but that it is a necessary social response to economic change over which government can have little positive influence in a market economy.

The evidence on this issue is far from conclusive, but my impression is that the evidence generally supports the view that the aggregate labour market does not clear at all times. Wage and employment

---

[3] These models have given rise to 'The New Economics of Personnel', *Journal of Labour Economics*, special issue, Oct. 1987.

[4] Any one individual may increase his chances of finding employment by greater search intensity. Because there are not enough jobs to go around, however, all job-seekers cannot improve their prospects by the same tactic.

rigidities are sufficient to create excess supply at some points in the business cycle and, perhaps, to create excess demand at other times as well. Kneissner and Goldsmith's (1987) recent review of the theoretical and empirical literature for the United States supports this viewpoint.

This impression does not diminish the contribution of equilibrium models of the labour market of the sort that Phelps (1970) and Lucas and Prescott (1974) have developed. First, the evidence is far from conclusive. Secondly, equilibrium models remain the basis for microeconomic analysis, even among many Keynesian economists concerned with a disequilibrium framework for macroeconomic models. Disequilibrium models are generally derived with reference to a particular equilibrium condition toward which the model will tend in the long run under stable conditions.[5] Thus underemployment problems are defined with reference to a situation of labour market equilibrium. Indeed, practical economic analysis and policy development remains a judicious blend of equilibrium and disequilibrium assumptions about market behaviour with some substantial variation in the blend across the economics profession.

The disagreement in macroeconomics concerning market equilibrium is also reflected in other areas of labour economics and the analysis of underemployment. Keynesians much more readily accept the view that job rationing occurs in various sectors of the labour market, adopting what has become known as the segmented labour market theory (Cain, 1976). Okun's (1981) career and auction labour markets are a good example of the Keynesian approach to labour market analysis. Career labour markets arise as a result of significant transaction costs including job training. These costs generate long-term agreements and job stability. Wages, career advancement, working conditions, and pension arrangements are attractive to discourage labour turnover. Auction labour markets, on the other hand, do not require job stability. In this situation wages, working conditions, and fringe benefits are generally unattractive leading to a high degree of worker dissatisfaction and turnover. Workers in career labour markets are generally protected from at least mild fluctuations in business activity. When a decline in activity occurs, wages are protected and, if the decline is sharp enough and workers are laid off, they are subject to

[5] An exception may be some efficiency wage models in which a wage above the equilibrium level is required in the long run to motivate workers. One such model is provided by Shapiro and Stiglitz (1984).

preferential recall when business activity rebounds. Workers in auction labour markets bear the brunt of the business cycle in terms of wages and employment. Underemployment over the typical business cycle is primarily a phenomenon of the auction labour market because only the auction market adjusts in the classical way. Underemployment also occurs throughout the business cycle because workers in the auction labour market have high turnover and seek jobs in the career market (Hall, 1971).

The concept of segmented labour markets remains controversial. Part of the reason for the controversy is the careless use of the term to reflect simple heterogeneity of workers and jobs. No one disputes that workers and jobs are heterogeneous. Indeed, the widely accepted problems of information in the labour market discussed in Chapter 3 are predicated on this heterogeneity. Workers in conventional human capital models follow a variety of career paths which do not give rise to the type of career labour markets to which Okun refers.[6] All 'segments' of the market remain auction markets responsive to changes in labour market conditions. In particular, entry to better jobs remains open to anyone willing to accumulate the necessary human capital.

Labour segmentation requires more than the simple observation that workers and jobs are heterogeneous. It requires the rejection of the market equilibrium assumption. Workers in long-term jobs in the career labour market are protected because their jobs are not subject to competition from outside the firm. A queue of qualified applicants will not lower wages or fringe benefits or displace workers in the career market. Their jobs are rationed, a distinct departure from the concept of competition and market equilibrium that prevails in the auction market. Thus Cain (1976: 1224) argues that 'noncompeting groups offer the single most basic criticism of the operations of the labor market and of the application of competitive assumptions by neoclassicists. This criticism is fundamental to the Segmented Labor Market challenge.' Doeringer (1986) also argues that the fundamental assumption of segmented markets is non-competing groups in the labour market.

We can see then why there is a natural alliance of Keynesian macroeconomic views with segmented labour market theory. Most Keynesians require a microeconomic foundation which accounts for wage inflexibility and labour market disequilibrium. Segmented labour market theories, including the new theories of efficiency wages,

---

[6] Heterogeneity of a more general nature can be analysed within Rosen's (1974) framework under perfect information.

have the same objective at the microeconomic level. There is, however, a difference of focus. Keynesians focus on macroeconomic stabilization and short-term cyclical underemployment. Segmented labour market theory is primarily concerned with long-term underemployment arising from the rationing of good (career labour market) jobs. The policies to combat long-term underemployment from the segmented labour market perspective usually include Keynesian aggregate demand expansion but usually go beyond the macroeconomy to recommend policies to alter job allocation in various labour market segments. We will examine this issue in Chapter 7.

The strength of the segmented labour market critique remains empirical. Numerous microeconomic theories of segmented markets are available[7] but little clear consensus has emerged. The equilibrium model of the labour market remains the preferred choice of recent textbooks in labour economics. Yet these textbooks must deal with several standard topics—collective bargaining, discrimination, and internal labour markets—for which the equilibrium approach seems unsuitable. The neoclassical theory of discrimination, for example, implies a progressive decline in earnings differences between whites and blacks and between men and women that has not been observed (Blau and Farber, 1987). Most analyses of discrimination add theories of discrimination that involve inferior access of certain workers (racial minorities or women) to good jobs. This requires a model with job rationing of the sort provided by the segmented labour market theories.

Our objective in this section has been to try to clarify the main issues in the underemployment debate. It seems clear from the macroeconomic literature and from the labour economics literature that market equilibrium (wage flexibility or job rationing) is the major issue. From this perspective we turn to the literature on urban underemployment.

6.2 UNDEREMPLOYMENT AND THE CITY

The underemployment debate has been applied to the analysis of urban underemployment in a number of instances. In most cases the nature and structure of cities is ignored. Cities have no effect on underemployment but reflect the consequences of various under-em-

---

[7] See Cain (1976) for a review of older theories and Akerlof and Yellen (1986) for a review of more recent efficiency wage theories.

ployment problems arising in the analysis of the previous section. Thus the previous section provides a useful framework to examine these views of the urban underemployment problem.

At the macroeconomic level the urban underemployment problem has been addressed by Keynesians. Their basic point is quite simple. All other discussions of the underemployment problem are secondary if there is a serious problem of deficient aggregate demand. A good example is Cheshire's (1979: 29) criticism of the Inner Area Studies in the United Kingdom:

In order to make my central argument quite unambiguous it is worth stating it at the outset. It will be argued that the most important single source of differences between spatial labour markets, such markets being spatial subdivisions of a national market, is differences in the level of excess demand for labour.

At the level of the *aggregate* labour market, this argument is the obvious starting-point given current evidence. Labour markets appear to suffer from deficient aggregate demand, at least periodically (Kneissner and Goldsmith, 1987). During recessions in business activity, involuntary unemployment arising from inadequate demand for labour may dominate all other forms of unemployment. Regional differences in the severity of the deficiency in labour demand create regional differences in the impact of the recession on unemployment. From this broad perspective of local labour markets, however, the urban underemployment problem is nothing more than a reflection of the general underemployment problem of deficient labour demand:

Primarily for economic reasons the areas in which the poor have been concentrated have been the inner cities. Spatial inequality may thus be just another and rather unimportant dimension of social inequality. It may consequently be best relieved by policies aimed at greater social equality and of these one of the most powerful and currently least favoured is managing the economy at the highest level of overall demand for labour compatible with other goals. (Cheshire, 1979: 41)

Cheshire's analysis is not restricted to fluctuations in aggregate demand over the business cycle, however. He argues that, at any point in the business cycle, differences in underemployment between regional labour markets primarily arise from differences in demand for labour. Thus regional disparities, however wide and persistent, can be explained by differences in regional labour demand. This argument is more controversial because it requires wage inflexibility and regional immobility of labour to generate long-term differences in the availability of jobs across regions.

Topel (1986) argues that recent evidence from the Current Population Survey in the United States does not support the view that wages are inflexible. He develops a model in which wages and employment adjust to changes in local labour market conditions in the island economy of Phelps (1970), Lucas and Prescott (1974), and Chapter 4 of this study. Changes in local (state) labour market conditions are changes in state employment, both anticipated and unanticipated. These changes in labour demand produce wage fluctuations because interstate migration is limited by mobility costs. Differences in excess labour demand across states do not persist because wage adjustments eliminate them. Note, however, that labour demand is the driving element in both Keynesian (disequilibrium) models and neoclassical (equilibrium) models. In Keynesian models, such as Cheshire's, deficient demand (negative excess demand) generates underemployment as wages do not adjust and jobs are rationed. In equilibrium models, such as Topel's, deficient demand generates real wage declines to clear the local market. In each case the effects of deficient demand arise because labour does not move rapidly to areas where demand conditions are better.[8]

It is worth noting at this point a further parallel with our earlier analysis. Topel points to migration studies which find that unskilled and older workers are less mobile. His model implies that wage fluctuations in response to a given demand shock will be greatest for this group. This implication is also supported by his empirical analysis. Our analysis in Chapters 4 and 5 maintained a similar focus on the immobility of unskilled workers within local labour markets rather than between them. We did not consider age, however, because the usual argument is that older workers are less mobile because of the shorter period for returns from investment in migration. Since we were not concerned with residential relocation in analysing workplace choice within urban labour markets we ignored age except in so far as it affects skill level through work experience. Thus our model is consistent with Topel's at a finer level of spatial detail.[9]

[8] One contention of many Keynesians, of course, is that deficient demand is at times a universal state of all local markets so that labour migration is futile. Equilibrium models reject this view.

[9] States may be convenient units for data collection but are there no mobility problems within states and within cities? We argue that this is an open question and an

The main distinction between the viewpoints represented by Cheshire and Topel is wage flexibility within local labour markets. Both models agree on demand fluctuations and labour immobility as the primary factors of influence. In Cheshire's analysis this leads to underemployment where demand is deficient, in Topel's analysis to wage declines. The evidence suggests some degree of wage flexibility (Topel) but perhaps not sufficient for rapid and complete market-clearing (Kneissner and Goldsmith, 1987). In this case demand deficiency would cause a combination of wage declines and unemployment, the extent of each effect depending upon the degree to which wages are flexible and the degree to which workers are mobile. Topel's island economy provides a useful framework in which to investigate local labour market issues even if we relax the assumption of wage flexibility, permit market disequilibrium, and investigate both wage and unemployment effects arising from demand shocks to local markets.

Related underemployment arguments from a disequilibrium perspective arise from a number of studies which employ some form of the segmented labour market theory. The arguments are related because the crucial factor in underemployment is job rationing. Job rationing implies deficient labour demand which may be reflected in discriminatory hiring decisions. Discrimination arises, however, because the queue of job applicants is too long.

Harrison (1972) provides perhaps the most thorough analysis of underemployment and poverty in cities from the perspective of segmented labour markets. He concentrates on racial minorities in the United States. His analysis takes issue with the neoclassical view that workers are paid according to the productivity generated by their human capital (their schooling, work experience, and on-the-job training). He argues in favour of the classical view that many workers are relegated to jobs with low productivity and low pay regardless of their own ability. He cites evidence of inflated job requirements that exclude poor ghetto residents from better jobs despite their ability to learn such jobs quickly and be productive (Harrison, 1972: 32–8). Moreover, the returns to education and training are inferior for non-whites, in terms of both earnings and unemployment, regardless of where they live in the city. We can see more clearly what underemployment involves in this context—minority workers are not only

important one for a complete analysis of the urban economy. Indeed, in some cases, the urban economy crosses state borders.

more likely to be unemployed but more likely to be employed in jobs which undervalue their capabilities in comparison with white workers.

Harrison sees little hope for improvement in minority economic opportunity until the current structure of labour demand is altered. The current structure contains a 'core' of profitable oligopolistic firms providing capital-intensive production jobs which offer good wages, working conditions, and career prospects. Core employment is limited, however, and non-whites are generally excluded by unnecessary job requirements or racial discrimination. Workers unable to obtain core employment are relegated to jobs in 'periphery' firms in competitive product markets. Economic conditions in these markets dictate poor wages and working conditions and offer little incentive for long-term job attachment. Capital investment is low both in physical and human capital terms. These are Okun's career and auction labour markets in another form.

The problem in general is the rationing of core jobs. The particular problem is what McCormick (1986) describes as 'unequal job rationing' that favours whites at the expense of non-whites. The policy prescription is selective demand creation rather than general demand creation. More core employment is required through selective job creation and more comprehensive economic planning. More core employment would decrease the supply of workers to peripheral firms resulting in higher wage levels in peripheral employment. Note that, in aggregate, the labour market can be in equilbrium even under most versions of the segmented labour market theory because there are enough jobs in the peripheral sector for everyone. Thus one can draw a distinction between the aggregate job-rationing concept of Keynesians or cyclical unemployment and the selective job-rationing concept of structural unemployment in segmented labour markets. In practice, the acceptance of wage inflexibility may often lead to the acceptance of both aggregate and selective job rationing.

Job rationing is clearly an important concept to examine in order to understand the underemployment problem. Yet there are many who have argued that urban spatial structure is not only a consequence but a cause of the underemployment problem. To dismiss these views without careful examination is unwise. Indeed, we have just argued that job rationing is not incompatible with a version of the island economy model in which some degree of wage inflexibility is assumed. Careful examination of these views requires a general model of urban structure and the labour market which, we have seen, has been lacking in the literature to this point. This has been one reason why the spatial mismatch hypothesis has been condemned:

The highly critical assessment of the Inner Area Studies' labour market analysis finally reached in this paper stems from this fundamental point that in the author's view at least, the Studies conspicuously failed to offer either a labour market analytical basis for their diagnosis or even, perhaps more surprisingly, an adequate basis in urban theory. (Cheshire, 1979: 29)

The previous chapters in this study have offered a theory of urban labour markets, based on the island economy, with supporting evidence on commuting. We now turn to its implications for underemployment and assess the empirical evidence on urban underemployment from this perspective.

6.3   URBAN STRUCTURE AND UNDEREMPLOYMENT

Most of the analysis of urban underemployment has maintained that local supply and demand factors are relatively unimportant. The exception has been proponents of the spatial mismatch hypothesis of Kain (1968a), including most recently the Inner Area Studies in the United Kingdom. The spatial mismatch hypothesis is assessed theoretically in this section by considering the implications for underemployment of the job–worker matching model of workplace choice. This is followed by an assessment of the empirical literature.

As in Chapters 4 and 5, we consider the urban area in terms of the island economy. The urban area consists, conceptually and empirically, of a series of urban subdivisions or local labour markets. Mobility among the islands is costly both in direct terms (travel costs) and in indirect terms (job information costs). All workers prefer the local labour market of their place of residence.[10] To this point our approach corresponds to Ellwood's (1986) model of the spatial mismatch problem.

More-skilled workers adopt more formal and spatially extensive search strategies in recognition of the effect of specific skill acquisition in reducing the density of job vacancies at all locations. Firms respond by adopting more extensive search practices when hiring more-skilled workers. Thus all search is spatially systematic but wor-

---

[10] The place of residence may be their current one or one to be chosen along with a workplace location. In practice, it is the residential location observed once the workplace location is established.

kers and firms differ in the intensity of their local search according to the skill level under consideration.

It is easier to ignore job rationing at first and return to the issue later. Thus, wages are assumed to be flexible and to adjust to clear each local labour market for each skill category. When local labour demand declines, however, declining wages may encourage search on other islands that would not occur if the local labour demand shock were neutral or positive. Thus spatial job search is influenced by skill level and by local labour market conditions.

The decision of a worker to accept a job offer depends upon its attractiveness, represented by the wage offer. The wage offer in turn depends upon local labour market conditions, represented by the ratio of jobs to workers in the local area as before. When local labour market conditions are good, local wage offers are high as firms compete for relatively scarce local workers. Workers quickly accept these offers and periods of unemployment are short. Moreover, good local labour market conditions for workers reduce turnover. Firms are less willing to discharge workers in a tight local market and workers are less willing to quit jobs when wages are improving. As a result unemployment, and underemployment arising from unsatisfactory employment opportunities, will be lower when local labour market conditions (jobs per worker in the local area) are good.

The effect of local labour market conditions on unemployment and underemployment also depends upon skill level. Skill level matters because more-skilled workers rely on local job opportunities to a smaller extent. Hence wage offers are less sensitive to local labour market conditions for more-mobile, more-skilled workers. When local labour market conditions are good for more-skilled workers, wage offers improve less than they do for those at lower skill levels because more-skilled workers are more easily attracted from other local markets. Decisions to accept local wage offers are influenced less by local labour market conditions and more by other factors, including labour market conditions elsewhere in the city. Thus unemployment and underemployment are less sensitive to local labour market conditions for more-skilled workers.

Workers in this model require information not only about general labour market conditions for the city and beyond but also about the intra-urban distribution of employment opportunities. There may be conflicting signals in this regard. Suppose that labour market conditions are good in a rapidly growing economy. Local firms may be expected to grow as well, but the growth may be concentrated in other areas of the city. Moreover, local firms are more likely to relocate in periods of rapid growth, particularly from inner cities, so that generally good economic conditions may not be reflected locally. Indeed, this is the plight of many inner cities discussed in Chapter 2. The point is that the useful information for workers is not just about general economic conditions but about the intra-urban spatial distribution of those conditions. Job search will provide that information in the form of wage offers at various locations within the city. Workers will learn about market conditions on various islands and eventually accept an offer of employment.

Workers is this model behave as they do in other island models. In Phelps (1970*b*) workers react to a deterioration of *general* economic conditions by declining what they perceive to be poor wage offers and seeking jobs elsewhere. When they leave their local market, they incur search costs in the form of unemployment. In Lucas and Prescott (1974) workers react to a deterioration of *local* economic conditions by declining local offers to seek better opportunities elsewhere, a process that requires some unemployment. In each case adverse demand shocks generate higher search unemployment—in Phelps's model because workers do not realize that the shock is a general one and in Lucas and Prescott's model because workers realize that the shock is island-specific but likely to persist for several periods. Either type of expectations on the part of workers will generate the postulated relationship between underemployment and local labour market conditions. And it is local labour market conditions, represented by jobs per worker in each local area, which provide a direct link with urban spatial structure.

One potential criticism is that we should distinguish unanticipated and anticipated changes in urban structure (jobs per worker in each local market). The analysis below, however, is limited to decennial census data. An examination of the trend in urban structure, which may be anticipated, and deviations from the trend, which may not be anticipated, is not possible. We must therefore assume that poor local labour market conditions reflect a recent series of adverse demand shocks and that good local labour market conditions reflect a recent series of positive demand shocks. To the extent that this is not universally accurate within the city, our empirical analysis can be improved by longitudinal data.

This model is a basic equilibrium model in the sense that wages are flexible on each island and workers choose when to leave an island to seek better employment opportunities elsewhere. The model is therefore useful as a foundation for more complex models of the urban labour market, much as the access–space trade-off model provides a useful basis for analysis of residential location. The model does not claim to be the complete story as far as urban labour market behaviour is concerned but the basis to examine other important issues, including job rationing, discrimination, segmented markets, unions, and imperfectly competitive firms. The focus here is the fundamental link between labour economics and urban economics, particularly urban spatial structure, and not a complete analysis of labour markets.

6.3.1 A model of urban structure and underemployment*

Consider a job-seeker with spatial boundary H defined by equation (4.3). Then the probability of not accepting a job in period of time Δt is

$$p(w) = 1 - \int_0^H f(w, x)\, dx, \qquad (6.1)$$

where, as in section 4.3.1, $f(w, x)$ is the probability of accepting a job involving commuting distance, x, and offering wage, w. If search is spatially systematic, then search will initially be confined to the local labour market. From section 4.3.1, we saw that local wage offers would vary with local labour market conditions, represented by variable s. In particular, we have that

$$\dot{w}_s > 0 \qquad (6.2)$$

from equation (4.22). Firms compete for scarce local workers and for workers from other islands, who must be compensated for the mobility costs involved, by bidding up wage rates to fill vacancies and reduce turnover. Thus, job-seekers find good local wage offers quickly where s is high such that

$$\frac{\partial f}{\partial s} > 0 \qquad (6.3)$$

for local jobs from equation (4.24) and

$$\frac{\partial p}{\partial s} < 0 \qquad (6.4)$$

from equation (6.1). When search is initially local, good local labour market conditions increase the probability of finding an acceptable job and reduce the likelihood of the extended unemployment required to search again locally or on other islands.

Individuals unable to find an acceptable offer may either lower their reservation wage as in conventional search models, or increase spatial search extent, or both. Note that if workers know the spatial distribution of local labour market conditions, and hence the spatial distribution of wages, across the city then workers living where local labour market conditions are poor would simply reduce their reservation wage and/or search elsewhere and avoid the higher probability of unemployment associated with local search. Since urban structure—in particular, the spatial distribution of jobs and workers—varies considerably over time, however, workers are in a perpetual state of imperfect knowledge about local and city-wide labour market conditions which can yield the type of search unemployment differentials described by the model. This approach is consistent with conventional models of search unemployment from the work of Phelps *et al.* (1970) and Lucas and Prescott (1974).

The effect of local labour market conditions on search unemployment of the type described above will decline with skill level because skill acquisition broadens the extent of search—that is, $\partial f_x / \partial G > 0$ from section 4.3.1. Since

$$\frac{\partial f_s}{\partial G} < 0 \ \text{ if } \ \frac{\partial f_x}{\partial G} > 0 \tag{6.5}$$

from equation (4.25), more-skilled workers are less likely to search locally regardless of local employment conditions. More-skilled workers are therefore less likely to search longer when local conditions are poor, or

$$\frac{\partial p_s}{\partial G} > 0 \tag{6.6}$$

from equation (6.1).

From equation (6.6) we may specify a model of individual unemployment probability for time interval Δt as

$$p = p(G, s), \ \frac{\partial p}{\partial s} < 0, \ \frac{\partial p_s}{\partial G} > 0, \tag{6.7}$$

where G represents skill level as before. Let $G_i \, (i = 2, \ldots, \Gamma)$ be a set of dummy variables representing skill categories as in equation (5.7) and let $Z = (Z_1, \ldots, Z_m)$ represent a set of individual characteristics other than skill level—such as sex, age, marital status, and number of children in Simpson's (1982) study. Then, if $g(Z_i)$ is the probability of a local labour force participant satisfying characteristic Z_i, $i = 1, \ldots, m$, and if $g(Z_i)$ and the probability of unemployment $p(\cdot)$ are independent, then the unemployment rate on any island may be expressed as

$$U(G, s; Z) = U_0(s) + \sum_{i=1}^{m} U_i g(Z_i) + \sum_{i=2}^{\Gamma} U_{m-1+i} G_i, \qquad (6.8)$$

where U_0 represents the rate of unemployment owing solely to local labour market conditions and U_i is the increased unemployment arising because individuals satisfy characteristic Z_i $(i = 1, \ldots, m)$ or fall into skill category G_i $(i = 2, \ldots, \Gamma)$. This specification permits a linear regression model of unemployment rate differences across islands to be formulated as

$$U = \delta_0 + \delta_1 s + \delta_2 s^2 + \sum_{i=1}^{m} \delta_{i+2} Z_i + \sum_{i=2}^{\Gamma} \delta_{m+2+i} G_i + \varepsilon_U, \qquad (6.9)$$

where ε_U is an error term. $U_0(s)$ is expressed as a quadratic form since, as discussed in section 4.1.1, workers may not only choose nearby locations but also locations with high values of s—such as the central business district and other large suburban employment centres—because these locations provide high arrival rates for job offers and hence the economies associated with multiple job searches. Hence local residents will have more competition from non-local job-seekers at locations where s is high. This implies that s overstates the probability of receiving an acceptable offer in these areas, or that

$$\frac{\partial}{\partial s}\left(\frac{\partial w}{\partial s}\right) < 0 \text{ and } \frac{\partial}{\partial s}\left(\frac{\partial p}{\partial s}\right) > 0. \qquad (6.10)$$

Hence,

$$\frac{\partial U}{\partial s} < 0 \qquad (6.11)$$

from equation (6.7), but

$$\frac{\partial}{\partial s}\left(\frac{\partial U}{\partial s}\right) > 0 \qquad (6.12)$$

from equation (6.10). This consideration implies that we should expect

$$\delta_1 < 0 \text{ and } \delta_2 > 0 \qquad (6.13)$$

in our regression model (6.9).

The hypothesis that less-skilled workers are more responsive to local labour market conditions given by equation (6.7) implies that

$$\frac{\partial}{\partial G}\left(\frac{\partial U}{\partial s}\right) > 0. \tag{6.14}$$

Simpson (1982) therefore respecifies $U_0(s)$ as

$$U_0(s) = \delta_{11}s + \delta_{21}s^2 + \sum_{i=2}^{r} \delta_{1i}(s_i - s_1) + \sum_{i=2}^{r} \delta_{2i}(s_i - s_1)^2, \tag{6.15}$$

where i is an index of ascending skill level as in Chapter 5. Then it is expected that

$$\frac{\partial U_0}{\partial(s_i - s_1)} = \delta_{1i} + \delta_{2i}(s_i - s_1) > 0 \ \forall \ i \tag{6.16}$$

and that this effect increases as i increases because, for more skilled workers, the negative partial correlation between local labour market conditions, s, and unemployment should be less important.

For married women, there is evidence that underemployment may take the form of reduced labour force participation as well as increased unemployment. If this is the case, then the effect of local labour market conditions on married female labour-force participation should be similar, but opposite in sign, to the effect on unemployment. Hence, Simpson (1982) also includes local labour market conditions in a regression model of married female participation rates across Greater London boroughs.

6.4 EMPIRICAL EVIDENCE

Several studies have examined unemployment and labour-force participation within cities. These studies have lacked a general model of urban labour market behaviour of the type postulated above. As a result much of the empirical analysis has concentrated on unemployment and participation gradients, relating unemployment and participation to the distance of the household from the city centre in some fashion. Siegel (1973) attempts to investigate the relationship between employment in the poverty areas of the New York SMSA and access to jobs. Using Kain's (1968a) approach, Siegel reasons that blacks are less residentially mobile than whites because of housing discrimination. Distance to employment should influence income and employment differentials more for blacks than whites. His regression results indicate that distance to employment, crudely approximated by central city and suburban dummy variables, are more important for blacks than for whites and for females than for males. Apparently blacks know about jobs in the suburbs but cannot afford to reach them, although Gayer's (1971) survey of two industrial parks in the same urban area showed that wage differentials were far more than adequate to compensate for additional commuting. Another weakness of Siegel's study is that, while he allowed for differences in education, age, and marital status within groups, he did not allow for skill differences between groups. Lack of skills among blacks, which arises from labour market discrimination rather than housing discrimination, constrains job search patterns to the local area according to our job–worker matching model. Even if distant suburban employment opportunities are available at rates of pay which more than compensate for commuting, unskilled black workers will not seek jobs there.

Mooney (1969) found that variations in the rate of employment per resident in the ghetto areas of twenty-five SMSAs in the United States were explained by the proportion of SMSA jobs in the central city as well as variations in aggregate demand, particularly for manufacturing employment for males. This again provides rough support for the hypothesis that separation of workers from employment opportunities increases unemployment and reduces participation, lowering employment per resident. Mooney uses the proportion of non-whites living in the central city who commute to the suburbs to estimate differences in transportation facilities between SMSAs. This variable may, however, represent differences in the occupational composition of urban areas that create differences in mobility according to our job–worker matching model and the supporting evidence in Chapter 5. Moreover, there may be an intervening effect of city size. In larger cities the proportion of non-whites (or whites) commuting from the central city to the suburbs falls because the central city is a much larger area. Since larger cities typically have worse unemployment and employment problems, there might be a spurious correlation between suburban commuting and central city employment rates because of city size. The reason for this correlation may not be transportation but factors related to the urban structure, namely the influx of blacks to large cities in the northern United States, their confinement to decaying inner-city areas, and the flight of industry and commerce from these inner cities. More disaggregated data, as well as more carefully developed theory, is required to reconcile these issues.

Lillydahl and Singell (1985) provide a recent review of the literature on unemployment and participation gradients. They find that a higher average commuting time and a higher proportion of non-movers in a census tract are associated with a higher unemployment rate and a lower female participation rate in that tract. While this evidence is consistent with the spatial mismatch hypothesis, their evidence on the unemployment and participation gradients is mixed. Female unemployment rates rise as distance increases, while participation rates fall; male unemployment rates fall as distance increases, while participation rates rise. They therefore conclude (p. 468) that

This work makes abundantly clear the need for a general theory of urban labour markets that takes cognizance of the enormous expansion in female labour force participation. While the traditional theory in labour and urban economics has provided important insights into each of these markets, a general equilibrium theory which allows for simultaneous job and residential choices in two-earner households is clearly necessary. Until such a theory is developed, the issues raised in this paper may never be completely resolved and policies will be formulated without adequate economic analysis.

The model presented in the previous section, and in Chapters 4 and 5, clearly addresses many of these concerns. Simpson (1982) has tested the model using observations on the thirty-two boroughs of Greater London from the 1971 Census of England and Wales. The results are summarized in Table 6.1. The analysis formulates a model of unemployment in an urban area based on labour as a quasi-fixed factor and a job–worker matching model in an island economy as specified above. Labour is a quasi-fixed factor because it includes fixed costs per worker employed as well as variable costs per hour worked (Oi, 1962). Skill, sex, age, the marital status of the worker, and the presence of children affect the unemployment rate in addition to urban structure.[11] Allowing for these worker characteristics in each borough, Table 6.1 shows that jobs per worker in the borough exerted a significant negative effect on the borough unemployment rate as predicted by the job–worker matching model. The effect was non-linear, declining as jobs per worker increased to reflect greater competition for jobs at large employment centres. The effect was also greater for less-skilled manual and non-manual workers than for skilled

[11]   No adequate variable reflecting racial composition of the borough was available. Metcalf and Richardson (1980) found no significant relationship between race and unemployment in Greater London when factors such as skill were included.

TABLE 6.1. *Regression estimates of unemployment rates by sex for Greater London, 1971* (method is OLS; *t*-values in parentheses)

Regressors	Males		Females	
Constant	8.44		9.09	
Skill	0.10	(2.9)	0.11	(8.0)
Marital status	− 0.22	(8.6)	− 0.08	(7.8)
Young	0.16	(1.0)	− 0.07	(1.3)
Old	0.19	(2.3)	− 0.07	(1.3)
Children	0.99	(3.2)		
s	− 1.42	(2.4)	− 1.38	(3.4)
s^2	0.27	(2.5)	0.18	(2.5)

Skill: proportion of workers unskilled / semi-skilled / personal-services
Marital status: proportion of workers married
Young: proportion of workers aged 15–20
Old: proportion of workers aged 55–64
s: jobs per resident for unskilled / semi-skilled manual workers and junior non-manual workers

Source: Simpson (1982).

workers as expected. In fact the results indicate no significant effect of urban structure on unemployment for skilled manual and non-manual workers. All regression equations were statistically significant and explained in the range of 89 per cent to 95 per cent of the variation in unemployment rates across Greater London boroughs.

Simpson's (1982) results indicate that a 10 per cent increase in unskilled jobs in a borough with an equal number of unskilled jobs and workers would lower the unemployment rate in the borough by 2.5 per cent for both males and females. Because the effect of urban structure on unemployment is non-linear, the results imply that a more equitable spatial distribution of existing employment would also be beneficial. A 10 per cent reduction in the variation in jobs per worker across boroughs would reduce male unemployment by 0.75 per cent and female unemployment by 0.5 per cent in Greater London according to these estimates. Thus the results suggest some modest scope for decentralization and other spatial redistribution of employment to alleviate unemployment.

Some underemployment may occur in the form of reduced labour-force participation, particularly for those with non-market alternatives to employment. Although workers may appear to choose not to participate in the labour market, they would participate if satisfactory employment opportunities were available. These 'discouraged workers' are the disguised unemployed, whose participation will increase as local economic conditions improve and local unemployment falls (Bowen and Finegan, 1969). This phenomenon may be particularly important for married females in response to local labour market conditions. Wabe (1969) and Lillydahl and Singell (1985) report what appear to be discouraged worker effects for females in response to local employment opportunities.

Simpson (1982) also estimates a model of labour-force participation for married females in Greater London in which jobs per worker in less-skilled non-manual and service occupations in a borough have a significant positive impact on participation in the borough after allowing for the influence of skill level for both males and females, children per family, and less-skilled male jobs per worker in the borough. The effect of jobs per worker is again non-linear indicating that the effect on participation declines as jobs per worker rises. This is not surprising because, when jobs are already plentiful, further new employment in the borough will have less effect. This non-linearity implies that a 10 per cent reduction in the variation in jobs per unskilled worker across Greater London boroughs would increase married female participation rates by 1.5 per cent. This suggests some further modest scope for the redistribution of urban employment to reduce underemployment.

Simpson (1977, ch. 5) estimated a similar model for the Toronto metropolitan area. Despite additional data problems, including fewer observations, the effect of local labour market conditions was found to be similar to that in Greater London. More jobs per worker in the local area reduced the local unemployment rate for males and females and increased the local participation rate for females. The results were often statistically significant despite the small number of observations.

One should hesitate to place too much reliance on these results. The data are aggregated to the level of the Greater London borough or Toronto census subdivision. Microdata of the type available in the transportation surveys discussed in Chapter 5 would provide a better test of the model but employment status in such surveys is either missing or unreliable.[12] Such data would avoid problems of aggrega-

---

[12]   The measured unemployment rate in the Greater London Transportation Survey was very small, e.g. much lower than the rate in the 1971 Census of England and Wales for Greater London.

tion bias and small sample size present in these results. The results provide additional corroborating evidence, however, that a relationship between urban structure and labour market behaviour of the sort predicted by the job–worker matching model is observed in different urban areas and requires further attention from those interested in understanding underemployment in cities.

Much of the empirical analysis of urban unemployment has concentrated on the effects of city size on unemployment (Vipond, 1974) or the unemployment gradient within cities (Vipond, 1984; Lillydahl and Singell, 1985). This analysis has proceeded without a clear model of urban labour market behaviour. The analysis provides some facts, but what type of model does it support and what policy implications does it have? The theory and evidence in this study implies that local labour market conditions can affect unemployment but the relationship to earlier analysis is not clear. Since jobs are more plentiful in the city centre, one might expect that unemployment would increase with distance from the city centre according to our model. An important factor, however, is the distribution of less-skilled jobs relative to less-skilled workers within the city and it may be that the jobs are more decentralized than the population for less-skilled workers. This is the essence of the spatial mismatch hypothesis, as well as one aspect of our model, and urban unemployment gradients may not tell us much about it. If employment decentralization, creating the mismatch problem, is more severe in large cities then one might also expect unemployment rates to be higher in large cities as Duncan and Reiss (1956) and Vipond (1974) found. The statistical link between city size and unemployment could arise from many sources, however, and requires a specific model of the sort developed in this study. In this regard, our model again appears to be consistent with the evidence.

6.5 EXTENSIONS: SPATIAL MOBILITY, JOB AVAILABILITY, AND UNDEREMPLOYMENT

The previous section has developed a simple model in which the spatial distribution of jobs and workers' places of residence affects the success that workers, particularly unskilled workers, have in finding employment because of limited information and mobility within the urban labour market. The model is consistent with evidence on the spatial distribution of unemployment and participation in Greater London and Toronto. It is also consistent with the earlier chapters and the analysis of commuting behaviour in Chapter 5. It provides a basis for further investigation of urban structure and underemployment.

Underemployment—whether actual unemployment, unemployment disguised as non-participation in the labour market, inadequate hours of employment, or employment at a job for which the worker is overqualified and underpaid[13]—may arise in this model from the supply side or the demand side. Local labour market conditions may deteriorate either because jobs are lost when an adverse demand shock occurs, or because there is an influx of workers. As wages fall, workers may prolong job search hoping to find more attractive offers. Once they realize that local labour market conditions have deteriorated they may seek jobs elsewhere, accept less satisfactory local employment, or drop out of the labour market. The process of expanding the job search is much more difficult for unskilled workers, who rely more heavily on the informal information network and local job contacts, than skilled workers using an extensive formal information network. Thus underemployment and local labour market conditions are linked, particularly for unskilled workers.

On the demand side jobs can be lost in any local labour market as an economy develops. Chapter 2 identifies an important trend in employment decentralization in large cities. Employment decentralization has left central cities with fewer jobs, although the story is not that simple. There are still plenty of jobs in central cities. The real problem is the selective nature of job creation and relocation. Wilson (1980) argues that the massive shift in production from goods to services has been especially pronounced in central cities, and Ellwood (1986) and Leonard (1987) provide more detailed evidence to support this position for Chicago and Los Angeles. The more rapid decentralization of goods production has left fewer manufacturing jobs within central city labour markets. These manufacturing jobs are the primary source of good jobs for unskilled central city residents, particularly young blacks in the case of the United States. Thus, Lewin-Epstein (1985) finds significant variation in the ratio of young workers to jobs, roughly the inverse of our measure of local labour market conditions, across seventy-four neighbourhoods in Chicago with the least favourable local labour market conditions belonging to black neighbourhoods. The labour market for unskilled workers in central cities

[13]   A worker's 'earnings capacity' may be measured in terms of his human capital (Garfinkel and Haveman, 1977). If labour market conditions are unfavourable, a worker may accept an offer of employment paying less than his earnings capacity rather than be unemployed.

has deteriorated, even if there are plenty of jobs there. Unless these unskilled workers can find suburban manufacturing jobs, they are likely to suffer from frequent or permanent underemployment.

On the supply side, an influx of workers can have a similar adverse effect on the local labour market if the workers are relatively immobile and depend on local employment to a large extent. Wilson (1980) traces the rapid growth of the population of young blacks in central cities in the United States. In the 1960s the black teenage population increased by 175 per cent in the central cities compared to 14 per cent for white teenagers. The black population 20 to 24 years of age increased by 67 per cent compared to 20 per cent for whites in that age category. This population explosion increased competition for local unskilled jobs since many young adults, particularly teenagers, are unskilled. Again it is important to note the selective nature of the local labour market shift. Central city residents who are successful in the labour market tend to move to the suburbs, leaving behind unsuccessful residents and newcomers from rural areas or other cities. The effect of urban residential location and migration decisions is the progressive accumulation of the unskilled and the unsuccessful in the central cities. Young adults must compete for local unskilled employment not only with other young adults, but also with older central city residents.

The combined effect of fewer central city jobs for the unskilled and more and more unskilled central city residents, both young and old, is a very substantial deterioration of local labour market conditions in central cities. The situation Wilson (1980) describes for the United States is likely repeated for minority groups in other countries as well, particularly for recent immigrants. Possible language difficulties, unfamiliarity with the local labour market, and lack of informal information sources about jobs leave recent arrivals particularly vulnerable to underemployment.

It is interesting to note that the spatial mismatch of workers and jobs need not be confined to the inner city. In Sydney, Australia Vipond and Beed (1986) find that workers in the outer suburbs have a higher probability of unemployment than inner-city workers with similar characteristics, including a measure of skill. They find that, in contrast to developments in most cities, population growth is outstripping employment growth in these outer suburbs. Our general analysis applies, but it explains a different spatial pattern of underemployment in this case.

The approach to urban labour market analysis and underemployment in this study may appear to contradict other prominent assessments of these problems based on the segmented labour market approach (Harrison, 1972; Wilson, 1980). These assessments focus on two aspects of the problem that have not been considered so far—the development of work habits in the peripheral and core sectors and the rationing of good jobs in the core sector. These aspects of the problem can, however, be considered as important extensions to our general approach along the lines indicated in the remainder of this section.

Many theories of the segmented labour market argue that work behaviour is developed through work experience which is very different in the core and peripheral sectors. Workers who obtain good jobs in the core sector are provided with good pay and fringe benefits, on-the-job training, a stable work environment, prospects for advancement and career development, and other incentives to perform well and remain with the firm. Punctuality, loyalty, and responsibility are stressed as part of the job. On the other hand, workers who are unable to obtain good jobs are forced into a peripheral labour market with low pay, little skill training or career development, poor working conditions, and often capricious supervision that promotes bad work habits, tardiness, absenteeism, carelessness, and a lack of dependability. Harrison and Sum (1979: 693) write that

The frequently heard argument that the major barrier excluding the poor from primary employment is their own lack of motivation to work ignores an important strand in labor market segmentation theory: Motivation, in particular, and worker behavior, in general, are formed in response to confinement. In acclimatizing themselves to local work arrangements, some workers may find it psychologically as well as technically difficult to move from one stratum of the economy to another. Embedded in the dual labor market is the hypothesis that productivity and stability increase as wages increase. Thus, at the low wages prevalent in the secondary segment, poor productivity and lack of motivation are to be expected.

Work habits acquired in employment in the peripheral sector do not prepare workers for the core sector. They make successful employment in the core sector more difficult and, from the employer's perspective, more expensive. For this reason, employers in the core sector generally prefer inexperienced, but well-educated, workers to experienced workers from the peripheral sector.

This argument is most forcefully made with regard to those at the bottom in terms of labour market success, the permanently poor and underemployed 'underclass' (Auletta, 1982). The underclass sees itself to be disadvantaged not only by immediate poverty but by a 'culture of poverty' which shapes its future. The underclass adopts a lifestyle of welfare dependency, lassitude, and often illegal activity that is cultivated by its local environment and limited work experience. The work habits developed in such an environment rule out employment in the core sector without substantial retraining in basic work skills.

The argument can be extended to the unskilled, working poor caught in the peripheral sector. Work habits developed on the job, or more likely in a succession of dead-end jobs, are generally superior to those developed by the welfare-dependent. They are none the less poor training for any good employment opportunities that might arise. The local environment is likely to reinforce the disadvantages in competition for good jobs. Opportunities for higher education, an important means of access to better jobs, are worse in poor neighbourhoods, for example. Thus poverty is transferred between generations by the residential and work environment.

The interesting urban question is the role that the spatial concentration of the poor in cities plays in this process. There is undoubtedly some link between the personal contacts and role models of the neighbourhood and the behaviour individuals adopt. If job instability, welfare dependency, educational deficiency, and criminal activity are the neighbourhood norm, these attitudes and activities will have a powerful influence on the lifestyles adopted by children and young adults in the neighbourhood. The extent to which spatial concentration of the poor creates a culture of poverty which transfers poverty from generation to generation is an important and difficult social problem beyond the scope of this study.

Our analysis does address this issue with regard to labour market behaviour, however. The analysis concentrates on job search and, in particular, the limited mobility of unskilled workers associated with informal search networks. These networks are a product of culture to a large extent. For the poor in inner-city areas in particular, the culture provides personal contacts and role models that contribute little to successful job search. The poor and long-term unemployed have less information about current employment opportunities and are not a good source of referrals for employers. The spatial concentration of the poor stifles the informal employment information network to reinforce joblessness among the local labour force.

Rees and Gray (1982) find that a youth is more likely to have a job if siblings also have a job. This may simply reflect the influence of local labour market conditions on job search success, as argued earlier, but it is likely that it also reflects the importance of personal contacts and referrals in finding jobs in the unskilled youth labour market. Holzer (1987) attributes 90 per cent of the difference in employment probability between white and black youths to differences in the ability of informal search methods—direct applications to employers and referrals from friends and relatives—to produce job offers. The black youth employment problem is a problem of overcoming the disadvantages of their informal information network of friends and relatives and the lack of local employment opportunities. While these studies are not placed in an urban spatial context, they are clearly relevant to the underemployment problem of unskilled youth in inner cities.

The argument helps to explain the process of slum formation and the perpetuation of poverty in inner cities in the spirit of cumulative disequilibrium models of other aspects of the urban economy (Oates *et al.*, 1971). Those who succeed in finding good jobs generally relocate in the suburbs, often because their jobs are in the suburbs as well or because of residential preferences. Their departure confines inner-city areas more and more to the underemployed. At the same time there are fewer and fewer good jobs in the inner cities, particularly for the unskilled. The informal information network deteriorates as the sources of information—successful firms and residents—leave.

The deterioration of the informal information network is likely to be most serious for youths. There is considerable evidence that career origin is an important determinant of career pattern and lifetime earnings (Bergmann, 1971; Edwards *et al.*, 1975). Youths lack job experience and have little labour market information. Information may be gained through formal education (Parnes and Kohen, 1975) but encouragement of education in poor neighbourhoods is often lacking. Financial pressures and the lack of educated role models may discourage even the most academically able. Without advanced education or other formal training youths are left to an unskilled labour market dominated by an informal information network. The information available from friends and relatives about remunerative careers with steady employment will be poor compared to youths in other, more prosperous areas of the city. Parnes and Kohen (1975) find that family socioeconomic status and urban residence are major determinants of occupational information along with education and ability. Inner-city youths begin at a disadvantage in every respect but ability, and it is very difficult to escape a bad career start.

Youths in poor neighbourhoods are likely to make poor career starts which will be perpetuated. Low pay will prevent escape from poor neighbourhoods. Dead-end jobs will offer little training or prospects for advancement and may cultivate poor work habits. Their labour market information network will not improve. Prospects for employment in the core sector will not improve with experience and may decline as work habits and lifestyle are modified by the local environment. Thus the spatial concentration of the poor, uneducated, and underemployed plays a role in the development of a new generation of the poor, uneducated, and underemployed. Poverty and urban slums are transferred intergenerationally.

This viewpoint, while hardly novel, is not an integral part of urban studies because the urban labour market is not an integral part of urban studies. The labour market and problems of underemployment and poverty are normally introduced as separate issues outside the scope of urban economics. These problems have implications for urban residential patterns but urban structure has no effect on the problems themselves. The analysis of the urban labour market in this study leads us to examine the possible effects of urban structure on poverty in cities and provides a framework within which these effects can be studied. It links urban studies to a wider set of studies of poverty and underemployment emphasizing the link between job search and labour market behaviour, neighbourhood conditions, and individual economic performance.

The effect of this broader viewpoint may be seen in discussion of urban renewal policy. Neighbourhood externalities—crime and deteriorating housing and public facilities, for example—are often cited as reinforcing the physical deterioration in inner cities and provide an argument for public intervention to reverse the process (Davis and Whinston, 1961; Thompson, 1965: 295–309). Yet physical renewal alone has proved disappointing in arresting the deterioration of cities. Since the deterioration is viewed as a symptom of poverty, this is not surprising. From our broader perspective, however, it may be more than a symptom of poverty. Our analysis points to externalities associated with deteriorating local employment conditions and a deteriorating local labour market information network in inner cities as well. This perspective raises questions about the direction of urban planning that will be considered further in Chapter 7.

There is a further important element of the approach to urban underemployment based on segmented labour markets that cannot be ignored. Wilson (1980), Harrison (1972), and others maintain that jobs are rationed. More specifically, they argue that good jobs—jobs in the core sector[14] providing high lifetime earnings, job stability, and good working conditions—are rationed to the disadvantage of black workers in the United States. While some black workers, particularly those with a good education, have been able to find jobs in the core sector, many less fortunate blacks have been left behind. Their analysis corresponds to McCormick's (1986) concept of discrimination arising from unequal job rationing. Unequal job rationing ensures that black workers will be underemployed at a higher rate than white workers regardless of urban location. As Harrison (1972: 116) puts it:

These findings are, of course, by no means conclusive. Further research with explicitly longitudinal data is needed . . . Nevertheless, from the resources at hand, it appears that urban nonwhites are severely constrained in their economic opportunities, regardless of where in the metropolis they reside. The implication is that there may be little to be gained from policies designed to rearrange the intrametropolitan spatial configuration of minority residences. In no part of the American city does the labour market 'work' for nonwhites.

The issue of job rationing and discrimination is important and merits serious attention. This should not, however, lead us to abandon the previous analysis in this chapter for several reasons. First, to test whether 'there may be little to be gained from policies designed to rearrange the intrametropolitan spatial configuration of minority residences' requires a clear specification of how these policies could be expected to reduce underemployment. The job–worker matching model in this study represents an attempt at such a specification and has some supporting empirical evidence to suggest that further investigation of the model is warranted.

Secondly, job rationing and the segmented labour market approach may not provide a general analysis of urban labour market problems. The approach certainly does provide a persuasive analysis of one

---

[14] Wilson (1980, ch. 5) refers to the core sector as the corporate and government sector. Doeringer and Piore (1971) originally called it the primary sector or primary labour market.

important aspect of underemployment in terms of unequal opportunities among racial groups (or between men and women). It is less clear that the approach offers a general analysis of urban underemployment of the type provided and tested in the previous section. Most versions of the segmented labour market model, including those of Wilson and Harrison, restrict job rationing to the core sector. The problem is that there are not enough good jobs, not that there are not enough jobs. Wages adjust to clear the local labour market in the peripheral sector. The job–worker matching model then at least applies to underemployment behaviour and other urban labour market issues in the peripheral sector.

Thirdly, it is not clear that an encompassing, or more general, model cannot be constructed which combines the job–worker matching model and the segmented labour market approaches to urban underemployment. Job rationing *per se* can be applied to the island economy used in this study by assuming that wages are inflexible and adjust slowly, if at all, to local labour market conditions. Deterioration of local labour market conditions then leads directly to underemployment rather than declining wage rates. Longer queues of available workers do not prompt employers to reduce wages. Underemployment does not arise when workers decide to refuse local offers to seek better employment opportunities elsewhere. Underemployment results from the lack of local employment opportunities at prevailing wage levels. As long as job search is restricted, particularly for unskilled workers, the implications of shifting labour market conditions are the same. The difference is in the potential magnitude and the involuntary nature of the underemployment problem, and in the scope for effective public intervention.

Rationing may be restricted to jobs in the core sector. This adds a new dimension—the distinction between core and peripheral employment—to the analysis. Underemployment for unskilled and immobile workers may then arise from two sources when local labour market conditions deteriorate. It may arise from a decline in local jobs and wages in the peripheral sector, which encourages workers to look elsewhere or to drop out of the labour force, and from a decline in local jobs in the core sector which leads to lay-offs and extended search for employment in the core sector. Workers who seek jobs in the core sector may seek and accept offers in the peripheral sector only reluctantly and after extensive search for core-sector jobs convinces them that they are unlikely to find one.

It should be noted that job rationing may occur in the peripheral sector of the local economy as well. Wilson (1980: 92) argues that there is no conclusive evidence that minimum wage rates limit employment but a more comprehensive survey of the effect of the minimum wage on employment provides good reason to differ with this judgement (Brown *et al*., 1982). Minimum wage rates may raise wage levels by rationing employment, especially among young workers. From the perspective of the island economy we are concerned not with the mean unskilled youth wage rate, which may be well above the minimum wage, but with the wage rate in local labour markets where conditions are particularly bad, such as many inner-city areas. The local labour market conditions in these areas may dictate equilibrium wage rates below the minimum wage. Compliance with minimum wage legislation then rations employment among job applicants.

Job rationing is a crucial and complex issue in the analysis of underemployment which cannot be resolved in this study. Consider, for example, Holzer's (1987) analysis of the informal information network and youth employment probabilities. The fact that the job search of black youths is less effective than that of white youths may be interpreted as nothing more than unequal job rationing arising from discrimination in employment. Black youth job search may not differ from white youth job search in any respect except that employer discrimination denies blacks some job offers, particularly some good job offers, that go to whites.[15]

In the absence of convincing evidence concerning the cause of urban underemployment the best course of action is to consider all of the above explanations. In particular, the job–worker matching model provides one explanation of urban underemployment, rooted in conventional economic analysis, which may be an important part of the story. The model is compatible with other explanations, including some of those arising from the segmented labour market analyses of urban underemployment. The extent to which these models explain urban underemployment and the nature of a more general model of the problem remain important issues on the urban agenda.

The absence of job rationing implies that sufficient jobs are available for all urban workers, which many scholars reject. In the island

[15] One could extend this argument to say that differences in job search behaviour are also attributable to discrimination in employment. Blacks who are frustrated by the lack of job opportunities may alter their search strategy, or give up in frustration, just as whites would do in the same circumstances.

economy, however, poor local labour market conditions generate poor local job offers. Proponents of the segmented labour market theory usually agree that there are enough poor job offers (for example, Wilson, 1980: 106). The question is whether there are enough good employment opportunities elsewhere *if workers seek them*. Because workers, particularly unskilled workers, are relatively immobile, good employment opportunities may not be found. The response of firms to scarce unskilled labour in the suburbs, where local labour market conditions for unskilled workers are good, is then to adopt production methods which economize on unskilled labour that is in short supply locally. Thus the same firm may use unskilled labour much less intensively in the suburbs because it is difficult to recruit and retain unskilled labour. Ginzberg (1985: 529) argues that New York City needs to connect inner-city workers with blue-collar and service jobs in the suburbs. Without this connection, there is a shortage of workers for the expansion of suburban firms. In such circumstances, jobs are not rationed even if they appear scarce. Thus the actual extent of job rationing is very difficult to determine.

Evidence of job rationing in the aggregate labour market (Kneissner and Goldsmith, 1987), job rationing in unionized jobs (Farber, 1983), and persistent inequality of employment opportunity by race and sex implies that the phenomenon of job rationing should not be ignored. In this section we argue that it should be an important component of a more general approach to urban labour market analysis based, in spatial terms, on the job–worker matching model developed in this study.

6.6 CONCLUDING REMARKS

Urban underemployment is a complex issue. Many scholars simplify it by arguing that underemployment is a labour market problem, or a general social problem, with urban spatial consequences. Urban structure, and spatial matching of jobs and workers, does not matter. This chapter provides a new analysis of the spatial mismatch hypothesis which questions this simplification.

The spatial mismatch hypothesis has suffered because of its weak theoretical foundations. If workers are aware of job opportunities elsewhere in the city, it is difficult to accept that commuting costs and residential immobility are sufficient to discourage workers from accepting them. Our approach has been to focus on the manner in which workers look for employment and to argue that it is important to understand that information about job opportunities in the city is costly. Workers have only fragmented, imperfect job information. For unskilled workers in particular, job search is orientated to the local labour market through an informal information network. Distant job opportunities, such as suburban jobs for inner-city residents, are not easily detected and, because of a shortage of applicants, may disappear. There do not appear to be enough jobs for unskilled inner-city workers because suburban firms adapt to local labour market conditions by using fewer unskilled workers. The problem, however, is worker immobility not job rationing *per se*.

The analysis in this chapter may be extended to other issues involving employment and mobility. One potentially important limitation on residential mobility in many countries is public housing. Hughes and McCormick (1987) report that 28 per cent of British households live in publicly owned accommodation, and this figure is probably higher in urban areas. Households relying on public housing may only be able to relocate if suitable public housing is available where they wish to relocate. It is inevitable, however, that shortages of public housing will coincide with surpluses of job vacancies in rapidly developing, typically suburban, areas of cities. This may not present a problem within cities if workers are able to move freely across labour market areas; workers may simply find jobs involving longer commuting until they can obtain nearby housing. It may be a more serious problem if job search is spatially restricted, however, because workers who cannot relocate may restrict themselves to local, unfavourable employment opportunities.

While public housing presents a potentially serious problem, there are reasons to discount its practical importance. Hughes and McCormick find the effect of housing tenure on interregional migration in the United Kingdom to be small because, they conclude:

Other socioeconomic characteristics of the population of council tenants, who are predominantly manual workers with few educational qualifications and are older on average than the whole population, mean their migration and movement rates are low relative to those for households in other tenure categories even after controlling for the influence of tenure. (Hughes and McCormick, 1987: 623)

This conclusion supports our analysis of intra-urban mobility—namely that other characteristics, particularly lack of skills, already restrict mobility for workers who are in public housing. Public housing may, however, reinforce this effect and frustrate policy initiatives to increase worker mobility. Where public housing is prominent, its potential effect on mobility, in addition to the effects analysed in this chapter, should be examined in future research. This chapter has provided a theoretical framework to investigate the effect of public housing on worker mobility and underemployment.

This chapter does not try to simplify the problem of underemployment by arguing that only worker immobility matters. Although the evidence presented is consistent with the job–worker matching model and spatial mismatch, it is hardly conclusive. Rather, our approach forces us to examine the general underemployment problem and to add an urban spatial perspective to it. Other explanations are not dismissed. Aspects of the segmented labour market approaches, such as behavioural modification and job rationing, are examined within the broader context of underemployment as an urban spatial phenomenon. No definitive answers about the importance of each explanation can be given. Hence each approach should have some influence on the formation of policies to deal with urban underemployment. Chapter 7 discusses urban employment policies from this perspective.

7

EMPLOYMENT POLICIES AND URBAN REDEVELOPMENT

ALTHOUGH a lot has been written about urban redevelopment and about employment policy, there have been few attempts to integrate employment policy and urban redevelopment. This is not surprising under the prevailing viewpoint that they are distinct issues. Employment policy is a national and regional issue while urban redevelopment is a local issue; labour is sufficiently mobile within cities to ignore local area effects. This study has provided an argument to dispute this viewpoint. The argument is based on conventional analysis of the labour market extended to the local area within cities; it is incorporated into the conventional analysis of the urban economy; and it is supported by a variety of evidence on spatial patterns of commuting and underemployment within large urban areas. The study provides a basis to consider the interrelationship between employment policy and urban redevelopment.

The link between employment policy and urban redevelopment is the theory of underemployment in the previous chapter. The theory relates underemployment problems to local labour market conditions. Improvement in local labour market conditions reduces underemployment and raises local income. Higher local income provides resources, both public and private, to address local urban redevelopment. If urban redevelopment is conducted without improvements in local labour market conditions, such that the local residents remain poor or the poor are relocated elsewhere within the city, then redevelopment will be temporary because the poor still do not have the means to sustain it. Hence social and physical renewal are complementary.

One way to circumvent employment policy is to argue that urban redevelopment problems arise from low incomes. The solution is to eliminate poverty by direct transfers of income to the poor rather than by trying to reduce underemployment. Income maintenance should be the focus, not employment policy. There are two standard objections to this argument. One is the problem of work disincentives that arise from direct income transfers. Evidence, particularly evidence from the four income-maintenance experiments in the United States (Robins, 1985; Basilevsky and Hum, 1984), supports this argument but it does not suggest that the work disincentives are large for modest income transfer programmes. These work disincentives may be offset to some extent by low tax rates for the poor to encourage work as a supplement to a basic guaranteed income.

The other objection to exclusive reliance on income maintenance arises from the externalities associated with underemployment and dependence on income transfers. In our work-orientated society good citizenship is associated with stable employment. Urban redevelopment requires good citizenship in terms of property maintenance, low crime rates, social involvement, and informed political decisions. Evidence for these externalities is anecdotal but provides a common argument, and political support, for governments to address underemployment as well as provide income assistance to the underemployed. In practice we observe a combination of income maintenance and employment policies to address poverty and underemployment. This implies that most governments deem employment policy to be one important element of the social policy mix and urban redevelopment. Ginzberg (1985: 654) summarizes the issue as follows:

The real choice the American people face is not greater or lesser support for employment programmes in the future, but rather the basic decision as to whether or not they desire to affirm the nation's long-term commitment to a society built on work. In the event that they affirm this commitment, they have no option but to support the further elaboration of employment policy and programming, which is a necessary if not sufficient condition for achieving this primary national goal.

New employment policies do not need to be developed to address problems of underemployment and development in cities. No new programmes are proposed, since a wide variety of programmes already exist. The emphasis of this chapter is on *local coordination* and on *evaluation of existing programmes* conducted in cities. Local coordination requires attention to the local labour market within the city in designing the policy mix. Local labour market conditions, in terms of the skill mix of jobs and workers within the local area, affect the success of different employment programmes and the optimal policy mix. Evaluation of employment programmes in terms of employment and urban development objectives requires data on local labour market conditions, which will vary from local area to local area within and between cities.

Programme evaluation is badly needed. As this study has emphasized at various points, labour economics remains controversial in many areas. These controversies often lead to dramatically different policy proposals. Economists who view the labour market in equilibrium terms tend to emphasize conventional employment programmes that try to improve the human capital of workers—their education and job skills, their job-information base, and their mobility. Economists who view the labour market in disequilibrium terms argue that conventional programmes are ineffective by themselves because jobs are rationed. Programmes to create jobs are needed, at least for selected workers.[1] Reconciliation of these competing approaches to labour economics and employment policy is incomplete and evaluation of specific employment programmes is needed as a guideline to what will work in particular circumstances. Moreover, these general approaches do not tell us what specific employment programmes work. Should more money go toward counselling or training? Should emphasis be placed on public or private job creation? Should programmes be administered locally, regionally, or nationally? Should programmes be administered publicly or privately? The questions, both economic and administrative, go on and on. Careful monitoring and evaluation can provide us with a more informed basis for shifting the programme portfolio to favour successful policies over unsuccessful ones. At the same time it may give us a better idea of the nature of the underemployment problem and the validity of various competing theories.

It is not possible, or productive, to try to provide a comprehensive analysis of employment programmes. Although modern employment policy is only three decades old, there have been regular changes in legislation and programme emphasis in most countries. In the United and the Comprehensive Employment and Training Act were enacted between 1962 and 1973 (Levitan *et al.*, 1981, ch. 17). Summarizing, never mind analysing, these programmes is a major task beyond the scope of this study. Our focus, therefore, is on generic employment programmes found in most developed market economies under a variety of legislative guises.

A useful distinction can be made between conventional employment, or 'manpower', programmes that focus on human capital development on the one hand and job-creation programmes on the other. We examine these policies in separate sections below in the context of local labour markets within cities.

7.1 CONVENTIONAL URBAN EMPLOYMENT PROGRAMMES

Conventional employment programmes try to improve the human capital of workers, including schooling, on-the-job training and work skills, job information, and mobility. The basic rationale for these programmes is the theory of human capital acquisition in a labour market that involves no job rationing. Wages adjust until the equilibrium levels of labour supply and demand are achieved. This occurs for each type of labour differentiated only by human capital characteristics. Because there are enough jobs at any level at the corresponding equilibrium wage, underemployment implies inadequate human capital to achieve some target in terms of earnings or employment stability. Workers who are released from declining industries and workers who habitually have trouble finding and keeping a satisfactory job may require new human capital to improve their employment prospects. Workers may undertake new human capital investment without government assistance, but governments may deem it necessary to intervene to provide public incentives for reasons of efficiency or equity. Thus governments provide free employment information and counselling services because there are inadequate incentives in the private sector for this activity.[2] They also subsidize job-training programmes, particularly for disadvantaged groups with special problems and limited financing.

It is important to realize that, in this view, employment programmes not only assist the programme participant but narrow the gap between

---

[2] Information is a public good in the sense that, once provided, others cannot be effectively excluded from sharing it without paying. Private agencies will charge a fee that will exceed the marginal cost of provision (negligible) and lead to an underutilization of employment information unless the government intervenes.

unskilled and skilled workers. Programme participants are generally unskilled or have skills that are obsolete. If they acquire new skills they are able to find better employment opportunities. They compete with skilled workers for available skilled vacancies and reduce the wages paid to skilled workers. Moreover, since they are no longer competing with unskilled workers for unskilled vacancies, the employment opportunities and wages for unskilled workers improve. Thus public subsidies to human capital investment can benefit all unskilled workers, both programme participants and non-participants, and reduce earnings inequality (Chiswick and Mincer, 1972).

This argument can be extended to the local labour market of our island economy only to a certain extent. In any local market in the absence of job rationing, employment programmes can reduce underemployment and earnings inequality in the manner described above. If local demand for labour is deficient, however, workers have to go elsewhere to find suitable vacancies. If workers are completely mobile this presents no problem. This study has argued, however, that urban workers, particularly less-skilled workers, are relatively immobile. If local demand for labour is deficient and workers are relatively immobile, then the surplus of applicants for scarce local jobs forces down wage rates. Some workers will decline low wage offers and search elsewhere or withdraw from the labour market in frustration; others will accept low pay. In each case underemployment arises from worker immobility. The available jobs in other areas of the city that remain vacant force wages for those positions to rise. In some cases, firms cancel positions rather than pay higher wages, although the position would have been offered and filled if workers were completely mobile. What appears to be a surplus of unskilled workers in certain local labour markets may be consistent with wage flexibility but worker immobility. If minimum wage rates or other arrangements limit the decline of wages, then an actual surplus of job applicants and job rationing occurs.

Employment programmes could provide skills to underemployed unskilled workers in excess supply in local labour markets. This has two effects. First, it qualifies the workers for skilled local jobs. Secondly, it also improves their information sources in the sense that skilled workers use formal information sources more intensively. Parnes and Kohen (1975) find that higher education is associated with better occupational information and higher earnings and occupational status among young men in the United States. They conclude that investment in education also involves investment in information about career options and employment conditions. Such information reduces underemployment by increasing the efficiency of occupational choice and the spatial extent of job search. Individuals with inferior information are more likely to err in the selection of an occupation and specific job, leading to dissatisfaction and repeated search.[3] Skills training other than formal education is likely to have similar positive effects on occupational and job choice, particularly if associated with career and job search counselling.

Let us be clear about the nature of the improvement in information identified by Parnes and Kohen. It is really job information associated with the formal network. As discussed at length in Chapter 2, more-skilled and educated workers use formal information sources much more intensively. Thus the causation implied by Parnes and Kohen may be incorrect—information does not lead to higher occupational status; rather, higher occupational status gives rise to better use of formal information networks. Formal information networks provide for a more spatially extensive search, leading to greater mobility among skilled workers. Thus employment programmes involving training and counselling can improve worker mobility through increased reliance on formal employment information networks.

It is tempting to argue that programmes can increase mobility directly. Employment information and counselling services for underemployed unskilled workers can assist them to find suitable job opportunities elsewhere in the city. This approach, while the most direct one, presents some problems because unskilled workers rely heavily on informal information networks rather than public services. There is clear evidence that the role of the government as a labour market broker and source of labour market information has declined sharply over the years in Canada (Employment and Immigration Canada, 1981, 76). Moreover, most users of the Canadian employment service for job information were dissatisfied with the service. Holzer (1988) presents empirical evidence which indicates that informal methods—friends and relatives and direct applications without referral—are the most productive source of job offers and acceptances among unemployed youth in the United States. It is therefore hardly surprising that these methods are used most frequently and that public

---

[3] If attitudes and work habits deteriorate in peripheral jobs, then the search may continue indefinitely.

employment services have relatively little influence. It will be difficult for employment information and counselling programmes to influence job search patterns under those circumstances.

Some reorientation of conventional urban employment programmes is warranted. In this regard our study indicates two directions. First, there should be a greater emphasis on local, intra-urban labour market differences in employment programme planning. Secondly, there should be more thorough evaluation of employment programmes taking account of the urban spatial dimension. Let us consider these issues in more depth.

Greater emphasis is needed on local labour market differences in employment programme planning if labour mobility is limited. There is little evidence that current planning gives serious consideration to the role that urban structure may play in underemployment problems. Labour markets are viewed as cities or regions between which mobility is limited but within which mobility is not a problem. A good example is the decentralization of employment programmes in the United States under the Nixon Administration. In 1973 the Comprehensive Employment and Training Act (CETA) designated local prime sponsors to plan, administer, and deliver employment programmes across the nation. Prime sponsors included officials at the city, county, or state level (Levitan *et al.*, 1981). Whatever the motives for this decision, there is no indication that this decentralization led to differentiation of local labour markets within cities or to recognition of mobility problems and the effect of urban structure on employment.

Mirengoff and Rindler's (1978) evaluation of CETA argues that the Act makes two major assumptions about effective employment planning:

The first assumption is that state and local sponsors, since they are familiar with varying local conditions and needs, are in a better position to plan than federal programme managers. The second assumption is that if the community is broadly represented in the planning process, the programs developed will be closely attuned to local needs. (p. 47)

Yet their evaluation provides no discussion of 'local conditions and needs' beyond the conventional focus on city and regional labour markets. Some decentralization of employment programme planning and delivery is required if local labour market differences are to be considered properly. This must be followed, however, with a serious assessment, within each city, of intra-urban labour market conditions and their implications for employment programme planning. This may take some time to involve community groups and reorientate programmes, but it may also require programme managers to focus on underemployment problems and labour market conditions in greater spatial detail than they have in the past.

Mirengoff and Rindler (1978: 9) describe local employment planning as 'passive' and 'largely routine for obtaining funding'. This might change over time as local planning councils adapt to their mandate. Yet local councils may continue to focus on city-wide employment conditions and ignore mobility problems and employment conditions within the city. As long as local labour markets are traditionally defined as city-wide or as regional markets, local councils may adopt the same standards without further investigation. This study has argued that the standard definition of a local labour market is too broad for large cities and requires a much more restrictive spatial interpretation. Only then will the effects of urban structure on local labour markets be properly addressed in planning and assessing employment programmes.

Employment policy has been more centralized in other countries and therefore even less likely to address local labour market conditions. In the United Kingdom, for example, the Manpower Services Commission has taken control of employment programmes since its inception in 1974. Prior to the formation of the Commission employment policy was administered by local education authorities under agreements with the Department of Education and Science. Employment programmes arc now administered by fifty-five Area Manpower Boards but with apparently little local autonomy to plan and set policy. Thus the Youth Opportunities Programme, begun in 1978, provided new money for youth employment programmes but with guidelines to reduce local autonomy in the content of those programmes (St John-Brooks, 1985).[4]

Hallman (1980: 95) provides further arguments for a local, or a neighbourhood, focus rather than a city-wide focus for employment programmes. Neighbourhoods may have special characteristics which can be incorporated in employment planning. Thus neighbourhood employment centres may be able to reduce alienation to government programmes and bureaucracy and improve recruitment, particularly

---

[4] Much of the controversy appears to have been over 'political' education of workers by local authorities (St John-Brooks, 1985: 14), but the Manpower Services Commission also appears to have adopted a narrow view that only skill training should be supported.

among disadvantaged workers in target areas. Local training programmes may be adapted to the racial or ethnic background of
the neighbourhood, including appropriate language training where
necessary and effective motivation and counselling of trainees. More
decentralized employment planning has allowed some local councils
to concentrate on special programmes for the Hispanic population in
the United States (Hallman, 1980: 45). At the same time we might
add that local employment conditions may be assessed and training
programmes may be aimed at providing skills for local job vacancies.
This may be much easier and more effective if local business repre-
sentatives are involved in the planning process.

Attention to local employment conditions is particularly important
where workers are relatively unskilled, as are most disadvantaged
trainees after short government-sponsored programmes, and have
strong preferences for employment within the neighbourhood. Where
local employment conditions are poor, planning must try to identify
the nearest jobs likely to attract trainees or try to attract more firms
to the local area (a matter we will discuss further in the next section).
A city-wide focus will be less effective in attracting and training the
disadvantaged and underemployed and less effective in finding them
long-term employment.

Decentralization of employment planning might be expected to
lead to greater diversification and experimentation in employment
programmes as councils develop independent local plans. Evidence
from CETA in the United States indicates a rapid shift from training
programmes to work experience and public service employment
programmes, although it is not clear if this reflects local needs or
administrative convenience (Mirengoff and Rindler, 1978, ch. 5).
Experimentation in employment programmes is widely supported in
the United States. Ginzberg (1985: 689), for example, argues that it
is an essential ingredient to better employment policies in the future.

Experimentation in employment programmes may involve various
target groups, including youth, single mothers, ex-offenders, and drug
addicts. It may also involve various combinations of services and
different types of organizations to deliver the services. In each case
a complex package of programmes is involved in terms of recruitment, counselling, training, basic education and motivation, and job
placement. These different parts of the package may also be subject
to experimentation. In each case some attention should also be paid
to local labour market conditions as a factor affecting experimental

outcomes. The outcomes of experiments may vary not only as a result of the particular treatment but also as a result of differences in local labour market conditions between different areas of a city or between local areas in different cities.

Experimental employment programmes are useful only in so far as they are evaluated carefully. On this score CETA programmes seem to have fared quite poorly (Hallman, 1980, ch. 5; Parnes, 1984) in part because the monitoring of local programmes has not been standardized and in part because evaluation procedures have not been standardized to facilitate comparisons. This may simply reflect poor data collection and evaluation procedures in employment planning in the United States (Ginzberg, 1985, ch. 47) and elsewhere.

Priority must be given to standardized, effective evaluation of employment programmes as an integral part of employment planning. Mirengoff and Rindler (1978: 269–70) call for 1 per cent of CETA funds to be used 'for a continuous research, evaluation, and demonstration programme both within government agencies and by outside, independent research organizations'. The proposed expenditure would have amounted to $57 million in 1976. This amount may be too modest, however. Effective evaluation of employment programmes must include evaluation of outcomes as well as processes. Where evaluations of CETA have been done, there has been far too little emphasis on evaluation of outcomes (Levitan *et al.*, 1981, ch. 20). This appears to be true of other programmes in the United States as well (Ginzberg, 1985: 639).

Evaluation of outcomes is costly if done properly. Eligible employment programme participants must be divided and enrolled both in a treatment group, receiving actual programmes, and a control group, not receiving any programmes. Enrolment must be in sufficient numbers to detect programme effects with adequate statistical reliability. Otherwise a simple comparison of programme participants before and after may yield misleading estimates of programme effects. Care must be taken to design a survey that captures treatments, outcomes, and any intervening variables which might affect outcomes. The survey should follow individuals not only through the programme but for several years afterward in order to obtain a good measure of the permanent employment effects. Multivariate statistical techniques should be used to estimate programme effects, allowing for such problems as selectivity bias arising from programme participation (Lalonde, 1986). An excellent review of the statistical issues involved in the evaluation of employment programmes is provided by Bloch (1979).

Enormous funds are being spent on employment programmes, many of which appear to yield benefits which exceed costs (Levitan *et al.*, ch. 20). Standardized outcome evaluations would provide a clearer indication of which programmes work best for which groups of participants to permit more efficient allocation of public resources to achieve employment targets.[5] Some programmes may be slowly phased out or restricted to certain groups while other programmes, showing larger outcome gains per dollar spent, are expanded. In this way slow but steady progress toward more effective employment programmes can be made while providing insight into the labour market process and problems of underemployment.

Decentralized employment planning still requires standardized and well-funded evaluation procedures. Planned experimentation[6] and programme diversification allows even greater opportunities for proper evaluation to uncover winners and losers among employment programmes, provided that comparisons between programmes and jurisdictions are possible. The problems involved in comparing programmes and jurisdictions are political as well as economic and statistical, since poor results can be threatening to politicians and bureaucrats. Care must be taken to avoid unproductive competition among jurisdictions, such as 'creaming' the most employable applicants and ignoring the more disadvantaged applicants to improve measured outcomes (Hallman, 1980: 52). Effective population targets or other measures must be used to ensure that this does not occur unduly. At the same time, there are enormous potential benefits available if proper evaluation procedures are incorporated in a decentralized employment planning system.

Evaluation of employment programmes should take account of local employment conditions. Some programmes—skill training and counselling—are likely to work better in tight local labour markets because they increase the mobility of trainees. Job search activities

---

[5] Some groups of participants may show worse results for all programmes. This does not necessarily imply that these groups should receive a smaller share of employment programme funds. Economic equity and political considerations may dictate otherwise. It does imply, however, that more funds should go to those programmes which yield the best results for these groups to raise the overall rate of return to employment programmes.

[6] Special programmes may be designed to encourage innovative demonstration projects by local employment planning councils.

of trainees and the control group should be monitored to see which search methods are productive and to see what effect employment programmes have on search methods. At least some job search data should include a *spatial dimension* assessing intra-urban search patterns which can be interpreted in terms of local labour markets. Far too little is known about job search activity within cities and the factors which improve its effectiveness. This study has argued that such activity is important and too often overlooked. Decentralized employment planning and careful outcome evaluations of programmes offer the best opportunity to learn about, and assess the importance of, worker mobility within urban areas. Indeed, the essence of decentralized decision-making and evaluation is to learn, largely through trial and error, what works and what does not in particular areas for particular groups. In this way progress can be made and repetition of mistakes can be avoided.

7.2 LOCAL JOB-CREATION PROGRAMMES

Conventional employment programmes have been criticized as ineffective because they do not create jobs for the underemployed. The argument implicitly or explicitly rejects the human capital model in which an increase in the supply of trained workers depresses the wage gap between trained and untrained workers until all trained workers are fully employed. Instead, a worker trained in a conventional employment programme either has difficulty finding steady employment using his skills or, if he does find steady employment, simply displaces another worker with comparable skills. Since the displaced worker is now underemployed, there are no social benefits to the programme even though there are measurable private benefits to programme trainees. Only job-creation programmes, alone or in conjunction with conventional employment programmes, can avoid this problem.

A clear statement of the case for job-creation programmes in the context of an urban economy is provided by Harrison (1972, 1974). He attacks the 'fallacious assumptions about the responsiveness of the economic system to improvements in the supply of ghetto labor' and the 'unjustified optimism about private corporate demand for ghetto labor' (Harrison, 1972: 154). Education and training are important objectives in the long run but poor policies to address underemployment in the short run. The reason is that the labour market is segmented and there are a limited number of good jobs in the core sector. The supply of good jobs is unresponsive to labour market conditions—despite an excess supply of willing and capable workers, the supply of good jobs does not expand and must be rationed. In the rationing process minority workers from urban ghettos are at a serious disadvantage, relegating them to unemployment or unrewarding jobs in the peripheral sector.

The problem Harrison sees is not unqualified workers in inner cities but an insufficient number of rewarding job opportunities. The solution is not training programmes but the development of new and broader urban job markets for inner-city residents. He advocates two measures: public employment programmes for disadvantaged workers and ghetto economic development, measures which are noticeably absent in the policy mix in the United States.

One can accept Harrison's argument that the underemployed need jobs not training and still question his policy recommendations. He dismisses other policy options, in particular the so-called 'ghetto dispersal' strategy advocated by Kain (1968*a*) and others. This strategy argues that the jobs required by inner-city residents are being created in the suburbs. The solution is to overcome the spatial mismatch by increasing the mobility of the inner-city underemployed. This can be accomplished by improving public transportation from the inner city to the suburbs to encourage inner-city residents to find and accept suburban jobs and by encouraging the relocation of disadvantaged inner-city residents in suburban areas. Rather than encourage the spatial concentration of disadvantaged minority workers, ghetto dispersal encourages their integration into the mainstream of economic life.

Although the argument for ghetto dispersal has been closely associated with John Kain, it has had many proponents. One of the earliest was Albert Rees (1966*b*: 346) who wrote:

Much of the growth of employment has been in the new, light industry of the suburbs and in services for rapidly growing suburban populations. Much of the unused and underused labour supply is in the slums in the heart of the central cities, among people who don't have automobiles. Better and faster public transportation would make employment accessible to many more in this group.

Reubens (1968) argued that money spent subsidizing firms to locate in New York City would be better spent relocating workers outside the city or providing sufficient transportation for them to find jobs in the metropolitan area outside New York City itself. A report by the Stanford Research Institute argued that the proposed Los Angeles rapid transit system would reduce unemployment by improving transportation to areas of labour shortage and save taxpayers $30 million annually (Peterson, 1975).

Harrison (1972) presents evidence that improvements in public transportation are not the answer. Subsidized reverse commuting experiments in major cities in the United States have had little success. Yet it is not clear that there are not job opportunities in the suburbs for inner-city workers, only that these jobs are not sought. Harrison's emphasis on inadequate job opportunities because of racial discrimination is one important consideration for minority workers. Another potential explanation, and one that can be applied more generally to underemployed workers, is the immobility of the underemployed. In this study we have argued that this immobility arises from the job search behaviour of unskilled workers, who rely on spatially restrictive informal methods. If unskilled workers in the inner city use referrals and direct application to find predominantly local jobs, then improvements in transportation to the suburbs will have little effect on their job search activity. The problem is not transportation, nor is it necessarily the lack of suburban job opportunities in many cases; the problem is the spatially restricted job search of inner-city residents. As Gayer (1971) found, there are job opportunities in the suburbs of New York City with sufficiently high pay to more than compensate for the costs of commuting from the inner-city without further public subsidization of transportation facilities. The problem is that underemployed inner-city workers don't look for jobs in the suburbs.

Harrison also argues that relocation of ghetto residents in the suburbs is not an effective strategy to reduce underemployment because governments, with the support of suburban residents, resist initiatives to integrate the poor and the rich. He writes:

In a study of two 'new towns' in California, Dr. Carl Werthman asked residents how they interpreted 'planning' and how they would react to the development of 'lower-priced' homes in the towns. His interviews . . . led him to the conclusion that 'planning' is thought to be a guarantee against . . . the lower priced home sold to the lower-income person. (Harrison, 1972: 166)

Other attempts to relocate ghetto residents in suburban areas have resulted in new concentrations of low-income housing with few local job opportunities. In other words, ghettos are reassembled in the suburbs at enormous public expense and limited social benefit.

The argument Harrison presents is a classic one in terms of regional analysis (for example, Richardson, 1969, or Stilwell, 1972). If there are regions with too few workers and regions with too few jobs, and if people cannot be moved to the jobs, then the jobs must be moved to the people. In the context of an urban economy, however, we are accustomed to thinking of a single labour market and ignoring intra-urban mobility problems. Harrison ignores mobility problems by concentrating on unequal access to employment opportunities by black Americans. A more general argument, which may also be a valid factor in the case of blacks, is that an urban economy is a set of 'regions' or 'islands' itself. This allows us to investigate mobility problems in the manner that is traditional in regional studies. The urban underemployed cannot be easily moved to suburban regions either daily or permanently. Hence local (inner-city) job-creation is the effective policy to combat underemployment.

This analogy to regional economics seems more direct in Harrison (1974). He sees the ghetto as a 'colony' or 'underdeveloped country' cut off from the economic mainstream. Like underdeveloped regions, the ghettos have some features to attract firms—a ready supply of inexpensive labour and suitable land in particular. Despite these apparent advantages over the suburbs, however, the ghettos have trouble attracting new employment opportunities. Migration, rather than helping, hurts the ghetto because it is selective. The successful residents and firms are likely to move to the suburbs, leaving behind a dearth of entrepreneurial expertise to create new employment opportunities.

The issue is whether to invest in people (ghetto residents) or to invest in places (the ghettos themselves). Harrison argues that those who advocate training programmes and ghetto dispersal ignore the discrimination and other market imperfections that limit job opportunities in the private sector for ghetto residents. They also ignore the 'neighbourhood effects' or externalities of ghetto development and underestimate the social returns. The return to any individual investor, whether an entrepreneur or a home-owner, is low unless others invest as well. Government must rebuild the infrastructure and stimulate private investment in ghetto areas to make them attractive to other investors.[7] This problem has been recognized with regard to housing

---

[7] The problem, known as the 'prisoner's dilemma', is that each individual's best choice is to invest elsewhere assuming that everyone else will do the same (the non-

and other aspects of physical redevelopment (Davis and Whinston, 1961, for example). It often appears in the concept of a 'growth point' or 'infant area subsidy policy' in which externalities can generate self-perpetuating growth beyond some point (Richardson, 1969: 415). The problem has been given less attention with regard to employment and social redevelopment. As argued in Chapter 6, the redevelopment of employment opportunities in ghetto areas can improve the informal information network for all ghetto residents about job opportunities inside and outside the ghetto and can provide a positive, work-orientated role model for others. We should not ignore the role that these factors can play in rebuilding the ghetto economy. The economy will, after all, be rebuilt by people not by the infrastructure. The challenge is for government to provide a critical level of physical redevelopment *and new employment* that will motivate regeneration of the community.

Harrison (1972: 1974) argues in favour of local control for economic development of the inner cities. He argues that programmes to employ the hard-core unemployed in private industry outside the ghetto are ineffective. The jobs are often menial and pay low wages, providing little incentive for job stability. Much of the funding available for the National Alliance of Businessmen's Job Opportunities in the Business Sector programme in the United States, for example, was not spent. On the other hand, Hall (1971) reports that efforts to induce large corporations to locate branch plants in ghettos and create good jobs for disadvantaged workers have met with some success. He argues that governments should encourage further private investment in ghettos by providing selective tax credits, by requiring such behaviour through federal contract provisions, and by legislating employment quotas. Harrison (1972: 186) notes, however, that business and government support for these programmes has waned. A better ghetto environment, including better public services and transportation, is needed before corporations are likely to play a willing role in further ghetto redevelopment. Harrison advocates locally controlled ghetto development through subsidies to black (that is, local) capitalism and housing renovation. He cites community economic development corporations as one vehicle for this policy.

Local or community economic development has become popular recently. Malizia (1985) notes that community economic development

cooperative game) but the best choice overall is for every individual to invest in the ghetto (the cooperative game).

was largely confined to underdeveloped countries before 1960. The Great Society programmes in the United States identified community economic development as a major policy goal to combat 'pockets of poverty' in inner cities. Ross (1986) argues that community economic development is the appropriate policy response to the current crisis of high unemployment in developed economies. The idea is not to focus on competition and short-run allocative efficiency but on innovation and growth. In other words, the idea is not to try to attract successful firms to the ghettos but to nurture new firms that will be successful in the future. This may require some short-run subsidization and protection to permit firms to innovate and achieve a critical size. Community economic development seeks to restore to inner cities their critical role as 'incubators' for economic growth.

Regeneration of inner cities will not be accomplished easily since capital and entrepreneurship has largely deserted ghetto areas in response to their decay. Community economic development corporations need to involve local business people and community leaders in identifying the needs of local business. Provided with government financial, legislative, and technical support, the community economic development corporation is expected to establish a local development plan that fits local needs. The community economic development corporation seeks entrepreneurs and organizers, conducts market or product feasibility studies, provides management consulting services, raises venture capital, and arranges loan packages and equity investments to act as the sponsor or catalyst for new enterprises (Booth and Fortis, 1984). Enterprises might also be encouraged by lower business and personal taxes in designated 'enterprise zones' of depressed communities (Auletta, 1982: 277).

Many argue that the community economic development corporation cannot succeed if its focus is too narrowly commercial. An effective local plan must deal with jobs, housing, community organizations, and public investment in infrastructure as well as commercial ventures. Otherwise entrepreneurs will continue to view depressed inner-city areas as hostile business environments and may resist strictly financial enticements. Many advocate public employment as an important initial source of job-creation. Ginzberg (1985: 678) summarizes the beneficial long-term outcome of public job-creation in the United States and the shift to public job-creation through community-based organizations in 1971. Harrison (1972) notes that public administration is now the most centralized industry in urban areas.

It is also growing rapidly and providing better jobs than the private sector. This makes public employment the best vehicle to replace departed manufacturing employment in inner cities.

Public employment may be particularly important in the early stages of urban redevelopment when local private employment opportunities are scarce. Jobs in the public sector provide a badly needed injection of income into depressed areas.[8] They also provide opportunities for the underemployed to gain work experience and to reorganize their lives around a steady job and source of income. A successful record of public sector employment can provide the basis for hiring into good jobs in the private sector, particularly with initial government support. Experimental employment programmes for disadvantaged workers can be developed and tested in the public sector and, where successful, extended to the private sector as well. In this way public sector employment can be used to rebuild the local workforce and the local private sector of depressed areas.

As in the previous section, we argue for a local focus and for careful evaluation of programmes. The local focus means not only an emphasis on local job-creation but attention to the interrelationship between the skill requirements of local jobs and the skill development of local workers. If local, underemployed workers depend on local employment opportunities, then training programmes need to develop skills that are in demand locally. Public sector employment programmes to provide work experience also need to develop skills that will help to obtain local jobs. In this manner local business opportunities can develop around local skills and local workers can play a major role in area redevelopment.

This local focus need not be viewed as permanent. Successful urban redevelopment leads to progressively stronger links with the surrounding economy. Similarly, urban redevelopment will provide job skills and more spatially extensive and formal job search networks which lead to employment opportunities elsewhere. Again the selective out-migration of successful firms and workers must be a concern as a brake on the momentum for further local redevelopment. Workers, in particular, must be convinced that the local area is an attractive place to remain even when employment opportunities arise in other parts of the city.

---

[8] One problem is that inner-city ghettos have very low employment and income multipliers until redevelopment succeeds (Harrison, 1974: 8).

Local job-creation programmes, like conventional employment programmes, need to be evaluated carefully. The methodology for evaluation of local job-creation programmes is not developed as well as it is for conventional employment programmes, but it should involve a clear analysis of the direct employment benefits and indirect employment benefits, or spin-offs, over a period of time. How well do private firms do under different public support programmes? What is the failure rate? Do successful firms stay in the area? How well do workers in subsidized private and public sector jobs do over time? Do they find good career paths? Are they able to find jobs in other firms? Are some programmes more effective than others in terms of employment and income generation for local residents?

Such evaluations are costly but not prohibitively so. They provide a unique and valuable source of information to analysts and planners about the local economy—how it works and what programmes work best. Since controversy will remain about the important economic issues for the foreseeable future, it is important that programmes that are tried out under different theories are also evaluated to distinguish good ideas from bad ones.

Nor need politicians and planners fear that evaluations will be uniformly negative and discourage funding according to Hallman's (1980: 70) assessment of the local role in job creation:

All available evidence indicates that community-based and neighbourhood organizations are valuable sources of job-creation in useful work. They are in touch with community needs, and they are less likely than government agencies to substitute public service employment money for other revenue sources. The work they undertake makes significant contributions to the low-income neighbourhoods they serve. By giving unemployed residents a chance to earn money, they help these individuals and also add to the neighbourhood economy.

7.3   FINDING THE OPTIMAL LOCAL POLICY MIX

Urban redevelopment and decentralized authority for employment policy are important developments in recent years. We have referred frequently in this chapter to the experience in the United States up to 1980 with CETA and local job-creation aimed primarily at depressed inner areas of large cities. To this we could add the earlier urban-specific employment programmes of the Model Cities programme and the Co-operative Area Manpower Planning Systems (Ruttenberg,

1970), although these programmes were narrowly focused on the delivery of services rather than local economic development (Harrison, 1974). In the United Kingdom, following upon the Inner Area Studies, the Thatcher government announced plans in 1986 to create a series of urban redevelopment councils to regenerate the inner cities with a combination of public and private financing. In Canada, the Forget Commission in 1986 called for the replacement of part of the support provided by unemployment insurance with, among other measures, community-based development projects involving the local community in identifying needs and potential markets and in planning, evaluating, and encouraging new ventures. The Forget Commission described community-based development as a powerful tool in the fight against unemployment. Also in Canada, the federal, provincial, and municipal governments have reached agreements to revitalize inner-city areas through community involvement, local job-creation, and complementary training programmes. One such agreement, the Winnipeg Core Area Initiative, is in its second five-year plan (Winnipeg Core Area Initiative Policy Committee, 1981).

The labour market plays an important role in urban redevelopment. Policy formulation must consider those features of labour market behaviour that are important in causing and curing urban decline. Traditional analysis considers the urban area to be one closely interconnected labour market in which local redevelopment is a problem of providing income and public services and in which employment policy has a city-wide focus. This study argues that there is good reason, both theoretical and empirical, to quarrel with this judgement.

The failure of many urban redevelopment and employment programmes provides ample reason to reconsider the traditional approach. Auletta (1982: 280) refers to the Atlantic City, New Jersey 'experiment'. Gambling was legalized and the city boomed. But the pockets of urban poverty remained. And the problems of education, training, discrimination, health, housing, transportation, and child care in these areas were untouched. Similarly Salinas (1986) shows that rapid economic growth *per se*, such as occurred in the Sunbelt states of the United States in recent years, does not reduce underemployment. The 'trickle down' approach to alleviating poverty does not work. What can other cities do with less favourable economic circumstances?

Because labour markets for the underemployed and largely unskilled are not city-wide, local planning and policy must be more spatially refined. Community economic development organizations are needed to identify local economic strengths and weaknesses and devise local plans. The needs of the local workforce and local business must be assessed and integrated. The focus must be not only on local job-creation but also on local jobs for local residents. If such programmes promote redevelopment and employment stability then reintegration of the local economy with the wider urban economy will follow.

All public authority should not be delegated to the community organization. Proper planning and budgeting procedures and technical expertise in employment programmes must be provided to local groups. Evaluation procedures and expertise must also be provided to ensure that programmes are evaluated properly and in a uniform manner to permit comparisons between programmes and across jurisdictions. Only in this fashion can effective local employment and urban redevelopment policies be identified, expanded, and transferred to other local areas with comparable problems.

8

FINAL THOUGHTS . . . FOR NOW

THIS study presents a theory of the spatial mobility of workers in cities to explain where workers find jobs and to improve our understanding of urban spatial structure and commuting patterns. This approach provides a useful extension to the conventional theory of residential location and urban spatial structure that forms the core of urban economics. In particular, it emphasizes the role of local employment conditions and skill acquisition in spatial job search and commuting behaviour and lays the groundwork for further analysis of such questions as wage and price gradients in cities with decentralized employment and the role of employment discrimination in commuting.

The theory also provides an explanation of the effect of urban structure on labour market performance. It emphasizes the importance of local labour market conditions within cities as the source of jobs for workers with limited formal skill training. Many scholars have cited local labour market conditions as a factor in the underemployment problems in cities. The spatial mismatch hypothesis has been both loosely formulated and crudely tested without adequate theoretical foundation heretofore. This study provides a theoretical foundation from modern labour economics that is consistent with evidence from Greater London, Toronto, and several cities in the United States. The evidence provides support for the spatial mismatch hypothesis but, more importantly, provides a basis for more careful empirical work in the future on this question. No longer can the spatial mismatch hypothesis be dismissed as vague and lacking a theoretical basis. Its empirical significance may be the subject of considerable future debate, but it should be taken seriously.

The analysis is far from complete, but it provides a clear link between urban economics and labour economics that has been almost totally ignored heretofore. It argues that many traditional issues in urban economics must be reconsidered to examine the impact of urban structure on the labour market. The labour market has been recognized to be important to urban problems but as a separate entity, generating income inequality and employment discrimination which affect urban structure and policy, rather than an *integral* part of the process of urban development. This study forces us to consider the labour market as an integral part of the process of urban development and raises new and interesting issues.

8.1 WORKPLACE CHOICE AND TRADITIONAL URBAN ISSUES

As we stated at the outset, this book is not a complete treatment of urban economics in the usual sense but an extension of traditional topics to include the urban labour market as an integral part of the urban spatial economy. Yet traditional topics are interrelated and, as one might expect, the analysis of urban labour markets must have some impact on these topics as well. An integrated approach, or textbook, should be on the agenda for future research. At this point, however, we will simply summarize the major areas of integration between the analysis in this book and traditional urban concerns.

8.1.1 Urban spatial structure

Clearly one major effect of our analysis is on the static theory of urban structure. As models of urban structure introduce employment decentralization, it is natural to consider workplace choice behaviour and to consider it in greater depth than is possible in the consumer choice model of residential location. The analysis in Chapters 3 through 5 then becomes a logical extension of residential choice models with decentralized employment. The three major components of urban structure are then an employment location model, a residential location model, and our workplace choice model.

One immediate effect will be a reinterpretation of wage gradients, as indicated in Chapter 2. As they arise from the residential location model they are simply the reservation wages of households that reflect the disutility and direct cost associated with commuting. As they arise from the model in this book, wage gradients are the product of the interaction of household reservation wages and the wage offers of firms which depend upon the spatial distribution of employment demand and labour supply. Moreover, labour market behaviour should reflect the spatial costs of information and job search, which can dramatically alter the predictions of economic theory. Thus wage gradients do not just slope downward in concert with land-rent gradients in cities as models now predict—they are expected to be steeper in cities with more centralized employment and steeper for less-skilled workers, other factors equal. Neither of these testable predictions can be derived from traditional models of urban structure without introducing, at least implicitly, the labour market model elucidated in Chapters 3 and 4.

Other, less obvious, effects of workplace choice behaviour on urban spatial structure remain to be investigated. Urban land-rent gradients, population gradients, employment-density gradients, and the location behaviour of firms in cities are all influenced by consideration of the urban labour market and the spatial mobility of workers.

8.1.2   Urban transportation

The speed and cost of urban transportation is an important determinant of urban structure in conventional models. Once employment is decentralized, we have argued that commuting patterns become more complex because workplace location must be determined. Our analysis implies that transportation costs are an important factor in workplace choice in the sense that workers prefer nearby jobs if they are available. Thus transportation infrastructure remains an important engine of urban spatial development. There are some caveats, however.

The simple view that urban transportation planning can overcome spatial mobility barriers within cities must be reassessed. Our analysis finds considerable support for the view that the mobility of workers is limited because of spatial restrictions on job search. Thus labour markets within cities are balkanized spatially to a considerable degree. The notion, discussed in Chapter 7, that improvements in transportation in areas of high underemployment will alleviate employment problems arising from the spatial mismatch of jobs and workers ignores the evidence that many workers have strong preferences to seek nearby jobs. It is unwise to confuse transportation availability with job accessibility when spatial barriers to job search exist. At the same time, transportation planning is obviously one important consideration in linking underemployed workers to available employment. Thus, transportation planning should work in concert with effective urban employment programmes, as discussed in Chapter 7.

Our analysis directs transportation planners to focus on the limited spatial mobility of less skilled workers in particular. Traditional urban economic models direct transportation planners to consider household characteristics such as income. Our perspective from the urban labour market, however, shifts the focus to individual skills as an important determinant of spatial mobility and workplace choice. To the extent that planning gives special weight to the needs of the underemployed, who are typically less skilled, it is crucial to consider the barriers to spatial mobility identified in Chapter 4 and tested with regard to commuting and underemployment in Chapters 5 and 6.

8.1.3   Housing and urban redevelopment

Few would disagree that earned income is the most important factor in housing decline and renewal. Yet traditional urban models have ignored any possible links between the labour market and urban structure of the sort addressed in this study. Thus physical deterioration has not been formally linked with labour market problems such as the spatial mismatch of jobs and workers and urban renewal has not been formally linked with local labour market renewal. The frustrating experience of physical renewal plans that ignore underlying labour market problems and other social problems should direct urban research to look for such links. Indeed, such links are now often made informally in assessing feasible redevelopment plans. Formal linkage is clearly desirable, however, and Chapters 4–6 provide a basis for this analysis.

The introduction of explicit links between housing and the urban labour market has important policy implications. It has been convenient to regard employment policy to be distinct from the analysis of housing and urban redevelopment policy so that urban redevelopment policy has generally been concerned with physical renewal alone, leaving poverty and employment as separate concerns. Even when comprehensive redevelopment plans have included employment programmes there has been no clear integration of these programmes with urban housing and commercial redevelopment. Such comprehensive plans have recognized that physical renewal is bound to fail unless employment and income problems are addressed, but the fundamental links between underemployment and urban decline have been ignored. Chapter 6 explores these links, focusing upon the job search behaviour of the underemployed. Evidence is presented to support the view that the city is rife with employment externalities as well as housing and commercial externalities—that finding employment is more difficult if the informal information network is poor as it is in slum areas where the underemployed are concentrated. Programmes to rejuvenate the local labour market, outlined in Chapter 7, are just as important as a basis for urban renewal as physical redevelopment plans and deserve careful attention. In particular, employment policies must meet the needs of the local labour force in the context of an overall redevelopment plan. Further analysis, experimentation, and evaluation is needed but first planners and policy-makers must adjust their focus to the community or neighbourhood level.

8.1.4 Urban dynamic models

The conventional theory of urban structure is formulated as a static model for analytical simplicity. Our extension of the theory to consider workplace choice and the urban labour market has also been formulated in static terms to facilitate integration with the conventional model and to facilitate model-testing using available cross-sectional data. Static models provide a useful simplification of a more complex, dynamic society to isolate important features of social behaviour.

Inevitably, urban models will be criticized for their static approach. An important question, then, is to identify the critical elements of a dynamic model, since we are unlikely to be able to leap from static models to a much more complex model with a full set of dynamic interactions. An early influential model of urban dynamics is provided by Forrester (1969), who concentrates on three subsystems: business activity, housing, and the working population. His model is non-spatial, however, since the entire urban area is the unit of analysis. Housing conditions and worker skills are differentiated but not situated within the city so that issues related to the spatial configuration of the city, which are central to this book and to urban economics, are ignored. Thus, the spatial dynamics of inner-city decay, employment decentralization, selective migration, and underemployment discussed in Chapter 6 *et al.* is ignored (Gray, 1972). Nevertheless, Forrester's model suggests that the dynamics of housing and workplace choice should be important elements of urban modelling and policy analysis.

The growing literature on urban dynamic models subsequent to Forrester's work is reviewed by Miyao (1987), who makes three important points from our perspective. First, he argues that 'the main reason for the delay in developing dynamic models of urban growth is because the theoretical foundations of urban economic analysis had not been solid enough to withstand a further elaboration of the system for dynamization' (p. 877). Thus dynamic models await solid static foundations, as we have argued. Secondly, urban dynamic models are either non-spatial models or spatial models of a monocentric city. Our approach, on the other hand, emphasizes the spatial interaction of households and firms when employment is decentralized. Thirdly, urban dynamic models have failed to integrate production and housing in a spatial setting. Hence current dynamic models are not ready to incorporate the job–worker matching model we have developed. Previous experience suggests, however, that static analysis of this model is required before more sophisticated dynamic models can be developed.

Vickerman's (1984) criticism of static urban models also concentrates on housing and workplace choice. He argues for a dynamic analysis which integrates residential location decisions and migration. This suggestion has been a common theme of recent empirical research on urban change in Europe (van der Veen and Evers, 1983; Evers and van der Veen, 1985, 1986; Congdon, 1987, 1988). Since migration arises from workplace relocation, and hence is one component of workplace choice behaviour, it is natural to consider the implications of workplace choice behaviour for the development of dynamic urban models.

Our analysis of workplace choice has been derived from the relatively recent economic literature on job search. As Mortensen (1986: 849) points out, one of the prime contributions of job search theory has been to provide a 'consistent portrayal of the dynamic dimensions of worker experience' ignored previously by economists. Job search theory examines the process by which workers move from one labour market activity to another during the course of their working life, from the search for a first job to learning about the job to search for alternative jobs. Thus job search theory is fundamentally dynamic in nature. Our analysis then extends this dynamic model to consider where jobs are found to describe the spatial aspects of a worker's career. Hence the model of workplace location decisions has been developed as part of a dynamic approach to worker behaviour that can provide a solid foundation for the study of urban change.

A dynamic model of urban structure should include a model of the life-cycle behaviour of households both as consumers and as workers. Quigley and Weinberg (1977) find that residential moves occur as housing requirements, household labour supply, and income change over the life cycle, as conventional residential location theory predicts, and as career progress dictates workplace relocation. While few would find it surprising that workplace relocation affects population movement, the previous literature has provided little theoretical analysis of this interaction. The theoretical analysis of workplace choice in Chapters 3–6 provides a basic framework to consider this issue.

What, then, are the elements of a dynamic urban model in which workplace choice and other labour market considerations are represented? First, the model must contain a mechanism, missing from current dynamic models, to generate employment decentralization in response to both endogenous elements of the model and external growth shocks. Initial steps in this direction are taken by White (1988) who concentrates on endogenous elements—wage and land-price gradients—to lure firms to suburban locations. There is an extensive literature on intra-urban employment location within cities, some of it reviewed in Chapter 2, to develop this submodel. Secondly, once the spatial distribution of employment demand has been determined, workplace and residential choices are made on the basis of the principles articulated in Chapters 2–5. This in turn determines the distribution of employment, earnings, and population within the city. Thirdly, employment relocation decisions may be made in response to changing spatial patterns of population and commuting in the fashion specified by Lowry-type models.

The contribution of our analysis is to provide a foundation for the specification of workplace and residential choice in dynamic models of cities with decentralized employment. In particular, the analysis in these chapters identifies three crucial elements of workplace relocation behaviour. First, workplace location responds to employment opportunities at both the local, intra-urban level and the inter-urban or regional level. Secondly, job search is spatially systematic. This principle implies that workers will prefer short moves and will be sensitive to local employment conditions within the city. Thirdly, skill acquisition broadens job search extent. This principle implies that the sensitivity to local employment conditions differs across skill groups —the lower the skill level, the lower is the spatial mobility of the worker. Hence urban mobility rates will be lower, and underemployment arising from spatial mismatch of workers and jobs potentially higher, for the less skilled. This feature provides a basis for the study of urban poverty and decay discussed in Chapter 6.

The analysis in these chapters provides a foundation for recent empirical work. It supports evidence of interdependency between workplace and residential location decisions (van der Veen and Evers, 1983; Evers and van der Veen, 1985, 1986). It also supports evidence that labour market structure and job availability are important aspects of urban change. Congdon (1987, 1988) finds that household migration responds to shifting job opportunities among London boroughs, but that this migration declines with the level of education. Congdon and Champion (1989) estimate a model of urban change in which an adverse change in labour demand in a London borough leads to selective out-migration of households, rising underemployment, falling incomes, and deteriorating housing conditions. This process may be reversed by improved local employment conditions followed by housing rehabilitation at a later date. This recent empirical work on residential and workplace location, commuting, and migration decisions supports both the static analysis of Chapters 3–5 and its extension to a dynamic analysis of urban change along the lines described above.

8.2 WORKPLACE CHOICE AND TRADITIONAL LABOUR MARKET ISSUES

If spatial theory falls into the domain of urban and regional studies exclusively, then this study has less to offer traditional analysis of labour markets. That analysis is decidedly non-spatial even where space is clearly an important underlying factor—such as the job search literature reviewed in Chapter 3. The one exception is migration, a topic which is shared by labour economics and regional science. In migration studies distance costs must be addressed in some fashion, and these studies, many by labour economists, do provide a useful starting-point to consider spatial mobility behaviour in Chapter 4.

Although migration is an important aspect of labour market adjustment, labour economists seem content to leave the topic to regional scientists because of its spatial nature. Pick up the most recent comprehensive review of labour economics by labour economists themselves—the *Handbook of Labor Economics* (Ashenfelter and Layard, 1986). In the topic headings of twenty-two chapters written by internationally recognized scholars, there is no mention of migration or any other spatial issue. Textbooks in labour economics are slightly better, often discussing migration in the context of regional wage differentials and unemployment, but nothing more.

Is this virtual exclusion of spatial issues by labour economists a wise decision? Labour economists traditionally examine labour market adjustment and barriers to mobility but seem content to ignore an important aspect of the market—its spatial character. Other barriers to mobility, such as discrimination and collective bargaining, are given much more serious treatment. Yet it is not clear why spatial barriers are not similarly important to the study of labour market behaviour.

In Chapters 3 and 4 we consider some of the spatial issues surrounding job search behaviour and labour market adjustment. This approach yields insights into the structure of cities and their labour markets with specific implications for commuting, underemployment, and employment policy. To the extent that this exercise has proved to be worth while, it should provide some impetus for further studies of the spatial dimension of labour markets and for the development of spatially detailed microdata on labour market activity. Whether these studies are done by 'labour economists' or 'regional scientists', they could yield important insights into traditional labour market topics. After all, if we limit our range of enquiry, we risk missing important new avenues of discovery.

REFERENCES

Abbott, Michael, and Ashenfelter, Orley (1976), 'Labor Supply, Commodity Demand, and the Allocation of Time', *Review of Economic Studies*, 43: 389–411.

Abraham, Katharine, and Katz, Lawrence (1986), 'Cyclical Unemployment: Sectoral Shifts or Aggregate Disturbances?', *Journal of Political Economy*, 94: 507–22.

Addison, John, and Siebert, W. Stanley (1979), *The Market for Labor: An Analytical Treatment*. Santa Monica, Calif.: Goodyear Publishing Co.

Aigner, Dennis, and Cain, Glen (1977), 'Statistical Theories of Discrimination in Labour Markets', *Industrial and Labor Relations Review*, 30: 175–87.

Akerlof, George, and Yellen, Janet (1986), *Efficiency Wage Models of the Labor Market*. New York: Cambridge University Press.

Alonso, William (1964), *Location and Land Use*. Cambridge, Mass.: Harvard University Press.

Arrow, Kenneth (1959), 'Toward a Theory of Price Adjustment', in Moses Abramovitz *et al.*, *The Allocation of Economic Resources*. Stanford, Calif.: Stanford University Press, 41–51.

—— (1973), 'Higher Education as a Filter', *Journal of Public Economics*, 2: 193–216.

—— (1974), 'Limited Knowledge and Economic Analysis', *American Economic Review*, 64: 1–10.

Ashenfelter, Orley, and Layard, Richard (eds.) (1986), *Handbook of Labor Economics*, i and ii. Amsterdam: North-Holland.

Auletta, Ken (1982), *The Underclass*. New York: Random House.

Banfield, Edward (1970), *The Unheavenly City: The Nature and Future of Our Urban Crisis*. Boston: Little, Brown & Co.

Barron, John, Black, Dan, and Loewenstein, Mark (1989), 'Job Matching and On-the-job Training', *Journal of Labor Economics*, 7: 1–19.

Basilevsky, Alex, and Hum, Derek (1984), *Experimental Social Programs and Analytic Methods*. New York: Academic Press.

Baily, Martin (1975), 'Dynamic Monopsony and Structural Change', *American Economic Review*, 65: 338–49.

Becker, Gary (1964), *Human Capital: A Theoretical and Empirical Analysis with Special Reference to Education*. New York: Columbia University Press.

Beckmann, M. J. (1969), 'On the Distribution of Urban Rent and Residential Density', *Journal of Economic Theory*, 1: 60–7.

Beesley, M. E. (1970), 'The Value of Time Spent in Travelling: Some New

184 References

Evidence', in R. E. Quandt (ed.), *The Demand for Travel: Theory and Measurement*. Lexington, Mass.: Heath-Lexington Books.

Beesley, M. E. (1973), *Urban Transportation Studies in Economic Policy*. London: Butterworth.

—— and Dalvi, M. Q. (1974), 'Spatial Equilibrium and the Journey to Work', *Journal of Transport Economics and Policy*, 8: 197–222.

Bergmann, Barbara (1971), 'The Effect on White Incomes of Discrimination in Employment', *Journal of Political Economy*, 79: 294–313.

Berry, Brian (1967), *Geography of Market Centers and Retail Distribution*. Englewood Cliffs, NJ: Prentice-Hall.

Blau, Francine, and Ferber, Marianne (1987), 'Discrimination: Empirical Evidence from the United States', *American Economic Review Papers and Proceedings*, 77: 316–20.

Blaug, Mark (1976), 'The Empirical Status of Human Capital Theory: A Slightly Jaundiced Survey', *Journal of Economic Literature*, 14: 827–55.

Bloch, Farrell (ed.) (1979), *Evaluating Manpower Training Programs, Research in Labor Economics*, Supplement 1. Greenwich, Conn.: JAI Press.

Booth, D., and Fortis, L. (1984), 'Building a Cooperative Economy: A Strategy for Community Based Economic Development', *Review of Social Economy*, 42: 339–59.

Borjas, George (1981), 'Job Mobility and Earnings over the Life Cycle', *Industrial and Labor Relations Review*, 34: 365–76.

—— and Rosen, Sherwin (1980), 'Income Prospects and Job Mobility of Younger Men', in Ronald Ehrenberg (ed.), *Research in Labor Economics*. Greenwich, Conn.: JAI Press, 159–82.

Bowen, William, and Finegan, T. Aldridge (1969), *The Economics of Labor Force Participation*. Princeton, NJ: Princeton University Press.

Brown, Charles, Gilroy, Curtis, and Kohen, Andrew (1982), 'The Effect of the Minimum Wage on Employment and Unemployment', *Journal of Economic Literature*, 20: 487–528.

Brueckner, Jan (1987), 'The Structure of Urban Equilibria: A Unified Treatment of the Muth-Mills Model', in Edwin Mills (ed.), *Handbook of Regional and Urban Economics*, ii. *Urban Economics*. Amsterdam: North-Holland.

Bulow, Jeremy, and Summers, Lawrence (1986), 'A Theory of Dual Labor Markets with Application to Industrial Policy, Discrimination, and Keynesian Unemployment', *Journal of Labor Economics*, 4 pt. 1: 376–414.

Burdett, Kenneth, and Judd, Kenneth (1983), 'Equilibrium Price Dispersion', *Econometrica*, 51: 955–70.

Cain, Glen (1976), 'The Challenge of Segmented Labor Market Theories to Orthodox Theory: A Survey', *Journal of Economic Literature*, 14: 1215–57.

Capozza, D. R. (1973), 'Subways and Land Use', *Environment and Planning*, 5: 555–76.

Cheshire, P. (1979), 'Inner Areas as Spatial Labour Markets: A Critique of the Inner Area Studies', *Urban Studies*, 16: 29–42.

—— (1981), 'Inner Areas as Spatial Labour Markets: A Rejoinder', *Urban Studies*, 18: 227–9.

Chiswick, Barry, and Mincer, Jacob (1972), 'Time-Series Changes in Personal Incom Inequality in the United States from 1939, with Projections to 1985', *Journal of Political Economy*, 80: S34–S66.

Clark, Colin (1966), *Population Growth and Land Use*. London: Macmillan.

Congdon, Peter (1987), 'The Interdependence of Geographical Migration with Job and Housing Mobility in London', *Regional Studies*, 22: 81–93.

—— (1988), 'Modelling Migration Flows between Areas: An Analysis for London Using the Census and OPCS Longitudinal Study', *Regional Studies*, 23: 87–103.

—— and Champion, Tony (1989), 'Trends and Structure in London's Migration and their Relation to Employment and Housing Markets', in Peter Congdon and Peter Batey (eds.), *Advances in Regional Demography: Forecasts, Information, Models*. London: Belhaven Press.

Dagsvik, John, Jovanovic, Boyan, and Shepard, Andrea (1985), 'A Foundation for Three Popular Assumptions in Job-matching Models', *Journal of Labor Economics*, 3: 403–20.

Davis, O., and Whinston, A. (1961), 'The Economics of Urban Renewal', *Law and Contemporary Problems*, 26: 105–17.

Denslow, D., and Eaton, P. (1984), 'Migration and Intervening Opportunities', *Southern Economic Journal*, 51: 369–87.

Doeringer, Peter (1986), 'Internal Labor Markets and Noncompeting Groups', *American Economic Review Papers and Proceedings*, 76: 48–52.

—— and Piore, Michael (1971), *Internal Labor Markets and Manpower Analysis*. Lexington, Mass.: D. C. Heath.

Duncan, Beverly (1956), 'Factors in Work-Residence Separation, Wage and Salary Workers, Chicago, 1951', *American Sociological Review*, 21: 48–56.

Duncan, O., and Reiss, A. (1956), *Social Characteristics of Urban and Rural Communities, 1950*. New York: John Wiley & Sons.

Edwards, Richard, Reich, Michael, and Gordon, David (1975), *Labor Market Segmentation*. Lexington, Mass.: D. C. Heath.

Ellwood, David (1986), 'The Spatial Mismatch Hypothesis: Are There Teenage Jobs Missing in the Ghetto?', in Richard Freeman and Harry Holzer (eds.), *The Black Youth Employment Crisis*. Chicago: University of Chicago Press.

Employment and Immigration Canada (1981), *Labour Market Development in the 1980s*. A Report of the Task Force on Labour Market Development. Ottawa: Employment and Immigration Canada.

Evans, Alan (1973), *The Economics of Residential Location*. London: Macmillan & Co.

186   *References*

Evans, Alan (1984), *Urban Economics: An Introduction*. Oxford: Blackwell.
—— and Richardson, Ray (1981), 'Urban Unemployment: Interpretation and Additional Evidence', *Scottish Journal of Political Economy*, 23: 107–24.
Evers, Gerard, and van der Veen, Anne (1985), 'A Simultaneous Non-Linear Model for Labour Migration and Commuting', *Regional Studies*, 19: 217–29.
—— —— (1986), 'Commuting, Migration and Labor Force Participation: Micro and Macro Economic Approaches', unpublished Ph.D. Dissertation (in Dutch), University of Tilburg, The Netherlands.
Farber, Henry (1983), 'The Determination of the Union Status of Workers', *Econometrica*, 51: 1417–37.
Feinberg, Robert (1977), 'Risk-aversion, Risk and the Duration of Unemployment', *Review of Economics and Statistics*, 59: 264–71.
—— (1978a), 'On the Empirical Importance of the Job Search Theory', *Southern Economic Journal*, 54: 508–21.
—— (1978b), 'The Forerunners of Job Search Theory', *Economic Inquiry*, 16: 126–32.
Fleisher, Belton, and Kniesner, Thomas (1984), *Labor Economics: Theory, Evidence and Policy*, 3rd edn. Englewood Cliffs, NJ: Prentice-Hall.
Flinn, Christopher (1986), 'Wages and Job Mobility of Young Workers', *Journal of Political Economy*, 94: S88–S110.
Forrester, Jay (1969), *Urban Dynamics*. Cambridge, Mass.: MIT Press.
Freeman, Richard (1982), 'Economic Determinants of Geographic and Individual Variation in the Labor Market Position of Young Persons', in Richard Freeman and David Wise (eds.), *The Youth Labor Market Problem: Its Nature, Causes and Consequences*. Chicago: University of Chicago Press.
Gal, Shmuel, Landsberger, Michael, and Levyson, Benny (1981), 'A Compound Strategy for Search in the Labor Market', *International Economic Review*, 22: 597–608.
Garfinkel, Irwin, and Haveman, Robert (1977), 'Earnings Capacity, Economic Status, and Poverty', *Journal of Human Resources*, 12: 49–70.
Gastwirth, Joseph (1976), 'On Probabilistic Models of Consumer Search for Information', *Quarterly Journal of Economics*, 90: 38–50.
Gayer, David (1971), 'An Index of Isolation for Metropolitan Labor Markets', *Land Economics*, 47: 356–64.
Ginzberg, Eli (1968), *Manpower Strategy for the Metropolis*. New York: Columbia University Press.
—— (1973), *New York is Very Much Alive: A Manpower View*. New York: McGraw-Hill.
—— (1985), *Understanding Human Resources: Perspectives, People, and Policy*. New York: University Press of America.
Gordon, I., and Lamont, I. (1982), 'A Model of Labour Market Interdependencies in the London Region', *Environment and Planning A*, 14: 237–64.

—— and Vickerman, R. (1982), 'Opportunity, Preference and Constraint: An Approach to the Analysis of Metropolitan Migration', *Urban Studies* 19: 247–61.

Gray, J., Pessel, D., and Varaiya, P. (1972), 'A Critique of Forrester's Model of an Urban Area', in Kan Chen (ed.), *Urban Dynamics: Extensions and Reflections*. San Francisco: San Francisco Press.

Greenwood, Michael (1975), 'Research on Internal Migration in the United States', *Journal of Economic Literature*, 13: 397–433.

—— (1981), *Migration and Economic Growth in the United States: National, Regional, and Metropolitan Perspectives*. New York: Academic Press.

Hall, Peter (1966), *Von Thunen's Isolated State*. Oxford: Pergamon Press.

—— (1981), *The Inner City in Context: The Final Report of the Social Science Research Council Inner Cities Working Party*. London: Heinemann Educational Books Ltd.

Hall, Robert (1971), 'Prospects for Shifting the Phillips Curve Through Manpower Policy', *Brookings Papers on Economic Activity*, 1971: 659–701.

Hallman, Howard (1980), Community-Based Employment Programs. Baltimore: Johns Hopkins University Press.

Hamilton, Bruce (1982), 'Wasteful Commuting', *Journal of Political Economy*, 90: 1035–53.

Hammermesh, Daniel, and Rees, Albert (1984), *The Economics of Work and Pay*, 3rd edn. New York: Harper & Row.

Hanushek, Eric (1981), 'Alternative Models of Earnings Determination and Labor Market Structure', *Journal of Human Resources*, 16: 238–59.

Harrison, Bennett (1972), *Education, Training, and the Urban Ghetto*. Baltimore: Johns Hopkins University Press.

—— (1974), 'Ghetto Economic Development: A Survey', *Journal of Economic Literature*, 12: 1–37.

—— and Sum, Andrew (1979), 'The Theory of Dual or Segmented Labor Markets', *Journal of Economic Issues*, 13: 687–706.

Hartwick, P. G., and Hartwick, J. M. (1972), 'An Analysis of an Urban Thoroughfare', *Environment and Planning*, 4: 193–204.

Hashimoto, Masanori (1981), 'Firm-Specific Human Capital as a Shared Investment', *American Economic Review*, 71: 475–82.

Hausman, Jerry (1978), 'Specification Tests in Econometrics', *Econometrica*, 46: 1251–72.

Hekman, John (1980), 'Income, Labor Supply, and Urban Residence', *American Economic Review*, 70: 805–11.

Henderson, J. Vernon (1985), *Economic Theory and the Cities*, 2nd edn. Orlando, Fla.: Academic Press.

Hensher, David (1976), 'The Value of Travel Time Savings', *Journal of Transport Economics and Policy*, 10: 167–76.

188   *References*

Hicks, John (1939), *Value and Capital*, 2nd edn. London: Oxford University Press.

Higgins, Joan, Deakin, Nicholas, Edwards, John, and Wicks, Malcolm (1983), *Government and Urban Poverty*. Oxford: Blackwell.

Holzer, Harry (1988), 'Search Method Use by Unemployed Youth', *Journal of Labor Economics*, 6: 1–20.

Hoover, Edgar (1948), *The Location of Economic Activity*. New York: McGraw-Hill.

—— and Vernon, Raymond (1959), *Anatomy of a Metropolis*. Cambridge, Mass.: Harvard University Press.

Hotelling, Harold (1929), 'Stability in Competition', *Economic Journal*, 41–57. Repr. in R. D. Dean, W. H. Leahy, and D. L. McKee (1970), *Spatial Economic Theory*. New York: Free Press.

Hughes, G., and McCormick, B. (1981), 'Do Council Housing Policies Reduce Migration Between Regions?', *Economic Journal*, 91: 919–37.

—— —— (1987), 'Housing Markets, Unemployment and Labour Market Flexibility in the UK', *European Economic Review*, 31: 615–45.

Hunter, Laurence, and Reid, Graham (1968), *Urban Worker Mobility*. Paris: OECD.

Inoki, T., and Suruga, T. (1981), 'Migration, Age and Education: A Cross-sectional Analysis of Geographic Labor Mobility in Japan', *Journal of Regional Science*, 21: 507–17.

Jackson, Jerry (1979), 'Intraurban Variation in the Price of Housing', *Journal of Urban Economics*, 6: 464–79.

Johnson, William (1978), 'A Theory of Job Shopping', *Quarterly Journal of Economics*, 92: 261–77.

Jovanovic, Boyan (1979), 'Job Matching and the Theory of Turnover', *Journal of Political Economy*, 87: 972–90.

—— (1987), 'Work, Rest, and Search: Unemployment, Turnover, and the Cycle', *Journal of Labor Economics*, 5: 131–48.

Kain, John (1962), 'The Journey-to-work as a Determinant of Residential Location', *Papers and Proceedings of the Regional Science Association*, 9: 137–60.

—— (1968a), 'Housing Segregation, Negro Employment, and Metropolitan Decentralization', *Quarterly Journal of Economics*, 82: 175–97.

—— (1968b), 'The Distribution and Movement of Jobs and Industry', in J. Wilson (ed.), *The Metropolitan Enigma*. Cambridge, Mass.: Harvard University Press, 1–39.

—— (1975), *Essays on Urban Spatial Structure*. Cambridge, Mass.: Ballinger.

Kerwin, R. S., and Ball, M. J. (1974), 'The Microeconomic Analysis of a Local Housing Market' in, *Papers from the Urban Economics Conference, 1973*, i. London: Centre for Environmental Studies, 115–99.

Kneissner, Thomas, and Goldsmith, Arthur (1987), 'A Survey of Alternative Models of the Aggregate U.S. Labor Market', *Journal of Economic Literature*, 25: 1241–80.

Kohsaka, H. (1986), 'The Location Process of Central Place System within a Circular City', *Economic Geography*, 62: 254–66.

Lalonde, Robert (1986), 'Evaluating the Econometric Evaluations of Training Programs with Experimental Data', *American Economic Review*, 76: 604–20.

Lapham, Victoria (1971), 'Do Blacks Pay More for Housing?', *Journal of Political Economy*, 79: 1244–57.

Leach, Richard (1985), *Whatever Happened to Urban Policy? A Comparative Study of Urban Policy in Australia, Canada and the United States*. Canberra: Centre for Research on Federal Financial Relations, Australian National University.

Leonard, Jonathan (1987), 'The Interaction of Residential Segregation and Employment Discrimination', *Journal of Urban Economics*, 21: 323–46.

Levitan, Sar, Mangum, Garth, and Marshall, Ray (1981), *Human Resources and Labor Markets: Employment and Training in the American Economy*. New York: Harper & Row.

Lewin-Epstein, Noah (1985), 'Neighborhoods, Local Labor Markets, and Employment Opportunities for White and Nonwhite Youth', *Social Science Quarterly*, 66: 163–71.

Lilien, David (1982), 'Sectoral Shifts and Cyclical Unemployment', *Journal of Political Economy*, 90: 777–93.

Linneman, P., and Graves, P. (1983), 'Migration and Job Change: A Multinomial Logit Approach', *Journal of Urban Economics*, 14: 263–79.

Lippman, Steven, and McCall, John (1976), 'The Economics of Job Search: A Survey', *Economic Inquiry*, 14: 155–89 and 347–68.

Lowry, Ira (1964), *A Model of Metropolis*. Research Memorandum 4035. Santa Monica, Calif.: Rand Corporation.

Lucas, Robert, and Prescott, Edward (1974), 'Equilibrium Search and Unemployment', *Journal of Economic Theory*, 7: 188–209.

McCall, B. P., and McCall, J. J. (1987), 'A Sequential Study of Migration and Job Search', *Journal of Labor Economics*, 5: 452–76.

McCall, John (1965), 'The Economics of Information and Optimal Stopping Rules', *Journal of Business*, 38: 300–17.

—— (1970), 'Economics of Information and Job Search', *Quarterly Journal of Economics*, 84: 113–26.

McCormick, Barry (1986), 'Employment Opportunity, Earnings, and the Journey to Work of Minority Workers in Great Britain', *Economic Journal*, 96: 375–97.

MacDonald, Glenn (1984), 'New Directions in the Economic Theory of Agency', *Canadian Journal of Economics*, 17: 415–40.

MacKay, Donald, *et al.* (1971), *Labour Markets Under Different Employment Conditions.* London: Allen & Unwin.

McKenna, C. (1985), *Uncertainty and the Labour Market: Recent Developments in Job Search Theory.* New York: St Martin's Press.

MacMinn, Richard (1980), 'Search and Market Equilibrium', *Journal of Political Economy*, 88: 308–27.

Macredie, Ian (1972), 'Job Search Patterns', *Notes on Labour Statistics 1971.* Ottawa: Statistics Canada, 72–207.

Maier, Gunther (1987), 'Job Search and Migration', in Manfred Fischer and Peter Nijkamp (eds.), *Regional Labour Markets: Analytical Contributions and Cross-national Comparisons.* Amsterdam: North-Holland, 189–204.

—— (1990), 'Modelling Search Processes in Space'. Paper presented to the 30th European Congress of the Regional Science Association, Istanbul.

Malizia, Emil (1985), *Local Economic Development: A Guide to Practice.* New York: Praeger.

Malm, F. Theodore (1954), 'Recruiting Patterns and the Functioning of Labor Markets', *Industrial and Labor Relations Review*, 7: 507–25.

Mellow, Wesley (1978), 'Search Costs and the Duration of Unemployment', *Economic Inquiry*, 16: 424–30.

Metcalf, David, and Richardson, Ray (1980), 'Unemployment in London', in A. Evans and D. Eversley (eds.), *The Inner City: Employment and Industry.* London: Heinemann Educational Books Ltd.

Mills, Edwin (1972a), *Urban Economics.* Glenview, Ill.: Scott, Foreman & Co.

—— (1972b), *Studies in the Structure of the Urban Economy.* Baltimore: Johns Hopkins Press.

Mincer, Jacob (1970), 'The Distribution of Labor Incomes: A Survey with Special Reference to the Human Capital Approach', *Journal of Economic Literature*, 8: 1–26.

Mirengoff, William, and Rindler, Lester (1978), *CETA: Manpower Programs Under Local Control.* Prepared for the Committee on Evaluation of Employment and Training Programs, National Research Council. Washington, DC.: National Academy of Sciences.

Miyao, Takahiro (1987), 'Dynamic Urban Models', *Handbook of Regional and Urban Economics*, ii: *Urban Economics*, 8. Amsterdam: North-Holland.

Mohan, Rakesh (1986), *Work, Wages, and Welfare in a Developing Metropolis: Consequences of Growth in Bogotá, Colombia.* World Bank Research Publication, New York: Oxford University Press.

Mooney, Joseph (1969), 'Housing Segregation, Negro Employment, and Metropolitan Decentralization: An Alternative Perspective', *Quarterly Journal of Economics*, 83: 299–311.

Morgan, Peter (1983), 'Search and Optimal Sample Sizes', *Review of Economic Studies*, 50: 659–75.

Mortensen, Dale (1970), 'A Theory of Wage and Employment Dynamics', in Edmund Phelps *et al.* (eds.), *Microeconomic Foundations of Employment and Inflation Theory*. New York: W. W. Norton, 167–211.

—— (1986), 'Job Search and Labor Market Analysis', in Orley Ashenfelter and Richard Layard (eds.), *Handbook of Labor Economics*: ii. Amsterdam: North-Holland, 849–919.

Moses, Leon (1962), 'Towards a Theory of Intra-Urban Wage Differentials and their Influence on Travel Patterns', *Papers and Proceedings of the Regional Science Association*, 9: 53–63.

Moynihan, Daniel (1968), *On Understanding Poverty*. New York: Basic Books.

Muth, Richard (1969), *Cities and Housing*. Chicago: University of Chicago Press.

Needham, B. (1981), 'Inner Areas as Spatial Labour Markets: A Comment', *Urban Studies*, 18: 225–6.

Nelson, Phillip (1973), 'The Elasticity of Labor Supply to the Individual Firm', *Econometrica*, 41: 853–66.

Oates, W., Howrey, E., and Baumol, W. (1971), 'The Analysis of Public Policy in Dynamic Urban Models', *Journal of Political Economy*, 79: 142–53.

Oi, Walter (1976), 'Residential Location and Labor Supply', *Journal of Political Economy*, 84: S221–S238.

Okun, Arthur (1981), *Prices and Quantities: A Macroeconomic Analysis*. Washington, DC: Brookings Institution.

Parnes, Herbert (1954), *Research on Labor Mobility: An Appraisal of Research Findings in the United States*. New York: Social Science Research Council, Bulletin 65.

—— (1984), *Peoplepower: Elements of Human Resource Policy*. Beverly Hills, Calif.: Sage Publications.

—— and Kohen, A. I. (1975), 'Occupational Information and Labor Market Status: The Case of Young Men', *Journal of Human Resources*, 10: 44–55.

Peterson, Thomas (1975), 'Cost-Benefit Analysis for Evaluating Transportation Proposals: Los Angeles Case Study', *Land Economics*, 51: 72–9.

Phelps, Edmund (1970a), 'Introduction: The New Microeconomics in Employment and Inflation Theory', in Phelps *et al.* (1970), 1–26.

—— (1970b), 'Money Wage Dynamics and Labor Market Equilibrium', in Phelps *et al.* (1970), 124–66.

—— (1985), *Political Economy: An Introductory Text*. New York: W. W. Norton.

—— *et al.* (1970), *Microeconomic Foundations of Employment and Inflation Theory*. New York: W. W. Norton.

Quigley, J., and Weinberg, D. (1977), 'Intra-Urban Residential Mobility: A Review and Synthesis', *International Regional Science Review*, 2: 41–66.

Reder, Melvin (1955), 'The Theory of Occupational Wage Differentials', *American Economic Review*, 45: 833–52.

Rees, Albert (1966), 'Information Networks in Labor Markets', *American Economic Review*, 56: 559–66.

——— (1966*b*), 'An Overview', in R. Gordon and M. Gordon (eds.), *Prosperity and Unemployment*. New York: John Wiley & Sons.

——— and Gray, Wayne (1982), 'Family Effects in Youth Employment', in Richard Freeman and David Wise (eds.), *The Youth Employment Problem: Its Nature, Causes and Consequences*. Chicago: University of Chicago Press.

——— and Shultz, George (1970), *Workers and Wages in an Urban Labor Market*. Chicago: University of Chicago Press.

Reubens, Beatrice (1968), 'The Hard-to-Employ: European Experience', in Eli Ginzberg (ed.), *Manpower Strategy for the Metropolis*. New York: Columbia University Press.

Rhodes, J., and Kan, A. (1971), *Office Dispersal and Regional Policy*. Cambridge: Cambridge University Press.

Richardson, Harry (1969), *Regional Economics: Location Theory, Urban Structure and Regional Change*. London: Weidenfeld & Nicolson.

——— (1971), *Urban Economics*. Harmondsworth: Penguin Books.

——— (1973), *The Economics of Urban Size*. Westmead: Saxon House, D. C. Heath Ltd.

——— (1977), *The New Urban Economics: and Alternatives*. London: Pion Ltd.

Robins, Philip (1985), 'A Comparison of the Labor Supply Findings from the Four Negative Income Tax Experiments', *Journal of Human Resources*, 20: 567–82.

Rosen, Sherwin (1974), 'Hedonic Prices and Implicit Markets: Product Differentiation in Pure Competition', *Journal of Political Economy*, 82: 34–55.

——— (1985), 'Implicit Contracts: A Survey', *Journal of Economic Literature*, 23: 1144–75.

Ross, David (1986), 'Local Economic Initiatives: An Overview', in David Ross, Gu Dauncey, and George McRobie, *Employment and Social Development in a Changing Economy*. Ottawa: Canadian Council on Social Development.

Rothenberg, Jerome (1970), 'The Impact of Local Government on Intra-Metropolitan Location', *Papers and Proceedings of the Regional Science Association*, 24: 47–81.

Rothschild, Michael (1973), 'Models of Market Organization with Imperfect Information: A Survey', *Journal of Political Economy*, 81: 1283–1308.

Rowe, Nicholas (1987), 'An Extreme Keynesian Macroeconomic Model with Formal Micro-Economic Foundations', *Canadian Journal of Economics*, 20: 306–20.

Ruttenberg, S. (1970), *Manpower Challenge of the 1970s: Institutions and Social Change*. Baltimore: Johns Hopkins Press.

St John-Brooks, Caroline (1985), 'Who Controls Training?—The Rise of the Manpower Services Commission', Fabian Tract 506. London: Fabian Society.

Salinas, Patricia (1986), 'Urban Growth, Subemployment, and Mobility', in Edward Bergman (ed.), *Local Economies in Transition: Policy Realities and Development Potentials*. Durham, NC: Duke University Press.

Samson, L. (1985), 'A Study of the Impact of Sectoral Shifts on Aggregate Unemployment in Canada', *Canadian Journal of Economics*, 18: 518–30.

Santomero, Anthony, and Seater, John (1978), 'The Inflation-Unemployment Trade-off: A Critique of the Literature', *Journal of Economic Literature*, 16: 499–544.

Schaeffer, Peter (1985), 'Human Capital Accumulation and Job Mobility', *Journal of Regional Science*, 25: 103–14.

Schuler, Richard (1974), 'The Interaction Between Local Government and Urban Residential Location', *American Economic Review*, 64: 682–96.

Schwartz, Aba (1973), 'Interpreting the Effect of Distance on Migration', *Journal of Political Economy*, 81: 1153–69.

—— (1976), 'Migration, Age, and Education', *Journal of Political Economy*, 84: 701–19.

Scott, Allen (1982), 'Locational Patterns and Dynamics of Industrial Activity in the Modern Metropolis', *Urban Studies*, 19: 111–42.

Seater, John (1977), 'A Unified Model of Consumption, Labor Supply, and Job Search', *Journal of Economic Theory*, 14: 349–72.

Shapiro, Carl, and Stiglitz, Joseph (1984), 'Equilibrium Unemployment as a Worker Discipline Device', *American Economic Review*, 74: 433–44.

Sheppard, Harold, and Belitsky, A. H. (1966), *The Job Hunt: Job-Seeking Behavior of Unemployed Workers in a Local Economy*. Baltimore: W. E. Upjohn Institute for Employment Research, Johns Hopkins Press.

Shultz, George (1962), 'Non-Union Market for White Collar Labor', in National Bureau of Economic Research, *Aspects of Labor Economics*. Princeton, NJ: Princeton University Press.

Siegel, Jay (1975), 'Intrametropolitan Migration: A Simultaneous Model of Employment and Residential Location of White and Black Households', *Journal of Urban Economics*, 2: 29–47.

Siegel, Philip (1973), 'The Location of Industry and Job Participation: An Econometric Study', *Economic Affairs*, 18: 54–8.

Simpson, Wayne (1977), *Imperfect Knowledge, Urban Structure and Labour Markets*. Unpublished Ph.D. Dissertation, London School of Economics.

—— (1980), 'A Simultaneous Model of Workplace and Residential Location Incorporating Job Search', *Journal of Urban Economics*, 8: 330–49.

—— (1982), 'Job Search and the Effect of Urban Structure on Unemployment

References

and Married Female Participation Rates', *Applied Economics*, 14: 153–65.

Simpson, Wayne (1983), 'On the Appropriate Spatial Unit for Labour Market Analysis and Policy Design', *Urban Studies*, 20: 487–9.

—— (1987), 'Workplace Location, Residential Location, and Urban Commuting', *Urban Studies*, 24: 119–28.

—— (1989), 'Urban Structure and Workplace Choice: Theory and Applications'. Paper presented to the 29th European Congress of the Regional Science Association, Cambridge, Aug. 1989.

Singell, Larry, and Lillydahl, Jane (1985), 'An Empirical Analysis of the Commute to Work Patterns of Males and Females in Two-Earner Households', *Urban Studies*, 23: 119–29.

Smith, James, and Welch, Finis (1987), 'Race and Poverty: A Forty Year Record', *American Economic Review Papers and Proceedings*, 77: 152–8.

Spence, A. Michael (1974), *Market Signaling*. Cambridge, Mass.: Harvard University Press.

Stern, Steven (1989), 'Estimating a Simultaneous Search Model', *Journal of Labor Economics*, 7: 348–69.

Stigler, George (1961), 'The Economics of Information', *Journal of Political Economy*, 69: 213–25.

—— (1962), 'Information in the Labor Market', *Journal of Political Economy*, 70: S94–S105.

Stiglitz, Joseph (1987), 'The Causes and Consequences of the Dependence of Quality on Price', *Journal of Economic Literature*, 25: 1–48.

Stilwell, Frank (1972), *Regional Economic Policy*. London: Macmillan.

Thompson, Wilbur (1965), *A Preface to Urban Economics*. Baltimore: Johns Hopkins Press.

Topel, Robert (1986), 'Local Labor Markets', *Journal of Political Economy*, 94: S111–S143.

van der Veen, Anne, and Evers, Gerhard (1985), 'A Simultaneous Model for Regional Labor Supply, Incorporating Labor Force Participation, Commuting and Migration', *Socio-Economic Planning Science*, 17: 239–50

Vickerman, R. (1984), 'Urban and Regional Change, Migration and Commuting—the Dynamics of Workplace, Residence, and Transport Choice', *Urban Studies*, 21: 15–29.

Vipond, Joan (1974), 'City Size and Unemployment', *Urban Studies*, 11: 39–46.

—— (1980), 'Intra-Urban Unemployment Differentials in Sydney, 1971', *Urban Studies*, 17: 131–8.

—— (1984), 'The Intra-Urban Unemployment Gradient: The Influence of Location on Unemployment', *Urban Studies*, 21: 377–88.

—— and Beed, Clive (1986), 'A Sydney and Melbourne Comparison of Intra-urban Differentials in Unemployment Rates', *Australian Geographical Studies*, 24: 41–56.

Wabe, J. S. (1966), 'Office Decentralization: An Empirical Study', *Urban Studies*, 3: 35–55.

—— (1969) 'Labour Force Participation Rates in the London Metropolitan Region', *Journal of the Royal Statistical Society, Series A (General)*, 132: 245–64.

Wachtel, Howard (1984), *Labor and the Economy*. Orlando, Fla.: Academic Press.

Wales, T. J. (1978), 'Labour Supply and Commuting Time', *Journal of Econometrics*, 8: 215–26.

Weber, Alfred (1928), *Theory of the Location of Industries*. Chicago: University of Chicago Press.

Webster, F., Bly, P., and Paulley, N. (eds.) (1988), *Urban Land-use and Transport Interaction: Policies and Models*. Avebury: Aldershot.

Weinberg, D. (1979), 'The Determinants of Intra-Urban Household Mobility', *Regional Science and Urban Economics*, 9: 219–46.

Weiss, Yoram (1971), 'Learning by Doing and Occupational Specialization', *Journal of Economic Theory*, 4: 189–98.

Wheaton, William (1977), 'Income and Urban Residence: An Analysis of Consumer Demand for Location', *American Economic Review*, 67: 620–31.

White, Michelle (1977), 'A Model of Residential Location Choice and Commuting by Men and Women Workers', *Journal of Regional Science*, 17: 41–52.

—— (1986), 'Long Commuting Journeys: Waste or Taste?', mimeo. Ann Arbor, Mich.: University of Michigan.

—— (1988), 'Location Choice and Commuting Behavior in Cities with Decentralized Employment', *Journal of Urban Economics*, 24: 129–52.

Wilson, William Julius (1980), *The Declining Significance of Race: Blacks and Changing American Institutions*, 2nd edn. Chicago: University of Chicago Press.

Winnipeg Core Area Initiative Policy Committee (1981), *Proposed Winnipeg Core Area Initiative*. Winnipeg: Winnipeg Core Area Initiative.

INDEX

access:
  to city centre 14
  to workplace 36

bid-rent schedule 23, 26–7, 39

community economic development 167–
  70
commuting: ·
  cost 14–15, 22–3, 37–8, 83–4, 117,
    128
  patterns 4, 6, 42–6, 101–14; by sex
    and race 109–14; by skill 83–9,
    101–5
  time, value of 24–8, 37, 42–3, 87, 97–9

decentralization:
  of employment 28–35; manufacturing
    29–34; offices 31; residential loca-
    tion and 35–41; retail trade 30–1,
    34–5; services 34–5; and underem-
    ployment 116–17, 140–1
  of population 30–3
discrimination 123, 126, 135, 146–9,
  166–7
  and commuting 109–14
dynamics 12–13, 34–5, 47–8, 91–2,
  177–80

employment policy 7, 152–72
  decentralization of 158–60, 169
  evaluation 161–3, 170
  job creation 163–70; public employ-
    ment 164, 169
  training 126–7
equilibrium:
  information and 51, 118–19
  labour market 64, 81–9, 118–23, 130–1
  location 23, 37–40

ghetto:
  dispersal 164–6
  economic development 164
gradient:
  land price 14, 22–8, 36–40, 42
  wage 36, 38–9, 41, 65, 86

housing 166–7, 176–7

public 150–1
human capital:
  and earnings 58, 155–6
  and employment policy 155–63
  and mobility 70–6, 157

information, economics of 50–2, 157
island economy 50, 58–62, 64–5, 76–8,
  84–9, 119, 125, 148–9, 156, 171
  and underemployment 58–9, 119,
    148–9

job matching 56–8, 62–5, 78
  and education 58
job rationing 120–3, 126–8, 146–9,
  156, 164
job search 50, 52–8, 61–5, 69–85, 84–9
  formal and informal networks 74–5,
    77–8, 157, 176–7
  sequential 53–6
  skill and 70–8, 81–4, 87–9, 97–9,
    128, 140
  spatial costs and 54–6, 59, 61–2, 65–
    7, 69–71, 76–8, 96, 128

labour cost:
  quasi-fixed 136
labour demand 82, 129
  monopsony 62–8, 84
  recruitment 78–81; information net-
    works and 78–81; skill and 78–81
labour markets 180–1
  in cities 5–7
  information and 51–2
  monopsony 64–8
labour supply 24–7
  of women 25, 134, 138
land prices 14, 22–8, 36–40, 42
local labour markets 9
  see also island economy

migration 71, 75, 178
minimum wage 148, 156

poverty 1, 3, 6, 143–5, 171
  income maintenance and 153

racial segregation 5, 117

residential location 3, 12, 14–28, 35–
41, 92–6, 174–5
children and 17, 21, 95
income and 15–19, 23–4, 41, 93, 95
number of workers and 19–21, 93, 95
preferences and 15, 19–20, 44
social agglomeration and 19–21

segmented labour markets 2–3, 7, 121–
3, 126–8, 142–9, 163
slums 1, 3, 144–6
spatial economics 3
spatial mismatch 3–4, 8–9, 117, 164
statics, comparative 13

transportation:
public 164–5, 167, 175–6

survey data 15–16, 31, 91–2

underemployment 3, 81–2, 116–51, 176
urban economic problems 1–5
urban growth 12–13, 34–5
see also dynamics
urban policy 1
urban structure:
definition 3, 12

wage gradient 36, 38–9, 41, 65, 86
worker mobility 4–5, 8–9
workplace choice/location 40–1, 46–9,
96–101
skill and 82–4, 87–9, 98–9